Object Solu

Managing the
Object-Oriented Project

The Addison-Wesley Series
in Object-Oriented Software Engineering

Grady Booch, Series Editor

Object Solutions

Managing the
Object-Oriented Project

Grady Booch

Rational Software Corporation
Santa Clara, California

ADDISON-WESLEY PUBLISHING COMPANY, INC.
MENLO PARK, CALIFORNIA • READING, MASSACHUSETTS
NEW YORK • DON MILLS, ONTARIO • WOKINGHAM, U.K.
BONN • PARIS • MILAN • MADRID • SYDNEY • SINGAPORE
TOKYO • SEOUL • TAIPEI • MEXICO CITY • SAN JUAN, PUERTO RICO

Executive Editor: Dan Joranstaad
Sponsoring Editor: Tim Cox
Assitant Editor: Laura Cheu
Senior Production Editor: Teri Holden
Associate Photo Editor: Lisa Lougee
Composition and Film Manager: Lillian Hom
Composition and Film Assistant: Vivian McDougal
Senior Manufacturing Coordinator: Janet Weaver
Copy Editor: Chris Grisonich
Proofreader: Elizabeth Gehrman
Text Designer: Kharibian & Associates
Illustrator: London Road Design
Compositor: London Road Design
Film Preparation: Lazer Touch
Printer: Courier Stoughton
Cover Designer: Yvo Riezebos

Photo Credits: Chapter 1, The Bettman Archive; Chapter 2, ©Richard Nowitz; Chapter 3, Courtesy of Paramount Pictures; Chapter 4, Courtesy of Grady Booch; Chapter 5, Printed by permission of Good Books, Intercourse, PA; Chapter 6, Courtesy of Lucasfilm Ltd.; Chapter 7, Erich Lessing/Art Resource, NY.

Library of Congress Cataloging-in Publication Data
Booch, Grady.
    Object solutions : managing the object-oriented project / Grady Booch.
    p. cm.
    Includes bibliographical references and index.
    ISBN 0-8053-0594-7
    1. Object-oriented programming (Computer science) 2. Computer
software--Development--Management.   I. Title.
    QA76.64.B67 1995
    005.1' 1--dc20   95-24671
                                                                      CIP

1 2 3 4 5 6 7 8 9 10—CRS—99 98 97 96 95

Addison-Wesley Publishing Company, Inc.
2725 Sand Hill Road
Menlo Park, CA 94025

To Jan
my friend, my lover, my wife

Preface

Early adopters of object-oriented technology took it on faith that object orientation was A Good Thing, offering hope for improving some ugly aspect of software development. Some of these primordial efforts truly flourished, some failed, but overall, a number of such projects quietly began to experience the anticipated benefits of objects: better time to market, improved quality, greater resilience to change, and increased levels of reuse. Of course, any new technology is fun to play with for a short while. Indeed, there is a part of our industry that thrives on embracing the latest fad in software development. However, the real business case for any mature technology is that it delivers measurable and sustainable benefits for real projects.

Object-oriented technology has demonstrated its value in a multitude of applications around the world. I have seen object-oriented languages and methods used successfully in such diverse problem domains as securities trading, medical electronics, enterprise-wide information management, air traffic control, semiconductor manufacturing, interactive video gaming, telecommunications network management, and astronomical research. Indeed, I can honestly say that in every industrialized country and in every conceivable application area, I have come across some use of object-oriented technology. Object-oriented stuff is indisputably a part of the mainstream of computing.

There exists an ample and growing body of experience from projects that have applied object-oriented technology. This experience – both good and bad – is useful in guiding new projects. One important conclusion that I draw from all such projects is that object-orientation can have a very positive impact upon software development, but that a project requires much more than just an object-oriented veneer to be successful. Programmers must not abandon sound development principles all in the name of objects. Similarly, managers must understand the subtle impact that objects have upon traditional practices.

SCOPE

In almost every project I have come across, be it a modest two- or three-person effort, to undertakings of epic proportions wherein geopolitical issues dominate, a common set of questions always appears: How do I transition my organization to object-oriented practices? What artifacts should I manage to retain control? How should I organize my staff? How do I measure the quality of the software being produced? How can I reconcile the creative needs of my individual programmers with management's needs for stability and predictability? Can object-orientation help me help my customers better articulate what they really want? These are all reasonable questions, and their answers strike at the heart of what is different and special about object-oriented technology.

This book serves to answer these and many other related questions, by offering pragmatic advice on the recommended practices and rules of thumb used by successful projects.

This is not a theoretical book, nor is its purpose to explain all the dark corners of object-oriented analysis, design, and programming. My previous work, *Object-Oriented Analysis and Design with Applications*, serves those purposes: it examines the theoretical underpinnings of all things object-oriented, and offers a comprehensive reference to a unified method of object-oriented analysis and design.

Object Solutions provides a direct and balanced treatment on all the important issues of managing object-oriented projects. I have been engaged in hundreds of projects; this book draws upon that broad experience. My intent is to explain what has worked, what has not, and how to distinguish between the two.

AUDIENCE

My intended audience includes project managers and senior programmers who want to apply object-oriented technology successfully to their projects, while avoiding the common mistakes that can befall the unwary. Professional programmers will find this book useful as well, giving them insight into the larger issues of turning cool looking object-oriented code into real products; this book will also help to explain why their managers do what they do. Students on their way to becoming professional programmers will come to understand why software development is often not very tidy in the real world, and how industrial-strength projects cope with this disorder.

ORGANIZATION

I have organized this book according to the various functional aspects of managing an object-oriented project. As such, it can either be read from cover to cover or selectively by topic. To make this material more accessible, my general style is to present an issue, discuss its implications, and then offer some recommended practices and rules of thumb. To distinguish these elements in the text, I use the following typographic conventions:

> This is an issue, usually stated in the form of a question followed by its answer, regarding some functional area of project management.

This is a recommended practice, which represents a generally acceptable way of addressing a given issue.

P #

This is a rule of thumb, which represents some quantifiable measure about a particular practice.

R #

I've numbered these practices and rules sequentially, so that specific ones can be referred to easily.

To reinforce certain lessons, I offer examples drawn from a variety of production object-oriented projects, whose details have been changed to protect the guilty. I highlight these examples in the following manner:

This is an example, drawn from some production object-oriented project.

ACKNOWLEDGMENTS

As a compendium of object-oriented wisdom, *Object Solutions* owes an enormous debt to the many professional managers and programmers whose contributions have advanced the state of the practice in object-oriented technology.

The following individuals deserve a special mention for reviewing my work in progress, and providing me with many useful comments and suggestions: Gregory Adams, Glen Andert, Andrew Baer, Dave Bernstein, Mike Dalpee, Rob Daly, Mike Devlin, Richard Dué, Jim Gillespie, Jim Hamilton, Larry Hartweg, Philippe Kruchten, Brian Lyons, Joe Marasco, Sue Mickel, Frank Pappas, Jim Purtilo, Rich Reitman, Walker Royce, Dave Tropeano, Mike Weeks, and Dr. William Wright.

A special thanks goes to my wife, Jan, for keeping me sane during the development of yet another book, and who always gently shows me that there is a rich life beyond all things object-oriented.

Contents

CHAPTER 1: FIRST PRINCIPLES   1

When Bad Things Happen to Good Projects   5
Establishing a Project's Focus   9
Understanding a Project's Culture   11
The Five Habits of Successful Object-Oriented Projects   22
Issues in Managing Object-Oriented Projects   29

CHAPTER 2: PRODUCTS AND PROCESS   33

In Search of Excellent Objects   37
Object-Oriented Architectures   43
The Artifacts of a Software Project   54
Establishing a Rational Design Process   63

CHAPTER 3: THE MACRO PROCESS   69

The One Minute Methodology   74
Conceptualization   80
Analysis   86
Design   108
Evolution   129
Maintenance   151

CHAPTER 4: THE MICRO PROCESS   154

I'm OK, My Program's OK   159
Identifying Classes and Objects   161
Identifying the Semantics of Classes and Objects   167
Identifying Relationships Among Classes and Objects   174
Implementing Classes and Objects   181

CHAPTER 5: THE DEVELOPMENT TEAM 185

Managers Who Hate Programmers, and the Programmers
   Who Work For Them 191
Roles and Responsibilities 194
Resource Allocation 206
Technology Transfer 212
Tools for the Worker 219

CHAPTER 6: MANAGEMENT AND PLANNING 225

Everything I Need to Know I'll Learn In My Next Project 229
Managing Risk 231
Planning and Scheduling 233
Costing and Staffing 236
Monitoring, Measuring, and Testing 237
Documenting 239
Projects in Crisis 244

CHAPTER 7: SPECIAL TOPICS 247

What They Don't Teach You in Programming Class 252
User-centric Systems 254
Data-centric Systems 257
Computation-centric Systems 260
Distributed Systems 262
Legacy Systems 265
Information Management Systems 267
Real Time Systems 270
Frameworks 274

EPILOGUE 277

SUMMARY OF RECOMMENDED PRACTICES 279

SUMMARY OF RULES OF THUMB 293

GLOSSARY 303

BIBLIOGRAPHY 307

INDEX 311

Chapter 1

First Principles

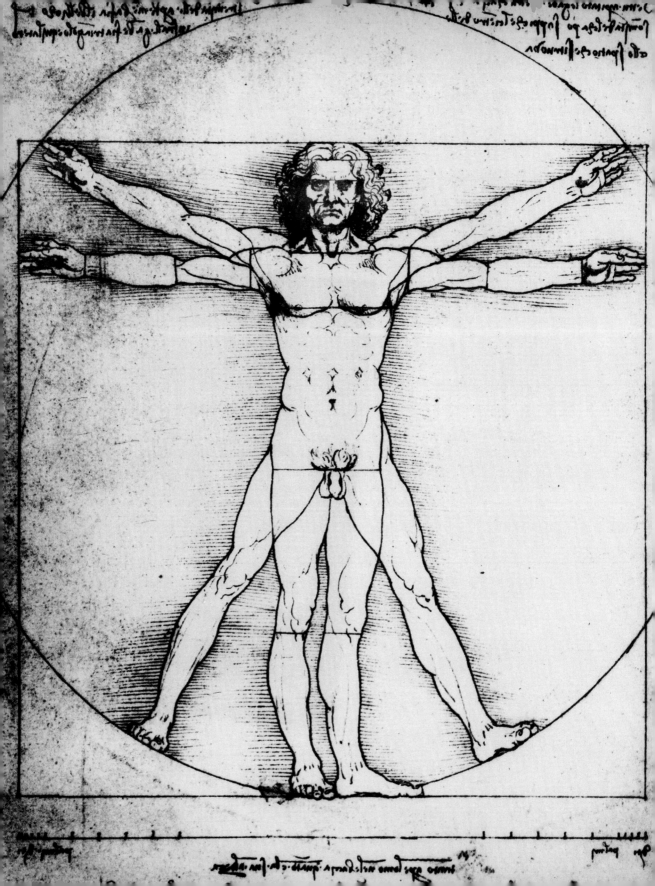

First Principles

Nature uses only the longest threads to weave her pattern, so each small piece of the fabric reveals the organization of the entire tapestry.

RICHARD FEYNMAN

First, some good news.

From the perspective of the software developer, we live in very interesting times. Consider all the software behind many of the activities that we take for granted in an industrialized society: making a phone call, buying shares in a mutual fund, driving a car, watching a movie, having a medical examination. Sophisticated software is already pervasive, and the fact that it continues to weave itself deeply into the fabric of society creates an insatiable demand for creative architects, abstractionists, and implementers.

Now, some bad news. It is not radical to predict that future software will be evolutionarily more complex. Indeed, two dominant forces drive this trend: the increased connectivity of distributed, high-performance computing systems and greater user expectations for better visualization of and access to information. The first force—increased connectivity—is made possible by the emergence of increasingly high-bandwidth conduits of information and is made practical by economies of scale. The second force—greater user expectations—is largely a consequence of the Nintendo generation that is socially aware of the creative possibilities of automation. Under the influences of both forces, it is reasonable for a consumer to expect that a movie ordered over cable television can be billed directly to his or her bank account. It is reasonable for a scientist to expect on-line access to information in distant laboratories. It is reasonable for an architect to expect the ability to walk through a virtual blueprint created by remote collaborators. It is reasonable for a player to interact with a game whose images are virtually indistinguishable from reality. It is reasonable for a retail business to expect there to be no seams in its mission-critical systems, connecting the event of a customer buying an item to the activities of the company's buyers (who react to rapidly changing consumer tastes) as well as to the activities of the company's marketing organization (which must target new offerings to increasingly specialized groups of consumers). The places where we find seams in such systems, those times when users ask "why can't I do *x*," hint at the fact that we have not yet mastered the complexity of a particular domain.

Even if we ignore the substantial amount of resources already being spent on software maintenance, the world's current supply of software developers would easily be consumed just by the activities of writing software that derive from the natural consequences of these two simple forces. If we add to this equation the largely unproductive tasks of coping with the microprocessor wars, the operating system wars, the programming language wars, and even the methodology wars, we find that scant resources are left to spend on discovering and inventing the next class of so-called "killer" applications. Ultimately, every computer user suffers.

On the positive side, however, software development today is far less constrained by hardware. Compared to a decade ago, many applications operate in a world of abundant MIPS, excess memory, and cheap connectivity. Of course, there are two sides to this blessing. On the one hand, this means that our hardware must no longer dramatically shape the software architectures that we craft. On the other hand, this embarrassment of riches tends to encourage an appetite for software than will never be satiated.

Thus, we are faced with a simple but fundamental truth:

> Our ability to imagine complex applications will always exceed our ability to develop them.

Actually, this is the most positive of situations: the demands of our imagination drive us continually to improve the ways in which we craft our software.

WHEN BAD THINGS HAPPEN TO GOOD PROJECTS

Most software projects start out for all the right reasons: to fill a market need, to provide certain much-needed functionality to a group of end users, to explore some wild theory. For many, writing software is a necessary and unavoidable part of their business, in other words, a secondary concern. A bank is in the business of managing money, not managing software, although software is an essential means to that end. A retail company achieves a competitive advantage in manufacturing and distribution through its software, although its primary business might be providing consumers with the latest fashions in clothes. For other people, writing software is their life, their passion, their joy, something they do while others focus on more mundane problems. In either case, developing software is something that consumes time and significant intellectual energy.

> Why do some software projects fail? Most often, it is because of:
> - A failure to properly manage the risks
> - Building the wrong thing
> - Being blindsided by technology

Unfortunately, as the work of a team unfolds, more than a few projects lose their way. Many projects fail because of a lack of adult supervision.* Increas-

---

* I don't mean to sound condescending. It is not that such projects fail because of poor management; rather, they fail because of *no* management.

ingly unrealistic schedules and plans are drawn up, cumulatively forming a succession of lies, with no one having the nerve to stand up and acknowledge reality. Petty empires form. Every problem is viewed as "a simple matter of programming," rather than as a reflection of a more systemic problem in the system's architecture or the development process itself. The project's direction and activities are set by the most obnoxious people in the group, because it is easier for management to let this group have its way than it is to make hard decisions when problems arise. Unmanaged projects such as these eventually enter into a "free fall" with no one taking responsibility and everyone waiting for the impact. Usually, the most merciful thing to do in these circumstances is to kill the project before it ruins everything in its path.

A company landed a major contract to supply a common suite of development tools which would ultimately be used by a variety of other contractors on a mission-critical space project. The company did a number of things right: it selected a seasoned architect, trained its people well, selected some good tools, and even instrumented their project so that management could tune the development process over time. However, once the project got going, upper management essentially stepped back and let the technologists on the project run amok. Free from the constraints of any clear goals or firm schedules for incremental releases, the programmers pursued what seemed to them some really cool, albeit irrelevant, implementation issues. While the project's managers spent their time playing political games, the programmers kept rolling forward their schedules, aided by the fact that there was no internal pressure to deliver anything real. In the meantime, end users kept demanding certain high priority deliverables, which were promptly brushed aside as things that would eventually be completed once the team had finished building all the necessary infrastructure. The testing team raised concerns about performance, warning that the framework being crafted would eventually collapse of its own sheer weight, once exposed to the demands of real users. After burning several tens of million dollars, the project was canceled, with hardly any deliverable software to show for all its effort.

There is a simple lesson to be learned from this project's demise:

Management must actively attack a project's risks, otherwise they will actively attack you.[*]

P 1

_____
[*] Gilb, p. 73.

Quite often, projects lose their way because they go adrift in completely uncharted territory. There is no shared vision of the problem being solved. The team is clueless as to the final destination, and so it thrashes about, throwing its scarce energies on what appear to be the most important technical tasks, which often turn out to be of secondary concern once the end users finally see the product. No one takes the time to validate what is being built with any end users or domain experts. Occasionally, so-called analysts capture the essence of the system's real requirements, but for a number of political and social reasons, that essence is never communicated to the people who must design and implement the system. A false sense of understanding pervades the project, and everyone is surprised when users reject the delivered software that was so lovingly crafted in a complete vacuum.

> A company was selected to develop a large interstate traffic control system. Early sizing estimates suggested the need for several hundred developers (in itself an early warning sign). Two new buildings were erected, one to house the project's analysts, and the other to house the project's designers and implementers. Not surprisingly, these artificial physical boundaries introduced significant amounts of noise in the communication of the user's requirements down to the level of the project's programmers. Memo wars raged, with analysts lobbing reports containing their view of the problem over the walls to the poor, isolated designers, who would from time to time fire back with reports of their own. The project's programmers were rarely exposed to any real end users; they were too busy coding, and besides, as the project's culture dictated it was thought that most of its programmers would not know how to deal with users anyway. As time unfolded and the project's real requirements became clear, there was considerable delay in communicating these changing needs from the users through the analysts to the designers, resulting in significant schedule slips as well as much broken glass in the customer/vendor relationship.

The experience from this project, and too many others like it, prompts the following recommended practice:

> Involve real users throughout the software development process; their presence is a constant reminder why and for whom the software is being crafted.

P 2

Occasionally, projects fail because they are blindsided by the very technology being employed to build the software itself. Tools break at the most inopportune moments, lacking the capacity to handle the project's exponentially increasing complexity. From time to time, the project's tools prove to be just plain erroneous, requiring programmers to perform unnatural acts to get around these limitations. Third-party software suppliers sometimes do not deliver what they originally promised; often some expected functionality is lacking, or performance is less than expected. In the worst of all possible scenarios, the supplier simply goes out of business, leaving the project totally exposed. Technology backlash happens most often when forces in the marketplace, beyond a project's local control, change the technology rules out from under it: a hardware platform vendor stops making a product, operating system interfaces and features are changed by their supplier faster than the project can meaningfully keep up, end user's tastes change and their expectations rise because of some other really neat program one of them recently saw mentioned in the latest trade magazine (even though that product later proved to be vaporware). Although the latest language/tool/method selected by a project might promise real benefits, extracting those benefits is usually much harder than it first appears. When blindsided by technology, there usually are not enough programming hours in the day to recover, without reducing the functionality of the system the project had promised to deliver. Ultimately, this is all very embarrassing for a software development organization: as professionals, the last thing to expect is for your own technology to turn on you.

A securities trading company made a significant investment in object-oriented stuff, buying the latest brand workstations and programming tools for all its developers. Shortly thereafter, the workstation vendor decided that it really was a software company after all, and so it stopped making any more of its hardware.

Too often, problems with the underlying technology take the blame for a project's failure when the real culprit is really non-technical, namely, the lack of active management that should have anticipated and planned contingencies for the technical risk in the first place. Still, we do not live in a perfect world, and thus:

P 3

Where possible, do not bind your project to any single-source technology, but if you must (such as when that technology offers some compelling advantage even in the face of its risk), build firewalls into your architecture and process so that your project will not unravel even if the technology does.

ESTABLISHING A PROJECT'S FOCUS

Despite these three failure modes, many software projects that start out for all the right reasons really do achieve at least some modest amount of success. However, even the most successful projects seem to take longer, involve more intellectual effort, and require more crisis management than we really believe they ever should. Unfortunately, as Parnas suggests, we can never have a completely rational development process because:[*]

- A system's users typically do not know exactly what they want and are unable to articulate all that they do know.
- Even if we could state all of a system's requirements, there are many details about a system that we can only discover once we are well into its implementation.
- Even if we knew all of these details, there are fundamental limits to the amount of complexity that humans can master.
- Even if we could master all this complexity, there are external forces, far beyond a project's control, that lead to changes in requirements, some of which may invalidate earlier decisions.
- Systems built by humans are always subject to human error.
- As we embark on each new project, we bring with us the intellectual baggage of ideas from earlier designs as well as the economic baggage of existing software, both of which shape our decisions independent of a system's real requirements.

Parnas goes on to observe that "For all of these reasons, the picture of the software designer deriving his design in a rational, error-free way from a statement of requirements is quite unrealistic." Fortunately, as Parnas observes, and as I'll discuss further in the next chapter, it is possible, and indeed desirable, to fake it. In one way or another, establishing the semblance of a rational design process is exactly what every successful project has to do.

Every successful project also entails the making of a plethora of technical decisions. Some of these decisions have sweeping implications for the system under construction, such as the decision to use a certain client/server topology, the decision to use a particular windowing framework, or the decision to use a relational database. These I call *strategic decisions*, because each denotes a fundamental architectural pattern. Other decisions are much more local in nature, such as the decision to use a particular programming idiom for iteration, the decisions that shape the interface of an individual class, or the decision to use a specific vendor's relational database. These I call *tactical decisions*. Together,

---

[*] Parnas, p. 251.

these strategic and tactical decisions shape the entire structure of a system under development.

However, technical decisions alone have little to do with mitigating the primary reasons that certain software projects fail. Managing risk, building the right thing, and defending against technological calamity are all largely economic decisions, not technical ones. Of course, the technology a project uses does impact each economic decision, by establishing a range of options and different values of cost, risk, and benefit to each decision.

As a result, before embarking on any new project, it is essential to explicitly identify those primary characteristics against which such economic decisions can be made. These characteristics include criteria such as:

- Time-to-market
- Completeness
- Performance
- Quality
- Fault tolerance
- Scaleability
- Extensibility
- Portability
- Architectural reusability
- Cost of ownership

It is impossible to optimize a system to address all of these criteria at once. If time-to-market is a project's primary concern, as it is in more than a few competitive shrink-wrap software domains, then completeness, performance, and all the various *-ilities* will likely suffer. If quality and fault tolerance are central, as it is in many human-rated systems such as in air traffic control and medical instrumentation, then time-to-market must play a secondary role. This is not to say that a project should not or cannot have multiple goals. Rather, the entire development team must recognize that for every technical decision, there is a cost—an economic tradeoff, if you will. In other words, you cannot have it all.

> The central task of the software management team is to balance a set of incomplete, inconsistent, and shifting technical and non-technical requirements, to produce a system that is optimal for its essential minimal characteristics.

This collection of essential minimal characteristics provides the focus for the software development team. Following through on this focus is effectively a management decision process, whose critical driver is ruthlessness.

P 4

> To be successful, the software development team must be ruthless: every technical decision must contribute to satisfying a system's essential minimal characteristics. Any decision that is counter to these characteristics must be rejected; any decision that is neutral to these characteristics must be considered a luxury.

To pull this off, the entire development organization must have a shared vision of the problem to be solved. As a project unfolds, the development team must continually ask itself, "are we still producing a system that satisfies the chosen characteristics?" If the answer is yes, then the team has effectively validated the path it is on. If the answer is no, then the team has only three choices:

- Retract the earlier decisions that have defocused the development effort. This is rarely a zero-sum game, for it usually require unwinding earlier work or, at the very least, dropping ongoing efforts.
- Relax some constraint. For example, explicitly slip the development schedule, eliminate some functionality, or reduce certain performance requirements.
- Abandon the project.

For a project to do otherwise means that it is just ignoring reality. Unfortunately, reality has a nasty way of sneaking up on a project, long after the development team thought that they had successfully hidden it under a sea of technical rubbish. Usually, the sudden awakening to the truth about a project's health comes in the form of irate or aggressively apathetic end users, who typically have a very unequivocal model of reality.

UNDERSTANDING A PROJECT'S CULTURE

Every software project, object-oriented or not, seems to follow one of several styles, depending upon its explicit or implicit choice of essential minimal characteristics. Each of these styles denotes a particular project culture, which I distinguish by its central focus.

Each software project has a particular focus:
- Calendar-driven
- Requirements-driven
- Documentation-driven
- Quality-driven
- Architecture-driven

Calendar-driven projects are characterized by an obsessive focus on the schedule. The operative word here is obsessive. Do not misread me: it is reasonable for every healthy project to keep an eye on its schedule when some sound requirement exists for delivering a piece of software at a particular time. However, in truly calendar-driven projects, decisions are made primarily according to what is expedient in the short term. Anything that does not contribute to meeting established schedules, including anything above some barely minimal acceptable functionality or performance, is abandoned, deferred, or worked around. As a result, completeness, quality, documentation, and conceptual integrity must suffer.

During the Desert Storm conflict, communication of battlefield information among the various allied forces proved to be far less than optimal, often owing to simple mismatches in protocols for and encoding of electronic data. Stuffing people in the system to deal with these impedance mismatches was just not an acceptable alternative because of human language issues and the real-time nature of the data. More than one programmer, called up from the reserves to the front lines, was given a simple and direct mission: armed with a laptop computer loaded with Object Pascal, develop a program to bridge those gaps in electronic communication. The challenge: this program had to be operational about by the time the programmer's transport plane landed in the Middle East.*

The only defensible and honorable reason for running an obsessive, calendar-driven project is that your organization will be out of business if your project does not deliver on time.

Obsessively calendar-driven projects usually embody no definable process, save for any informal discipline that derives from the local programming culture.‡ Unfortunately, far too many software development teams toil in this state of continuous chaos and are kept alive only through the efforts of a few heroic programmers. A start-up company can get away with this strategy for a short while, because it may be the only way to break into the market. A modest-sized company can tolerate this strategy for a little bit longer. If the business is continually opening new markets, then the aggregation of all its various software projects appears as a collection of smaller start-ups. A really big company can

---

* The programmer who relayed this story to me added a new phrase to my vocabulary: He called his mission "combat coding." The urgency of mission this programmer faced is not unlike a number of projects I encounter in various financial centers around the world, except that, in these latter cases, their enemies aren't shooting at them (although some may feel that way).

‡ Found written on a white board at a calendar-driven organization: *Real programmers don't use methods.*

get away with this strategy for the longest time, because if it can throw enough people at a problem, probability suggests that a tolerable number of these projects will succeed through the valiant efforts of a few off-scale programmers, giving the illusion that the company knows what it is doing. In fact, the very heat and smoke put off by the sheer motion of all these projects will inject sufficient fear, uncertainty, and doubt into the end user's domain. This strategy sometimes yields a psychological advantage that overcomes all its technical liabilities by throwing all competitors off balance.

The problem, of course, is that a completely calendar-driven development policy does not offer a sustainable business solution. Because the resulting software products are rarely scaleable, extensible, portable, or reusable, the long-term cost of ownership of such products is intolerably high. Calendar-driven projects also have a high social cost. From time to time, it is genuinely fun to be part of a tightly focused, high-energy, independent band of software outlaws, but it is definitely not a lifestyle that can be endured forever. As a result, organizations that are always under schedule pressure usually have lousy morale. When a developer is capable of making good or even profound technical decisions, there is little satisfaction in always having to make expedient ones.

> If the majority of the projects in your organization are obsessively short term, calendar-driven projects, there is something very, very wrong, indeed. Radical changes in the organization's software development process are in order, before the company or its people are ruined.

R 1

Requirements-driven projects are characterized by a rigid focus on the system's outwardly observable behavior, sometimes expressed as its function points. Decisions are made primarily according to the local needs of each requirement. Meeting established schedules is still valued, although timelines are usually secondary to the importance of completeness. All things being equal, a project employing a requirements-driven policy will be more likely to slip schedules to reach certain levels of functionality, than it would be willing to cast off functionality for the sake of preserving schedules. Quality, including performance, is important only insofar as there exist tangible requirements. The documentation produced by such projects generally adds little value beyond mechanically tracing requirements to implementation. Conceptual integrity sometimes suffers because there is little motivation to deal with scaleability, extensibility, portability, or reusability beyond what any vague requirements might imply.

> A telecommunications company set about to improve its customer service software by developing a completely new system with a modern graphical user interface. Analysis yielded a set of requirements that modeled the business process, which was best described in terms of the various windows and menus that its

end users would see. To the general satisfaction of its users, the system was delivered reasonably complete and in a timely fashion. However, the system proved to be a challenge to maintain. As end users requested new functionality and as the business model changed over time, developers found that these new requirements shook certain fundamental assumptions they had made about the system, and so they were difficult to satisfy without adding large amounts of new infrastructure. Whole new branches of the application had to be crafted, paralleling elements in the older architecture, because certain new components did not integrate just right with the earlier, locally optimized parts. Although the system was operational and reasonably functional, code bloat was diagnosed, with the long-term prognosis suggesting that the entire system would have to eventually be rewritten once the introduction of enough new requirements passed some threshold that caused the cost of maintenance to exceed the cost of throwing the system away and starting all over.

A requirements-driven style of development is often the best match for crafting systems whose outwardly observable behavior is well-defined and largely unchanging. In such projects, completeness is typically the driving force. A requirements-driven process often yields a system that is fairly optimal to a given static set of requirements.

Requirements-driven projects typically observe the following process:

- Enumerate all of the system's functions.
- Design components for each of these threads.
- Implement each component.

These activities are commonly called analysis, design, and implementation, the traditional phases of a waterfall life cycle.

To some degree, a requirements-driven style of development is an ancient vestige of structured programming techniques as scaled up to analysis and design. This is not to say that requirements-driven development is a bad thing. Indeed, many mission-critical systems were successfully developed and fielded during the 1970s and 80s (and still in the 90s) using this style. However, as the earlier example suggests, there is a dark side to this model: requirements-driven projects are easily thrown off balance as requirements change.

Studying the canonical software architecture produced by projects that employ this style of development reveals why this is so. As Figure 1-1 shows, requirements-driven architectures typically have a small substrate, containing only a few common support elements shared by all threads of the system. Common databases and utility components typically populate this infrastructure. On top of this substrate are largely parallel structures, aligned with each major system function.* In a simplistic way, this is a very natural structure for some kinds of applications. Certain transaction-oriented applications are often designed in this manner, because each transaction can be articulated as a fairly independent, sequential activity. This structure also encourages parallel paths of development, because there is little worry about the activity of one thread corrupting another.

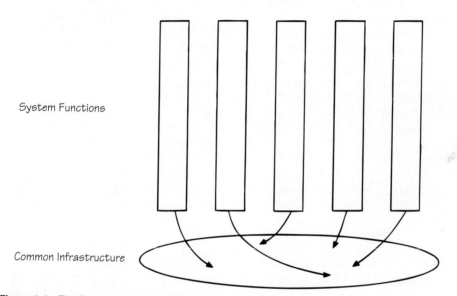

Figure 1-1   The Structure of Requirements-Driven Projects

On the positive side, requirements traceability is fairly easy to achieve with this model; each requirement can in theory be mapped to one component, again a vestige of the structured programming culture. On the negative side, this model does not encourage simple architectures, which exploit common patterns that exist among the various system functions. Furthermore, this model is not very responsive to change. Because each branch of the architecture tends to be locally optimized to individual system functions, new requirements either end up invalidating earlier assumptions, which must then be repaired in numerous arms of the system, or introducing new features which further dilute the amount of real reuse, because more arms must be added to the system.

---

* The resulting shape yields what some call a *stovepipe* architecture. In practice, such architectures rarely look even this clean. Rather, they are characterized by vertical pipes of varying lengths, some short and fat and others tall and skinny. Especially for long-suffering legacy systems, cross-connecting pipes tend to spring up, further complicating the picture.

This is why, over time, such architectures tend to collapse of their own weight. Even though they may have been adequate for the problem as initially perceived, they are not enduring artifacts. Of course, for certain domains, this is simply not an issue. For example, when crafting the control system of a deep space probe, completeness and quality (especially performance) are usually dominant.* Time-to-market is far less of a consideration except for launch window constraints, which are literally set by the alignment of the planets. If the software is not ready, you cannot go on with the launch and hope for the next upgrade. Furthermore, such applications are largely disposable and so maintenance takes a very different form than that found in terrestrial management information systems. Uploading new software to a probe is a common activity, but it is usually done only to work around some hardware failure or a change in mission.

This suggests a rule of thumb:

R 2

If 90% or more of your system's requirements are expected to be stable over the software's lifespan, then applying a requirements-driven policy has a fair chance of yielding a reasonably optimal solution. Anything less than this degree of stability requires a different development approach to achieve a tolerable value for the system's total cost of ownership.

A documentation-driven style of project management is generally not a very sound way to develop software, but I mention it here only because unfortunately it is very common, especially among certain government projects and really large commercial organizations whose misguided efforts to follow certain software development and quality standards lead them astray. Documentation-driven approaches are essentially a degenerate form of a requirements-driven process, a case of bureaucracy gone mad in the face of software. Development decisions are made primarily according to what documentation has to be delivered next. Often, as the deadline for delivering the next document looms on the schedule, all significant development work ceases until the document is pushed out the door, usually to a customer who never reads it anyway. The development team then has to rush madly to catch up on its real work, until these activities are again interrupted by the apocalyptic approach of the next piece of documentation that has to be written.

This European country's government desired to provide electronic access to all the materials in its public library system.

---

* Software for satellites and space probes operates under the most severe of time and space-constraints. Reliability concerns (stray cosmic rays that flip bits in electronic devices are a very real issue), power constraints, and hard-real time requirements demand that developers craft very clever algorithms. Curiously, weight constraints limit even the size of programs: Every byte of object code requires a tiny bit of physical memory, which adds up to some real mass for large programs.

Given the sweeping vision of this project, the team started with an object-oriented analysis, which sought to specify an enterprise-wide domain model. After an exhaustive analysis phase, the team delivered an 8,000 page requirements document, which no one could understand.

Projects that start out with noble intentions to follow a requirements-driven path can easily be sidetracked onto the documentation-driven rut. This generally happens when management, uncertain how to manage the creative aspects of the software process, imposes a heavy-handed form of control by requiring a plethora of what it thinks are essential documents.

> If your project has more writers than programmers, or if the cost of updating your documentation is greater than the cost of making a change to your software, then your project has certainly fallen into the black hole of documentation-driven development.

R 3

Thus, the existence of documentation-driven projects in your organization is usually an indication that your management is basically insecure about its ability to control its developers. This is not to say that all documentation is useless.* As I discuss in the next chapter, certain documents offer an essential management tool, and serve as an important legacy of the software development process. However, what is to be avoided is gratuitous documentation, documents for the document's sake. In the ocean of paper generated by a software project, only a few documents really prove to be critical for a healthy project not perverted by paper envy.

In all fairness, however, a few circumstances exist in which the paper output of a project may be allowed to exceed its software output. For example, when crafting a shrink-wrap class library, documentation of the library's architecture and its patterns of use is essential for end users to understand and apply that library. The process of developing such a library may reasonably be documentation-driven, because all external documentation is absolutely central to the approachability and usability of the library. This, of course, is another economic tradeoff: sometimes it is more cost effective for a company to ship a technical consultant to explain the software (and so gain revenues for his or her time) than it is to write the proper documentation.

Quality-driven projects are characterized by an almost obsessive focus on certain quantifiable measures. Some of these measures concentrate on external, system-wide behaviors. For example, an air traffic control system might demand less than one second of down time per decade. A commercial banking application might require its system to process several hundred transactions

---

* Found written on a white board at another organization in crisis: *Real programmers don't document.*

per second during peak periods. A network management system might expect a mean time between failure on the order of several months. Other measures may focus on internal, software specific characteristics, including the relative complexity of individual classes, the depth and width of class lattices, and quality measures such as defect discovery rates and defect density rates.

In quality-driven projects, decisions are made primarily to optimize the selected measures. Completeness is usually a given, although schedules will be allowed to yield for the sake of quality. The documentation required by such a project is often quite detailed—and occasionally involves a significant amount of hairy mathematics—to demonstrate that the required measures of goodness or correctness can be achieved. Scaleability, extensibility, portability, and reusability are always secondary considerations (these characteristics cannot easily be measured anyway). Quite often, to achieve the required quality goals, it is necessary to vigorously optimize certain elements of the system, with the result that the final solution is often very brittle: touching one part of the system tends to breaks the delicately crafted and highly optimized components in other parts of the system.

A medical electronics company set out to produce a family of pacemaker products.[*] Object-oriented technology was selected to assist in crafting a simple framework that could be applied across the entire product line. This approach did help to reduce the overall cost of software development in that line of business, although individual products required tuning to meet quality requirements.

A quality-driven style of development is essential in certain domains. For example, software controlling a nuclear power plant's cooling system must be fail-safe, that is, it must not fail in catastrophic ways. Flight control software for aerodynamically unstable aircraft must tolerate certain failure modes, yet continue to operate correctly. Telephone switching systems must continue to operate even in the presence of hardware failure. Similarly, software for medical equipment must often be certified to be correct.

If even a single human life were to be jeopardized by the failure of your software system, a quality-driven approach to development should be considered.

R 4

Quality-driven projects are by their nature very conservative beasts. Typically there is a great reluctance to change things that have already been com-

---

[*] In this example, C and C++ rather than Smalltalk were selected as implementation languages. This was probably a very wise decision: Unscheduled garbage collection, typical of most Smalltalk environments, would be more than slightly inconvenient to a pacemaker's owner.

pleted, largely because of the high cost of verification and validation. In the extreme, such projects may resort to ultra-conservative practices, such as verifying the binary compatibility of new releases; even upgrading a compiler becomes a major moral decision. Especially where human lives are involved, formal proofs of correctness may be employed to increase the project's level of confidence in the system's behavior. There is a simple measure for the success of such quality-driven projects: if a cadre of lawyers has to sort out the damage from a system failure, than the project has indeed failed in a very big way.

Although a quality-driven development style is essential in certain domains, it is simply not affordable in many others. This is not to say that software projects can ignore quality considerations altogether. Rather, this is a recognition that in software development, achieving a certain level of quality is always an economic decision. In the best of cases, a project will strike a suitable balance between satisfying these quality considerations and the cost of achieving them. Quite often, even slightly relaxing certain quality constraints (such as mean down time or mean time between failure) has an enormous impact on reducing the cost of development, and so it is important for management to constantly question the authority of any quality requirements that appear to be too constraining. Still, sacrificing quality for a short-term development advantage is usually always false economy, so the wise manager will always consider the cost of ownership of software when making such tradeoffs.

In the worst case, quality-driven projects end up optimizing all the wrong things. For example, if external requirements for transaction throughput are the dominant consideration, then all work will be focused on achieving this throughput, often to the detriment of simplicity and changeability.* If over time other performance concerns prove to be more important issues, redirecting the system to this new focus is often quite painful. Similarly, where external requirements are impossible to satisfy solely through software—usually because they involve interaction with hardware—the development team has the tendency to turn its attention to more microscopic issues that can be measured, such as the local quality of individual components. Such a local focus typically does not end up satisfying the more global concerns of the system.

Architecture-driven projects represent the most mature style of development. These projects are characterized by a focus on creating a framework that satisfies all known hard requirements, and yet is resilient enough to adapt to those requirements that are not yet known or well understood. In every sense of the word, architecture-driven policies are an evolutionary step beyond requirements-driven policies. In many ways, these two approaches are similar, except that, with object-oriented technology, architecture-driven policies seek to mitigate the dark side of requirements-driven policies.

---

* In a similar fashion, database analysts must occasionally denormalize their schemas to achieve certain performance goals, at the cost of tainting the purity of the solution.

Time-to-market is definitely not a forgotten consideration under this style of development, but whereas calendar-driven projects tend to optimize only for the next milestone, architecture-driven projects tend to optimize for the long term. Importantly, immediate time-to-market considerations can still be addressed, by instituting an incremental and iterative process that evolves the architecture and establishes a rhythm of releases whose schedule is well-defined yet whose delivered functionality may vary slightly in the short-term as needed to reflect feedback from earlier releases. This situation is not unlike that of a business that focuses on quarterly financial results, as opposed to one that focuses on overall performance and health of the company. In the first case, the business will tend to make decisions that may make short term financial performance look good, but often at the expense of fumbling long term, strategic opportunities. In the second case, the business will tend to make decisions that are not necessarily optimal for every quarter's performance, but in the long term builds a solid, healthy, and enduring business.

Completeness is indeed an important consideration under this style of development, but only in a very large sense of the word. Recognizing that completeness is in the mind of the end user and that a system's real requirements are often not known until users try out a system in industrial settings, architecture-driven projects strive to accommodate this reality by building frameworks that are adaptable. Thus, the decision process used in architecture-driven projects involves asking if a given technical decision will satisfy existing requirements, as well as offers reasonable degrees of freedom to address future requirements as they are discovered. Issues of performance and quality are treated in a similar fashion: architecture-driven projects seek to build frameworks that can properly be tuned in the context of real use, at which time the system's real requirements can be better articulated.

All the *-ilities*—scaleability, extensibility, portability, and reusability—are central to architecture-driven approaches, because the focus is on crafting enduring artifacts. These *-ilities* are all essentially different attributes that contribute to the resilience of a software system.

A company experienced in developing control systems for ships sought to dominate a certain segment of its market. Using object-oriented methods, the organization developed a framework that it could adapt to the particular requirements of its expected customers. The resulting architecture, made up of well over a million lines of code, was applied to ships from five different countries. Using this framework, the company has to date not lost a single major competitive bid, thus representing a substantial return on investment for the company.

An architecture-driven style of development has all the benefits of a requirements-driven style, as well as the favorable characteristic of encouraging the creation of resilient frameworks that can withstand shifting requirements and technological calamity. In short:

> An architecture-driven style of development is usually the best approach for the creation of most complex software-intensive systems.

Architecture-driven projects typically observe the following process:

P 5

- Specify the system's desired behavior through a collection of scenarios.
- Create, then validate, an architecture that exploits the common patterns found in these scenarios.
- Evolve that architecture, making mid-course corrections as necessary to adapt to new requirements as they are uncovered.

I call these activities analysis, design, and evolution, the phases of an object-oriented life cycle. In a very real sense, an architecture-driven style of development represents the marriage of object-oriented technology and traditional software engineering. This life cycle is discussed in detail in the next three chapters.

As Figure 1-2 shows, architecture-driven approaches tend to yield structures that are similar to those of requirements-driven approaches (which is good) but that have a larger substrate (which is even better, because this is where the resiliency of these architectures becomes important).

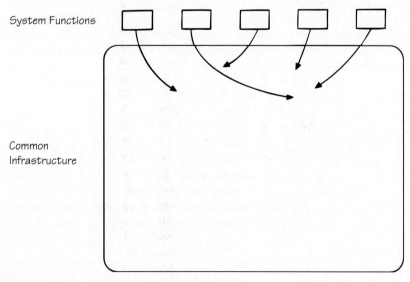

Figure 1-2   The Structure of Architecture-Driven Projects

As in a requirements-driven architecture, above the common infrastructure are parallel structures that align with each major system function, thus preserving the ability to trace from requirements to implementation. These elements serve as the "top" of an object-oriented architecture. However, unlike requirements-driven architectures, these parts are often very small, because they leverage off the facilities of a much richer substrate that serves to codify the common patterns found in the application's domain.[*] Many kinds of applications are better suited to this model than in requirements-driven projects, because each of the system's requirements can be satisfied by a much smaller component, and new or changed functionality can be introduced with minimal effort.

The most striking feature of the structure of an architecture-driven project is that its components tend to map to the abstractions we find in the real world, in a hierarchy that starts close to the implementation and rises to the vocabulary of the problem domain.

THE FIVE HABITS OF SUCCESSFUL OBJECT-ORIENTED PROJECTS

In a book about object-oriented stuff, this may sound a bit heretical, but it is true: the success of a project is orthogonal to its object-orientedness. I have seen many successful projects whose developers would not recognize a class or an object if it hit them in the face. I have also seen more than a few whopping failures among projects whose developers are so into this technology that they dream of object-oriented utopias in polymorphic Technicolor. Why bother with object-orientation then, you may ask? To answer that question, let me start with a definition of success:

> A successful software project is one whose deliverables satisfy and possibly exceed the end user's expectations, was developed in a timely and economical fashion, and is resilient to change and adaptation.[‡]

This is a technology-neutral definition: many paths can lead to project success. However, of the successful projects I come across, far more of them use

---

[*] Chapter 2 examines each of the elements of a canonical object-oriented architecture in greater detail.

[‡] For most commercial organizations, there is a simple but brutal slant on this definition: A successful project is one that makes lots of money.

object-oriented technology than do not. Furthermore, most of the failures I have seen and most of the dysfunctional projects in crisis that I have tried to rescue had not even a whit of object-orientation about them.

Now, this is a startling observation: in the business of writing complex software, you take whatever advantage you can, and if object-orientation works—and it does—then you grab it. However, just saying a project is object-oriented does not make it so, and thus we must consider the issue around which this whole book revolves:

> How does a project effectively apply object-oriented technology to achieve the benefits that lead to success?

There are several aspects to this question. First, what are the benefits that an object-orientation provides? Among the most successful projects that I encounter, there are at least four such benefits that I find:

- Better time to market
- Improved quality
- Greater resilience to change
- Increased degree of reuse

To a large extent, these benefits directly address different aspects of the essential minimal characteristics that every project must consider.

An entertainment company required a system to model sales at its theater concessions. Simple spreadsheet programs were insufficient to deal with the analysis and visualization of complex scenarios involving pricing strategies vis-a-vis different audiences, markets, and products. From conceptualization to initial delivery, the project took only six weeks. The project team attributed much of this success to the use of object-oriented technology.

A software company set out to develop a domain-specific class library, using object-oriented methods. Development took almost 18 months and generated around 50,000 lines of C++. Even after production use by several hundred customers, less than ten severe bugs were ever reported, and each of these required only about one person-day each to correct.

A securities trading firm located in Sydney selected Smalltalk as the basis of its software development. Given the almost rabid competition, the constantly shifting collection of securities they had to manage, and the globalization of their markets, they found it essential to develop a framework that could be used to rapidly lash together new applications, only to tear them down as changing market conditions warranted. Experienced with objects since 1989, the team matured to the point where their usual development life cycle could be measured on the order of about 6 hours. The half-life of the software—in a sense a measure of how often these applications were turned over—averaged about 2 months.

A systems integration company did a domain analysis of a spectrum of billing applications, and from this information, they developed a library of C++ and Smalltalk classes that modeled various common aspects of these applications. Using this library, they were then able to generate specialized billing applications without having to start from scratch each time.

Many more success stories exist that illustrate the benefits of an object-orientation. In the bibliography, I provide references to a number of such case studies.

Again, just saying that these benefits exist for some projects does not make it so for every project, which leads to a second question: what is it about an object-orientation that creates these benefits? Stated another way, how does an object-orientation mitigate the three primary reasons that projects fail?

Let me suggest a short answer to this question:

Why do certain object-oriented projects succeed? Most often, it is because:
- An object-oriented model of the problem and its solution encourages the creation of a common vocabulary between the end users of a system and its developers, thus creating a shared understanding of the problem being solved.
- The use of continuous integration creates opportunities to recognize risk early and make incremental corrections without destabilizing the entire development effort.
- An object-oriented architecture provides a clear separation of concerns among disparate elements of a system, creating firewalls that prevent a change in one part of the system from rending the fabric of the entire architecture.

There are many other aspects to this answer, such as issues of simplicity, localization of structure and behavior, and the expressiveness of inheritance among classes, but I will defer these topics to later chapters, since they pop up again when I talk about the object-oriented process.

Whenever I step in to an object-oriented project, it is not hard to quickly assess if the development team is on the right path, or if this is a project in crisis. Indeed, there are a number of practices that I find common among successful object-oriented projects. Perhaps just as important, the absence of these practices in a project is a good predictor of potential failure.

The five habits of a successful object-oriented project include:
- A ruthless focus on the development of a system that provides a well-understood collection of essential minimal characteristics.
- The existence of a culture that is centered on results, encourages communication, and yet is not afraid to fail.
- The effective use of object-oriented modeling.
- The existence of a strong architectural vision.
- The application of a well-managed iterative and incremental development life cycle.

At first glance, some of these habits seem to have nothing to do with objects; they are just sound practices that every project should follow. To some degree this is true: there is much common sense implied by these practices. However, in the presence of an object-orientation, there are some subtle yet important entanglements.

Earlier, I mention that the critical driver of every successful project is its focused ruthlessness. This is true no matter if the project is object-oriented or not. However, what an object-orientation brings to a project is the ability to better react to a changing understanding of the real problem, which becomes manifest in a different set of essential characteristics. A successful object-oriented project will generate solutions that are tunable—within reason—without requiring a significant amount of rework.

> The project was tasked with creating a new inventory control system, in itself not an activity requiring any rocket science. For a variety of social and technical reasons, the team decided to use object-oriented methods to drive the development process. Early successes by the team did not go unnoticed, so well into the development process, the customer added significant new requirements (but did not provide any new resources or schedule relief). Despite this change of focus mid-stream, the team was able to recover by adding a few new abstractions and assembling

them in clever ways within the existing framework. Much to the customer's surprise, the team completed the work ahead of schedule.

From this follows a simple recommendation:

P 6

> A successful object-oriented project must be both focused and ruthless, but it must also not be blind to opportunities for simplifying its problem by identifying general solutions that can be specialized to solve its particular problem.

This is precisely why an architecture-driven policy helps: it can lead to the creation of simple, general solutions that can be tuned to specific problems as needed.

Regarding culture, well, there are object-oriented cultures and then there are non-object-oriented ones. A quick study of a project's architecture will reveal the team's biases: a project lead by a relational database guru will often revolve around the database schema, a project lead by an application engineer will typically revolve around the various threads of the system's functions, a project lead by an object-oriented architect will typically revolve around a set of classes and mechanisms that model the problem domain. Frankly, none of these architectures are necessarily wrong: it all depends upon the context. A cultural issue that transcends context, however, is the team's focus on results, healthy communication, and an absence of fear of failure. The importance of the focus on results is fairly obvious. The need for effective communication comes as no surprise, either. Indeed, an object-orientation seems to facilitate communication in two ways. First, many of the objects found in a well-structured object-oriented application reflect an abstraction of the problem that is shared by both end users and developers. This benefit seems to derive from the very nature of classes and objects, which provide the unification of some piece of data together with the behavior associated with that data. Second, most object-oriented programming languages permit a clear separation of concerns between an abstraction's interface and its implementation, thus facilitating different yet integrated views of the same abstraction.

> Images from the Hubble Space Telescope encompass terabytes of data, and it is critical that astronomers accessing this data have a simple yet powerful means of finding and manipulating the information. The project tasked with building this system applied object-oriented methods and found that diagrams of class structures and object scenarios proved to be an excellent vehicle for the astronomers and developers to communicate about the expected behavior of the application.

A fear of failure typically results in two horrible outcomes: an overemphasis on analysis, and an underemphasis on experimentation. The reality, in all engineering disciplines, is that there is much to be learned from an examination of why something fails. Studying the circumstances under which a certain bridge collapsed advances the practice so that the next bridge will be better. Thus, a hard lesson to accept in crafting object-oriented software is this:

> There is no such thing as a perfect class or a perfect class structure.

But, that's OK. The successful development team seeks to build good (and occasionally profound) abstractions that are suitable to a given context.* If the use of a particular class or a whole collaboration of classes reveals that things are not right, this is a sign of a failure of the abstraction, and it represents a forcing function that drives the team to improve the abstraction.

This suggests the following practice:

> Crafting good abstractions is difficult, and furthermore, there is no such thing as a perfect abstraction. Successful projects realize this, and they are not afraid continually to improve their abstractions as they learn more about the problem they are trying to solve.

P 7

Let me be clear, however. I condemn the practice of unrestrained hacking and rabid prototyping; an absence of fear is not a license to blindly ravage a system all in the name of building the perfect abstraction.‡

The statement that the effective use of object-oriented modeling is a habit of successful object-oriented projects may at first seem redundant. However, the operative word here is "effective." An effective use of classes and objects is much more than just using the syntactic sugar of object-oriented programming languages.

> In one early object-oriented project at a telecommunications company, the developers were taught C++ largely by osmosis (to be exact, by handing them a book). Their efforts to use C++'s object-oriented features were noble but futile: a number of their classes consisted of exactly one member function, named with variations of the verb phrase "do it." This is a classic example of putting an object-oriented veneer over a functional decomposition.

---

* How individual developers achieve this is the topic of Chapter 4.

‡ Found written on yet another white board: *Give me Smalltalk, a laptop computer, and a place to stand, and I can move the world.*

I have more to say about effective modeling in subsequent chapters, but there is one practice that I find common among the more sophisticated and successful object-oriented projects:

P 8

> Remember that the class is a necessary but insufficient means of decomposition. For all but the most trivial systems, it is necessary to architect the system not in terms of individual classes, but in the form of clusters of classes.

Continuing, if I were to distill the lessons from this book into just one recommendation, it would be this:

P 9

> To be successful, an object-oriented project must craft an architecture that is both coherent and resilient and then must propagate and evolve the vision of this architecture to the entire development team.

This recommendation is largely a consequence of the benefits of an architecture-driven policy.

A system that has a sound architecture is one that has conceptual integrity. It is only through having a clear sense of a system's architecture that it becomes possible to discover common abstractions and mechanisms. Exploiting this commonalty ultimately leads to the construction of systems that are simpler, and therefore smaller and more reliable. Building a system in 10,000 human-generated source lines is far better than an equivalent system that takes 100,000 lines.[*]

> A large, international computer company, faced with rightsizing and the pressures of business process reengineering, sought to achieve some uniformity among its myriad information management systems by applying object-oriented technology. A key feature in this strategy was the creation of an architecture guide for the whole project, which served to capture the mind of the chief architect and communicate the basic structure and common patterns of collaboration found among these key abstractions.

Because the notion of an object-oriented architecture is so central to the success of a project, I discuss what constitutes a good object-oriented architecture in the next chapter.

Lastly, the successful object-oriented projects I have come across follow neither anarchic nor draconian development life cycles. Rather, I find that the process that leads to the successful construction of object-oriented architectures

---

[*] This is in fact a compelling reason for using object-oriented technology because it aids in developing concise systems.

tends to be both iterative and incremental.* Such a process is iterative in the sense that it involves the successive refinement of an object-oriented architecture, from which we apply the experience and results of each new release to the next iteration of analysis and design. The process is incremental in the sense that each pass through the analysis/design/evolution cycle leads a project to gradually refine its strategic and tactical decisions, ultimately converging upon a solution that meets the end user's real (and usually unstated) requirements, and yet is simple, reliable, and adaptable.

> During development of a modest size application involving only a few hundred classes, the development team crafting this particular class library found it necessary to tear apart and then reassemble the system's central class hierarchy some 5 times. Each time, the change could be made without seriously disrupting any clients of this hierarchy (because public interfaces were left largely unchanged), yet each change tended to make the resulting application smaller, not larger (because each time, new opportunities for exploiting the existence of common structure and common behavior were uncovered).

This suggests this chapter's final recommendation:

> To reconcile the need for creativity with the demand for rigor, a successful object-oriented project must apply an incremental and iterative process, which rapidly converges upon a solution that meets the system's essential minimal characteristics.

P 10

In short, an incremental and iterative process helps to reconcile the art and science of object-oriented software engineering.

ISSUES IN MANAGING OBJECT-ORIENTED PROJECTS

Let me say one last time: Just because a project is object-oriented does not guarantee its success.

> A market leader in EDA (electronic design automation) decided to further its ownership of that market by employing object-oriented technology. The expectation was that it would reduce its development and maintenance costs and create a suite of applica-

---

* Chapters 3 and 4 discuss this iterative and incremental life cycle in detail.

tions that could be more flexibly packaged to meet rapidly changing market tastes, thereby blowing away its competition.
Management really did do many things right. It trained or hired
some really excellent C++ programmers. It planned a strategic
architecture. It tried to use object-oriented stuff in all the right
ways. However, it failed. Ultimately, the project took far longer
than expected, resulting in a significant erosion of the company's
market share, which it only began to recover a few years later
after they managed to wrestle the project back on track. As in any
large failed project, the reasons for failure are usually complex,
and derive from an interaction of technical, economic, political,
and social problems. However, a post-mortem analysis of this
project suggested that a major cause of the failure was simply
that the team had lost control of the object-oriented architecture.

I am not relaying this horror story to scare you away from object-orientation.
As with any powerful, expressive technology, object-orientation brings significant opportunities to enhance the success of a project, and to enable its members to tackle more complex applications than they could otherwise (consider
building a single-family house: I would much rather use a power saw than a
hand saw to cut all the lumber). Of course, with power comes responsibility
(every year, a few people lose appendages to power saws, however, it is rather
unusual to accidentally cut off your finger with a hand saw). The difference,
especially with an object-orientation, is the effective use and active management of the technology.

Many elements of actively managing a software development project are a
careful application of common sense lessons that apply no matter what technology we are using.[*] However, as I have already shown, object-orientation
colors these lessons in different ways. Comparing projects that use structured
analysis techniques versus object-oriented techniques versus projects that have
no identifiable techniques, there are subtle and significant differences in the
products that are created and the processes that lead to these products. This is
the central theme of the next three chapters.

Similarly, there are differences in the make up of the development team that
a project would assign to projects using these different technologies. Chapter 5
addresses these issues, with a discussion of the roles, responsibilities, allocation, and education of the object-oriented project team.

Furthermore, the leverage points that project managers have to control their
projects is different with object-oriented technology. Chapter 6 addresses these
management issues by considering some recommended practices and rules of

---

[*] In particular, check out the section in Chapter 6 titled "Everything I Need to Know I'll Learn In
My Next Project."

thumb for costing, staffing, planning, scheduling, monitoring, measuring, testing, and documenting.

Finally, some special situations occur regularly in object-oriented projects, with each of these cases tending to modify the general object-oriented practices and rules. I examine these issues in Chapter 7.

Products and Process

Products and Process

Those of us who have been trained as architects have this desire perhaps at the very center of our lives: that one day, somewhere, somehow, we shall build one building which is wonderful, beautiful, breathtaking, a place where people can walk and dream for centuries.

CHRISTOPHER ALEXANDER

If I am building a new house, discussions with my architect are important to me because they help us to reach a shared vision of the product that meets my family's needs, within our budget and time constraints. Blueprints are important to both of us; they help us to communicate our intent more formally and precisely. Power tools and tape measures are needed by all the skilled carpenters, electricians, plumbers, and painters to carry out this plan. Visiting the site from time to time and having building inspectors study the work independently is essential to verify that what is being built conforms to my original intent as well as to standard practice. In the end, however, what's most important to me and my family is the finished house itself—everything else is secondary, an unavoidable step in the process that leads to that end product.

As the needs of my family change (perhaps I need to convert part of the basement to an office or a bedroom) and things wear out (I may need to refinish the kitchen, or repair a leaky faucet in the bathroom), the next most important product to me is some tangible or intangible remembrance of my home's underlying architecture. Is a particular wall load-bearing, or can I safely knock it out to expand a room? Where does the plumbing run, so that I can tap into it to add a new sink? What is the overall style that I am trying to present with this house, and does aluminum siding really go with a French country style house?

This development process is analogous with software. A successful software development organization never loses sight of its primary mission: to efficiently develop, deliver, and maintain software products that delight the end user and that satisfy all stated or imagined requirements. To be blunt, a piece of executable software that does something useful is the most important product of every healthy project. The activities of analysis, design, implementation, quality assurance, and documentation are important only insofar as they contribute to that goal. Everything else that goes on—all the meetings, the discussions at the white board, the programming, the writing, the testing—is entirely secondary.

Second in importance only to the delivered software itself, the most important product of the healthy project is some tangible or intangible remembrance of the software's architecture, which is essential for the continued evolution and maintenance of the system. As new requirements are discovered and lingering bugs stamped out, all changes must be accomplished in a manner that is harmonious with the original architecture. Otherwise, over time, the organization will be left with a shoddy, much-patched piece of software the original structure of which is so obscure that it is effectively unmaintainable. Brittle systems such as these are always a real burden to the organization that must preserve them, sometimes costing the organization more to keep alive than it would be to start over from scratch.

If a complete outsider paid a visit to your software development organization, what would he or she find? Would he or she come to the conclusion that the primary activity of your developers was to sit in meetings and talk? Would this visitor think that paper was your most important product? Would he or she leave without ever talking to a programmer, because the programmers were only visible from their back side, hunched over a hot workstation, never coming up for air, and definitely never talking to anyone other than another programmer? In the healthy project, none of these things can be found.

To the technologist, industrial-strength software development would seem much more tractable if everything were just a simple matter of programming. Unfortunately, it is not so. Requirements are rarely if ever complete, correct, unambiguous, and never changing. Business rules fluctuate. Technology changes. Developers come and go. For this reason, every non-trivial project, and especially those that seek to build lasting artifacts, must create a set of intermediate products that facilitate this end goal, namely, the delivery of a quality software system. Furthermore, every organization that wants to deploy and support software on a reoccurring basis must have in place a process that is sufficiently well-defined, so that even as new and more complex applications are tackled, the project team can continue to improve its software development process, making it continually more efficient and more responsive to the ever-changing needs of the business.

In this chapter, we consider the products and process of the successful object-oriented project.

IN SEARCH OF EXCELLENT OBJECTS

If the delivery of a quality software system is in fact the aspiration of every healthy project, we must ask the simple question, what makes for a quality piece of software? Not surprisingly, the answer we find depends upon who is doing the asking.

From the perspective of the individual object-oriented programmer, there is first a brutally objective answer to this question: a quality piece of software is one that works and that does what it is expected to do, nothing more and nothing less. From the perspective of the end users and the development team as a whole, there is next an equally brutal subjective answer: a quality piece of software is elegant.

Elegance is that elusive quality of coolness that every programmer admires and strives for, yet cannot name. Elegant software is simple. Elegant software is clever, yet not obscure. Elegant software solves complex problems through wonderfully inventive mechanisms that are semantically rich enough to be applied to other, perhaps totally unrelated problems. Elegance means finding just the right abstraction. Elegance means using limited resources in novel ways.

A transportation company, faced with the problem of routing hundreds of thousands of packages through its network of ships, planes, trains, and trucks, crafted an object-oriented system to manage global day-to-day operations. An object model proved to be an excellent match for this problem: both the network and the physical packages being transported across this network were all obviously objectifiable things. With this architecture in place, it was possible to incrementally add some rather exotic approaches to calculating least-cost and least-time paths for individual packages, both intractable problems, given the volume of shipments per day. Using genetic algorithms running on a separate supercomputer, software agents constantly surveyed the global network and offered advice to operational personnel. As it turned out, these basic algorithms could be used to discover optimal routes for local pick up and delivery, as well as the packing of containers aboard transport vehicles.

This example addresses the importance of an object-oriented architecture. Let me discuss the meaning of architecture, starting from simple things (classes) up to more macro things (frameworks).

For the individual object-oriented programmer, the primary unit of decomposition is the class. This is in stark contrast to the non-object-oriented programmer, for whom the algorithm is the primary unit of decomposition. As I discuss further in Chapter 4, this difference greatly affects how the individual programmer views the world, and how he or she goes about the daily business of writing software. For now, it is worth stating this as a practice of all healthy object-oriented projects:

For the object-oriented project, remember that the primary unit of decomposition is the class, not the algorithm.

P 11

Of course, as I discuss in the previous chapter, this is only a starting point: classes are a necessary but insufficient element of decomposition. Nonetheless, with the class as the focus of the individual developer, then it is reasonable to expect that quality object-oriented software comes in part from building quality classes.

A well-designed class:
- Provides a crisp abstraction of some thing drawn from the vocabulary of the problem domain or the solution domain.
- Embodies a small, well-defined set of responsibilities, and carries them all out very well.
- Provides a clear separation of the abstraction's behavior and its implementation.
- Is understandable and simple yet extensible and adaptable.

A class denotes set of objects that share a common structure and a common behavior. Thus, in a quality object-oriented software system, you will find many classes that speak the language of the domain expert. In a billing system, one would find classes representing customers, suppliers, bills, and products. In a health care system, one would find classes representing patients, providers, and services. In both of these examples, as we turn to the implementation, we will find classes that speak the language of the programmer: for example, we might find classes representing transactions, lists (of products or services), and tables (of suppliers and providers). In other words:

> Every class in an object-oriented system should map to some tangible or conceptual abstraction in the domain of the end user or the implementer. Actively challenge all classes that fail this test.

P 12

When I speak of building "crisp" abstractions, I mean that each class must have well-defined boundaries. A class representing all expensive providers in a health care system is probably not a good abstraction, because the meaning of "expensive" is fuzzy and subjective. Separate classes representing all full-care providers and all limited-care providers are probably much better representations that speak to the system's users.

Another major element of crispness relates to the structure and the behavior embodied by a class. For example, a class representing customers in a billing system will encompass attributes such as the customer's name, address, and phone numbers. Directly including a list of employees as a customer attribute is probably wrong for this application because it is certainly not part of the vocabulary of the billing domain. Similarly, the behavior associated with this class might include the ability to ask a customer for its payment history and credit rating, information which must be calculated rather than just simply retrieved. However, asking a customer for the names of his or her children is entirely irrelevant to this domain, and so should not be part of the abstraction.

How then do we know when we have a quality class? The answer is wrapped up in a measure of the abstraction's responsibilities. Simply stated, a responsibility is some behavior for which an object is held accountable. In other words, a responsibility denotes the obligation of an object to provide a certain behavior. Since every object is an instance of some class, this means that each class must embody all the responsibilities of all of its instances.

The distribution of responsibilities in an object-oriented system is a critical decision. It is wrong to have too few classes causing each to do too much, just as it is equally wrong to have too many classes where each does too little. This suggests another rule of thumb:

R 5

Every class should embody only about 3-5 distinct responsibilities.

Of course, this is just a general rule. Some classes (such as a window class in a graphical user interface framework) are so fundamental that they must embrace many more responsibilities. A few classes (such as classes representing physical valves and gauges in a factory automation system) may embody only one or two responsibilities. The important philosophy behind this rule is that for the sake of understandability and resilience, most of the classes in a quality object-oriented systems will generally embody only a handful of responsibilities. Classes that have significantly more or less than the average are not necessarily wrong, but they are certainly suspect of being under- or over-abstracted.

Do not confuse the responsibilities of a class with its operations, however. A responsibility represents a general obligation of behavior, and each responsibility might be carried out by a set of cooperating operations. For example, in a billing system, our abstraction of a customer might embody just three primary responsibilities: managing contact information (including the company's name, address and phone numbers), managing credit information (including payment history and credit rating) and tracking associations with all current and past orders. For each of these responsibilities, we probably have a handful of concrete operations that clients can perform upon instances of each class. Thus managing credit information probably requires several distinct operations for updating lines of credit, registering payments, and calculating payment history.

From the point of view of the individual object-oriented programmer, each quality class must also have a clear separation between the abstraction's behavior and its implementation. For example, exposing the binding of a customer class to its underlying representation in a particular relational database is wrong because it requires clients of this class to understand database details that they really need not know, and furthermore it makes it difficult to change the implementation of the class without violating low-level assumptions that clients may have already made because the bones of the implementation poked through the interface of the abstraction.

If we have done a good job in distributing responsibilities throughout a system, a quality class will also be understandable and simple. By building primitive classes that have crisp boundaries and yet expose operations that allow the structure and behavior of that class to be tuned by other classes, we end up with extensible and adaptable classes as well.

As I suggest in the previous chapter, developing a single class in isolation is difficult. Crafting a quality object-oriented system goes far beyond crafting individual high-quality classes. The reason for this is very simple: in a complex system, no class stands alone; rather, classes collaborate with one another to carry out the desired behavior of the system. Therefore, from the perspective of the software architect, building quality systems requires the consideration of software structures that transcend the individual class.

Indeed, rarely does a class carry out its responsibilities in isolation. For example, managing a customer's credit information requires that a customer object collaborate with payment objects, whose classes are responsible for managing the details of payment history. By delegating responsibilities across peer classes in this manner, the developer ends up with individual classes that are relatively simple, although not too simple. Similarly, a developer can achieve elegance and simplicity by delegating responsibilities up and down a hierarchy of classes. For example, in a billing system, we might find a hierarchy of customer classes, rooted with a general customer class that carries out the responsibilities we describe above, followed by concrete subclasses, such as commercial customers, government customers, and international customers. In this example, each class specializes these general responsibilities and perhaps provides a few new ones of its own.

> MacApp is perhaps the quintessential example of a quality object-oriented framework. First available in early 1985 in the language Object Pascal, MacApp represented one of the first commercially available object-oriented application frameworks. Its domain was quite general, intended to aid the creation of all applications that conformed to the Macintosh look and feel. Not surprisingly, early versions of this library were quite unapproachable, largely because the whole library was presented as a vast sea of classes, whose collaborations had to be discovered by each hearty developer that dared journey through this unchartered territory. Furthermore, responsibilities for system behavior were not crisply distributed through the library, making it difficult to adapt individual classes. After considerable real use, the library was altered radically in the late 1980s: classes were changed, hierarchies altered, responsibilities redistributed. Around 1990, the library was entirely rewritten in C++, and further changes were made to the class structure. A relatively stable version was finally release in 1992. By this time, the library was much more approachable, understandable, and adaptable. No

longer presented as just a sea of classes, the library's architecture was made explicit, and key collaborations were well-documented.

As I discuss in more detail later in this chapter, building quality systems such as MacApp requires an incremental and iterative process. With the distribution of responsibilities as a focus of the architect, then, it is reasonable to expect that quality object-oriented software comes in part from building quality collaborations of classes.

> A well-designed collaboration:
> - Involves the contribution of a small set of classes that work together to carry out some behavior.
> - Provides a behavior that is not the responsibility of any one abstraction, but rather derives from the distributed responsibilities of the community.

All well-designed object-oriented systems embody a collection of quality collaborations. For example:

In the Smalltalk class library, MVC (model-view-controller) is perhaps the most important collaboration. This mechanism is quite pervasive, and it is, in fact, central to the architecture of almost every well-structured Smalltalk program. In this collaboration, we have three abstractions: a model class, generally representing elements in the problem's data modeling domain, a view class, responsible for rendering these elements textually or graphically, and a controller class, acting as a mediator between the model and its views and responsible for coordinating updates to both. The presence of the MVC collaboration is an important unifying factor in the architecture of the Smalltalk library.

As I discuss in the next chapter, crafting the important collaborations in a software system is a central activity of the architect during design. These collaborations represent the soul of the architecture, because they are strategic decisions that anchor the basic shape of the software.

This discussion suggests another practice of all successful object-oriented projects:

Distribute the behavior in an object-oriented system in two ways: up and down class hierarchies, representing the generalization/specialization of responsibilities. and across peer classes that collaborate with one another.

These two dimensions—class hierarchies and peer collaborations—represent the basic elements of every well-structured object-oriented architecture.

Thus, let me return to my initial question: what makes for a quality piece of software? Ultimately, there are two answers. Local quality comes from the crafting of quality classes; global quality comes from crafting quality architectures.

OBJECT-ORIENTED ARCHITECTURES

I have continued to emphasize the importance of architecture in crafting quality object-oriented systems. What exactly is the nature of the well-structured object-oriented architecture?

> A well-structured object-oriented architecture consists of:
> - A set of classes, typically organized into multiple hierarchies.
> - A set of collaborations that specify how those classes cooperate to provide various system functions.

For example:

> A company responsible for processing credit card transactions defined an object-oriented architecture for its family of applications. This system included a set of classes defining a domain model of all the things relevant to the domain, such as accounts, institutions (responsible for issuing accounts and qualifying transactions against them), and purchases (representing debits against an account). Along with these hierarchies, the architecture provided well-defined patterns of collaboration among these classes, including mechanisms for verifying an account, approving a transaction, routing a transaction to an institution, and dealing with exceptional conditions.

Every well-structured object-oriented architecture must consider both of these dimensions.* This leads to the following recommendation:

---

* There are other dimensions to every non-trivial software system, but these two are perhaps the most important. For a more complete discussion on all the views of software architecture, see Kruchten, P. *Software Architecture and Iterative Development*. Santa Clara, California: Rational Software Corporation, 1995.

P 14

Craft architectures so that they encompass all the abstractions relevant to the given domain together with all the mechanisms that animate these abstractions within that domain.

The first dimension of an object-oriented architecture—a set of classes organized into multiple hierarchies—serves to capture the static model of the abstractions that form the vocabulary of the domain. I speak of this as a vocabulary because each abstraction represents something in the language of an end user or an implementer. For example, in the credit card processing example above, we find several nearly independent hierarchies relevant to domain experts, including classes representing accounts, institutions, and purchases. Each of these represents a hierarchy, not just a single class. For example, there exist corporate accounts, individual accounts, and joint accounts, as well as accounts whose balance may be carried over (with interest) every month and accounts that must be paid off every month. Modeling these different kinds of accounts as one class is wrong because this offers a poor distribution of responsibilities. A better approach is to define a hierarchy of accounts, starting at the most general kind of account and then providing more specialized kinds of accounts through subclassing.

I emphasize the use of multiple hierarchies because of the following rule of thumb:

R 6

A single class hierarchy is suitable for only the most simple application; every other system should in general have exactly one hierarchy of classes for every fundamental abstraction in the model.

Ultimately, using independent hierarchies for semantically distant abstractions provides a better distribution of responsibilities in the system.

Each independent hierarchy, together with all its close supporting classes, represents a natural grouping of abstractions in the decomposition of a system. I call such groupings *class categories* because they denote architectural elements that are bigger than a class or even a hierarchy of classes.* Indeed, as I mentioned in the previous chapter, the class is a necessary but insufficient means of decomposition: it is the class category that provides this larger unit of decomposition. Within each cluster there will be classes that are semantically close (such as corporate accounts and individual accounts). Between these clusters there will be classes that are semantically more distant (such as accounts versus institutions versus transactions). In general, class hierarchies rarely cross class category boundaries.

---

* I have borrowed this concept from Smalltalk, although Smalltalk itself provides only minimal enforceable semantics for class categories. In C++, namespace semantics provide the equivalent of class categories.

This leads to the following recommended practice and its associated rules of thumb:

> For the larger object-oriented project, remember that the primary unit of decomposition is the class category, not the individual class.

P 15

> If your system has only a few classes, then class categories are generally architectural overkill. If, however, your system has more than about 50 to 100 classes, to manage the growing complexity, you must decompose your system in terms of class categories, not just individual classes.

R 7

> The typical class category will consist of a dozen or so classes.

R 8

This first dimension is important in architecting an object-oriented system, but it is also insufficient because it reflects only the static elements of a system. The second dimension of an object-oriented architecture—a well-defined set of collaborations—serves to capture the dynamic model.

Each collaboration represents some behavior that arises from a set of distinct yet cooperative objects, often cutting across class category boundaries. For example, consider how information about accounts, institutions, and purchases is made persistent.[*] Clearly, it is in our best interests to devise a consistent approach: the persistence of all these kinds of objects should use the same mechanism, and this mechanism should be hidden from clients that want to use these objects. A reasonable solution to this problem is to define a set of classes that provide a lower-level form of persistence for atomic values and then to have each persistent class use this mechanism to stream out values (for storage) or stream in values (for reconstructing the object from its persistent store). We would expect that such a mechanism would also be responsible for handling the caching of objects and resolving references or pointers, which cannot be stored directly. This mechanism fits the definition of a collaboration: there is no one class that provides this behavior, but rather, persistence in the system derives from the collaborative activity of several classes working together.

This suggests the following practice and a corresponding rule:

> Remember that a class rarely stands alone. Thus, especially when considering the dynamics of a system, concentrate on how certain groups of objects collaborate so that common behavior is handled through common mechanisms.

P 16

---

[*] By *persistent*, I mean that its value persists for an indefinite time. Relational databases and object-oriented databases are typically the machinery behind persistence mechanisms in object-oriented systems.

Most object-oriented systems require less than 10 to 20 central mechanisms.

R 9

A central mechanism is one that has sweeping architectural implications, and thus represents a strategic decision. For a large class of systems, there is a set of common mechanisms that every architect must consider.

Many object-oriented systems must include central mechanisms for:
- Persistence
- Storage management
- Process management
- Messaging
- Object distribution and object migration
- Networking
- Transactions
- Events
- Exceptional conditions
- Common look and feel

This list is not exhaustive, but it does represent the most common kinds of mechanisms that are found in many different systems. For each of these issues, there is generally a range of possible solutions, and the task of the software development team is to decide upon and then carry out a single approach to each, suitable to all the non-technical requirements of the system including performance, capacity, reliability, and security. For example:

A transportation company, building a distributed system to track shipments, required access to information from several hundred cities scattered around the world. A shipment might be initiated in one city (for example, Hong Kong) and concluded in another (for example, Chicago) with several intermediate stops in-between to change carriers. Not surprisingly, a study of data traffic in the existing system showed that most accesses to shipping information happened from the shipment's current local city or next destination. Thus, as a shipment moved around the globe, its focus of access would follow. To accommodate this pattern and to ultimately balance the load on the global network, the system's architects devised a mechanism for object migration: objects (representing shipments) would literally move about the network, invisible to each application, and would migrate along with the physical shipment. This mechanism consisted of a set of classes that extended the behavior of yet a lower-level mechanism for messaging.

Selecting an approach to object migration is indeed a strategic decision, because it has implications for the very backbone of the architecture. However, not every decision the development team makes is strategic. Some decisions are much more tactical and therefore local in nature. For example, the exact protocol every client uses to force the migration of a shipment object is a tactical decision, made in the context of the more strategic one. However, it is often said that the devil is in the details, and carrying out all the tactical decisions of a system in a consistent manner is just as important as making all the right strategic ones.

> A particular software company devised a tool for program development whose architecture was beautifully simple. However, investigation of the code for individual classes revealed that the implementation of this architecture was very messy, and reflected the inconsistent coding styles of different programmers. For example, some programmers used C++ exceptions to denote exceptional conditions, whereas others used the C idiom of returning an integer value. Even worse, some classes were well-encapsulated and thus exported no public member objects (instance variables), whereas others broke all the rules of information hiding by making all of an object's state public. Mainly because of the small size and the close coupling of the original team, the project managed to meet its early schedules. However, once the team grew, new developers extending the system found it to be very fragile and difficult to build upon. Ultimately, the project took a schedule hit of several months while the team rewrote many details of the system so that they would reflect a consistent style.

This story, and many others like it, suggests the following recommendation:

P 17

> The architecture of a well-structured, object-oriented system denotes its logical and physical structure, forged by all the strategic and tactical decisions applied during development. Be certain to make all strategic decisions explicitly with consideration for the tradeoffs of each alternative. Similarly, do not neglect the myriad of tactical decision that must be made: establish tactical policies for the project, and put controls in place so that these policies are followed consistently.

There is also a related and equally important recommendation:

P 18

> Seek to build simple architectures, wherein common behavior is achieved through common mechanisms.

The key point here is that all well-structured object-oriented systems are full of patterns, ranging from patterns such as mechanisms for object migration that shape the system as a whole to more local patterns such as idioms for handling exceptional conditions that reflect more tactical concerns. The most successful projects make the selection of these patterns an explicit part of the development process.

> A pattern is a common solution to a problem in a given context; a pattern also serves to capture its author's intent and vision. A well-structured object-oriented architecture typically encompasses a range of patterns, from idioms to mechanisms to frameworks.

Each pattern that forms an object-oriented system represents a part of the overall architecture. For this reason, patterns are often called a system's microarchitecture.

As I suggest above, there is a spectrum of patterns that every development team must consider. At the bottom of the food chain, closest to the code, there are idioms. An idiom is an expression peculiar to a certain programming language or application culture, representing a generally accepted convention for use of the language. Idioms represent reuse in the small.

The C++ culture in particular is full of idioms, some of which grew out of the C culture, and some of which are new to C++. For example, returning an integer value to indicate the success or failure of some function is a common C idiom, sometimes adopted in C++ as an alternative to exceptions. The importance of this idiom is that it represents a commonly accepted style, such that any developer who sees this style immediately knows its conventions (for example, the convention that any positive value denotes success). Violate an idiom and you will be treated like an outsider whose code may be perfectly legal, but incomprehensible to those who are inside the culture.

In all fairness, every programming language has its own set of idioms, and part of the effort of learning a new language is learning its idioms along with its syntax and semantics. Similarly, every development team has its own idioms, specific to that team's experience and culture, and preserving these idioms across the team's products is equally important in maintaining some degree of local consistency. This suggests the following practice:

P 19

> Early in the development process, agree upon a set of idioms that your team will use to write its code. Document these decisions in the form of

a style guide, and enforce these idioms through the use of tools (which unequivocally demand conformance) and through walkthroughs (which achieve convergence through peer pressure and mentoring).

I have more to say about documentation in Chapter 6, but one lesson is important to state here: have your project's style guide written by a few of your best developers, and not by those people who just happen to have the free time to do it. To do otherwise usually results in a style guide that is overly detailed and not grounded in the pragmatic idioms of that language.

The typical developer will only be able to absorb a few dozen new idioms, and thus the best style guides are simple, averaging about 30 pages, and serve to document idioms important to the project.

R 10

If your project's style guide is too large, developers will get lost in its details, no one will bother reading it completely, and ultimately, it will fall into disuse.

Many developers learn idioms best by sharing examples, and so it is useful to back up your project's style guide with a set of examples which individual developers can study and plagiarize. In this manner, you can achieve some degree of conceptual integrity in the details of your project's implementation.

Next up the food chain of patterns are mechanisms, which build upon idioms. A *mechanism* is a structure whereby objects collaborate to provide some behavior that satisfies a requirement of the problem; a mechanism is thus a design decision about how certain collections of objects cooperate. As I describe earlier, mechanisms are important because they are strategic decisions that anchor the basic shape of the software system.

The ten mechanisms I mention earlier are ones that I come across in a wide variety of application domains. For each one of these problem areas, there are a variety of solutions, and it is the role of the development team to choose one. As I discuss in the next chapter, choosing and validating these mechanisms are an important part of the design phase.

Some mechanisms are heavyweight, such as patterns for persistence or for object migration, because they involve the participation of a large set of objects or involve a significant amount of behavior. Other mechanisms, although they are more lightweight, are equally important in crafting successful object-oriented systems. For example, consider the problem of creating new instances of shipment objects in the problem above. A different kind of shipment object may be created in a given scenario depending upon the current state of the system. I might create a normal shipment object in one case, and a shipment object for hazardous materials in another, with each of these objects as an instance of some class in a hierarchy of shipment classes. This problem is actually a specific instance of a more general problem, namely, defining a factory object that creates a particular instance from some class hierarchy, depending upon certain external conditions. Since our system might have many such hierarchies, the same problem crops throughout, and so it is wise to define a common factory object mechanism.[*]

The architecture for even the most complex systems can be made simpler by codifying common behavior through common mechanisms. This suggests the following practice and its associated rule of thumb:

P 20

During architectural design, agree upon a set of mechanisms responsible for providing the system's central behavior that results from collaborations of objects. Validate these mechanisms with prototypes, document these decisions in the form of an architecture document, and enforce these mechanisms through the use of tools and walkthroughs.

R 11

The best architecture documents are simple, averaging far less than 100 pages, and they serve to document the key class structures and mechanisms important to the project.

As I discuss further in Chapter 6, an architecture document is a living document and is evolved during the development effort.

At the top of the hierarchy of patterns are frameworks, which build upon idioms and mechanisms. A framework represents a collection of classes that provide a set of services for a particular domain; a framework exports a number of individual classes and mechanisms which clients can use or adapt. Frameworks are thus a kind of pattern that provides reuse in the large.

Frameworks are usually specific to the major functional parts of a system or to entire vertical application domains. For example, a graphical application might use an off-the-shelf framework for a particular windowing system, or a framework for process synchronization across processors. All such frameworks typically consist of a set of classes and mechanisms specific to those classes. Similarly, an organization might forge a framework specific to its own line of business. For example, a trading company might take an off-the-shelf framework for securities trading and then adapt it to its specific business rules.

By using mature frameworks, the effort of the development team is made even easier, because now major functional elements can be reused. Equally important, mature frameworks have sufficient knobs, slots, and tabs, so to speak, so that they can be integrated with other frameworks and adapted as necessary to the current problem. The existence of these knobs, slots, and tabs largely derives from the ability to subclass from the hierarchies of classes in the framework, and then override existing behavior or add new behavior.

P 21

Where possible, employ existing mature frameworks in your system. If such frameworks do not exist, and if you expect to build a family of programs for your domain, consider creating your own framework.

---

[*] Gamma *et al.* provides the codification of around two dozen such patterns.

But beware: building good frameworks is hard.

> A framework does not even begin to reach maturity until it has been applied in at least three or more distinct applications.

R 12

By viewing architectures in terms of the patterns that they embody, there emerges a remarkable similarity among many well structured object-oriented systems. In Figure 2-1, I expand upon the diagram in Chapter 1 to reveal the functional parts of many such systems.[*] Each of these parts represents some framework, consisting of a set of classes and associated mechanisms.

A canonical object-oriented architecture typically includes the following elements:
- Base operating system
- Networking
- Persistent object store
- Distributed object management
- Domain-independent framework
- Application environment
- GUI desktop environment
- Domain model
- Domain-specific framework

At the bottom of this infrastructure, we find common platform services:

- Base operating system
- Networking

These two layers serve to insulate the rest of the application from the details of its hardware. For some applications, the base operating system may be a large component that provides many common services (such as with Windows 95 or UNIX), but in others, it may be very small (such as in embedded controllers), providing only simple programmatic interfaces to external devices. Similarly, the networking element of this substrate furnishes all the primitive communication abstractions required by the application. This may be a major functional component in certain domains (such as in an electronic funds transfer system), but non-existent in others (such as in a stand-alone computer game).

---

[*] This division of components was inspired by the work of Foley, M. and Cortese, A. January 17, 1994. "OS Vendors Pick Object Standards," *PC Week*, p. 43.

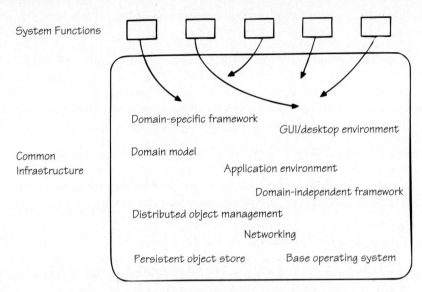

Figure 2-1   A Well-Structured Object-Oriented Architecture

Built on top of these facilities, we find the resources that manage object storage and distribution, which collectively define the application's plumbing:

- Persistent object store
- Distributed object management

In traditional terms, the persistent object store constitutes an application's database, although to some degree an object store is at a slightly higher level of abstraction than a simple relational database, because an object store embodies the storage properties of a database together with some of the common behavior that characterizes these objects. Distributed object management builds upon these services and lower ones in the substrate to provide abstractions for the administration of distributed as well as mobile data in a networked environment. For example, consider a chemical engineering application that encompasses a web of computers scattered about the manufacturing floor. Some of this application's data, such as information about the inventory of various chemicals used in the process and recipes for various substances to be produced, may live on a specific node that acts as a central server for the system. Other kinds of data, such as the records about a particular production run, may be physically scattered across the network, yet appear as a logical whole to higher layers of the application.

Ultimately, the value of these two layers is that they provide the illusion to applications that objects live permanently in a large, virtual address space. In reality, an object lives on a particular processor and may or may not be truly persistent. By granting this illusion, the applications at the top of a system are ultimately much simpler, especially in geographically distributed situations.

At the next highest level in the infrastructure, we find frameworks that cover domain-independent abstractions (such as various collection classes), application objects (which handle common client services such as printing and clipboard management on workstations), and the GUI facilities (which provide the primitive abstractions for building user interfaces):

- Domain-independent framework
- Application environment
- GUI/desktop environment

Just above this level of abstraction, we find all the common abstractions that are peculiar to our given domain. Typically, these abstractions are packaged in two components:

- Domain model
- Domain-dependent framework

The domain model serves to capture all the classes of objects that form the vocabulary for our problem domain. For mission-critical management information systems, for example, this might include our specific abstractions of things such as customers, orders, and products, together with the business rules that apply to these things. For technical applications such as telephone switching systems, this might include things such as lines, terminals, conversations, and features, together with a specification of their behavior.

The domain-dependent framework provides all the common collaborations of these things that are specific to our domain. For example, in certain management information systems, this framework might include classes that collaborate to carry out transactions; for switching systems, this framework might provide classes that define common features such as plain old telephone service (POTS) as well as more advanced features such as call waiting, call conferencing, and caller ID.

In Chapter 7, I discuss how this canonical architecture adapts to certain kinds of applications, such as real-time systems and data-centric applications. Still, no matter what the application, it is essential to preserve the architectural integrity of a system. How this is done is one of the topics of Chapter 3.

A well-structured architecture:
- Is constructed in layers of abstraction.
- Has a clear separation of concerns among these layers.
- Is simple.

As Figure 2-1 suggests, all well-structured object-oriented architectures have clearly-defined layers, with each layer providing some coherent set of services through a well-defined and controlled interface. Each layer builds upon equally well-defined and controlled facilities at lower levels of abstraction. Such architectures are ultimately simple, because they reuse patterns at various levels in the system, from idioms to mechanisms to frameworks.

THE ARTIFACTS OF A SOFTWARE PROJECT

During the construction of a house, many artifacts beyond the physical house itself must be created, either as byproducts of the construction process or as aids to construction. For example, the builder and the owner will sign a contract that specifies what is to be built. For some houses, a scale model may be developed. General blueprints will be drawn showing the layout of the house, and some detailed blueprints may be drawn for the house's electrical and plumbing services. Construction workers may erect scaffolding, only to dismantle it when their work is done. Photos or sketches of features from existing homes may be used as a guide to the individual craftsmen. At the end of construction, the owner may be left only with the house itself, a set of keys, some general blueprints, and maintenance and warranty information.

The process of developing software is similar. A successful software development organization will generate just the right amount of artifacts beyond the application itself, either as byproducts of the development process or as aids to development. Too many prototypes, test scaffolding, or documentation, and the team will have wasted precious resources. Too few prototypes, test scaffolding, or documentation, and the team runs the risk of building the wrong thing or being blindsided by technology.

> The reusable artifacts of every software project include:[*]
> - Architecture
> - Design
> - Code
> - Requirements
> - Data
> - Human interfaces
> - Estimates
> - Project plans
> - Test plans
> - Documentation

---

[*] Jones, *Analysis and Control of Software Risks.*

In the next two chapters, I will explain the process by which these artifacts are created.

Jones refers to these artifacts as *reusable* in the sense that are important beyond the lifetime of the individual project that created them. Code may be lifted from one project and reused in another. The look and feel defined by the human interface of one application may be applied in a different program. Frameworks may be architecture to serve as the foundation for an entire family of programs.

Every legitimate product generated by a software development team must ultimately exist to satisfy some clear purpose for a specific audience. In fact, I find that each of these ten artifacts can be grouped according to the three primary clients that they serve: the development team itself, end users, and the management team.

For the most part, the artifacts of interest to the development team encompass the project's architecture, its tactical design, and its code. As I discuss in the previous section, the project's architecture is this group's most important artifact, because it defines the very shape of the system and endures long after an application has been delivered. Depending upon the formality of the project, this artifact manifests itself in intangible as well as very tangible ways. Intangibly, an architecture simply exists in the structure of the software itself as well as in the minds of its architects. More tangibly, an architecture may be captured in the form of an architectural prototype or in a document that describes the system's key hierarchies together with its most important mechanisms.

> An organization developed an object-oriented framework for securities trading applications. Because it expected this framework to be adapted to many different organizations around the world, the team documented the system's key class hierarchies and its strategic mechanisms, and then delivered these online in a model that could be interactively browsed and queried. This approach made it easier for clients to explore the underlying architecture in unstructured ways.

Design artifacts typically encompass more tactical things, such as the design of individual classes or categories of classes, or the design of major subsystem interfaces. Intangibly, design artifacts are found in the idioms and some of the mechanisms used by a project. More tangibly, tactical design decisions may be documented in high-level style guides, interface control documents, or in the same kind of document as the system's entire architecture (but with a more limited scope).

> This project, which focused on delivering a front-end programming tool, anchored its development by writing and then evolv-

ing an architecture document. Individual developers were assigned responsibility for certain class categories. As they further refined their part of the system, each would write another small document that captured the architecture of that class category. This strategy proved to be useful because it forced individual developers to build a framework understandable to the clients of that class category. Additionally, by imposing this policy across the system, it exposed common mechanisms that could be exploited in other categories, ultimately simplifying the entire system.

Code artifacts ultimately represent the most tangible products of the development team, for they represent the raw output of the programmer's labor. At the very least, in an object-oriented system, these artifacts are manifest in the interfaces and implementation of individual classes, collectively forming a class library. In more formal projects, these artifacts may be documented by explaining the semantics of each important operation or attribute in all the interesting classes.

This project was tasked with developing a cross-platform class library, consisting of several hundred classes. Along with an architecture document, the development team provided online help, consisting of the "one manual page per class" style, wherein each class was documented with a synopsis of its interface, a description of its general semantics, a description of the semantics of each public operation, cross references to other related classes, and references to examples using that particular class.

The artifacts of interest to the end user encompass the project's requirements, its data, and its human interfaces. Ultimately, an end user's most important artifact beyond the delivered software system itself is the project's requirements, for a number of reasons:

- Requirements bind the scope of the solution.
- Requirements force end users and the development team to communicate about the implications of user's expectations.
- Requirements, together with an appropriate risk assessment, provide the basis for all project planning.
- Requirements form the foundation of most testing activities.

Intangibly, requirements exist in the minds of end users. Where possible, these requirements should be captured in a very tangible yet living document. Indeed, the very purpose of requirements analysis is to extract as many as possible of these unstated requirements from the minds of users and make them explicit. Unfortunately, as I have already mentioned, this is never a perfect process and so, except for the most simple of systems, we must expect that a system's requirements are never complete, may be incorrect, are likely to be ambiguous, and are certainly open to change. For this reason, it is essential that a project's requirements never be treated as something that is decided upon once at the beginning of a project and from that point is a closed topic. Rather, a project's requirements should indeed represent a living statement, always open to clarification and negotiation, with the decision process being driven by business decisions. Thus, it is the task of the software project manger to make progress despite these uncertainties. What tangible form should requirements take? From my experience, I favor scenario-based requirements, backed up by prototypes that provide operational models of the system's desired behavior.

> Initiated because of a corporate-wide business process reengineering activity, one company's development organization was tasked with updating its entire suite of software, with the requirement that older applications would continue to be supported until a relatively painless transition to the new applications was possible. The team bound the expectations of its many end users by first conducting a series of interviews with various groups of users, and then by documenting their requirements in a series of business scenarios that collectively described the behavior of each of the new applications. This collection of scenarios was formally reviewed, yet was evolved as users were exposed to prototypes and early releases that caused them to clarify their earlier requirements and exposed previously-unstated expectations.

Data artifacts encompass the raw information that may be used within or across applications. Too often, as an organization expands and the reach of its software grows, data becomes fragmented across applications and redundancies crop up. This is especially true if an organization's data artifacts are not described tangibly, but rather are retained as second-class citizens of each application project. By tangibly documenting critical data artifacts, it is possible to exploit patterns of use across applications.

> A telephone company pulled off a software coup by offering the first marketing program that gave discounts to members for calling certain other family members and friends. This was a true win-win situation: members received real discounts for calling people they would call regularly anyway, and the telephony company gained many new members, because to receive the discount, each family member and friend had to sign up to the program as well. The reasons for the success of this program were

many, but technically it hinged upon the fact that billing data was relatively centralized and was easily available to applications far beyond the application that initially created this data.

Human interfaces as reusable artifacts constitute the general look and feel of a family of programs. Although general windowing systems for personal computers and workstations offer their own particular look and feel, they still provide considerable degrees of freedom in the look and feel of individual applications, especially as it relates to the use of various controls and the overall work flow by which users interact with an application. Intangibly, a human interface exists in the style of user interface used by a running application. Especially in the case of families of closely related programs, having a tangibly documented user interface style guide is an essential artifact. Not only does such a guide provide a basis for building consensus between end users and developers, user interface style guides provide continuity in future applications. Indeed, there is a high and hidden training cost in delivering applications with inconsistent human interfaces.

An organization downsizing from mainframes chose the use of object-oriented technology to architect its client-server architecture. Because they were also moving to more modern graphical user interfaces, the team developed a corporate human interface style guide to document the look and feel of its forthcoming suite of applications. This style guide consisted of sample screen shots and textual scenarios, backed up by a few executable prototype user interfaces that users could play with long before the final application was delivered.

The artifacts of interest to the management team encompass various estimates, project plans, test plans, and documentation. Especially for the mature software development organization, many such estimates and plans derive from the experience of earlier projects, tuned to that organization's particular culture and modified as necessary to meet the unique needs of each new project. Estimates especially must be tuned to the organization, because—as virtually all software estimation experts have observed—the capability of the development team as a whole has the greatest impact upon an organization's productivity. However, because this technology is still relatively new, there does not yet exist a large body of experience that allows us to calibrate traditional estimation models such as COCOMO or Price-S to object-oriented systems. As such, most projects today must rely upon informally gathered estimates, calibrated to a few pilot projects.

Starting out with its first production object-oriented system, this organization initiated a pilot project for one small piece of the system, which it planned to throw away. Management carefully instrumented this activity, and measured the productivity of individual developers in terms of function points and numbers of classes developed within a specified time frame. Management then used this data to calibrate individual members and project schedules for the production system. As the project continued, management continued to collect data to refine these estimates.

In simple terms, project planning encompasses all the infrastructure of a software project that relates to scheduling and staffing. In the most chaotic projects, scheduling is *ad hoc*, and staffing consists of little more than assigning to a project those people who are otherwise unengaged. In the more mature projects, project planning is deliberate, and involves the explicit scheduling of releases and other artifacts, as well as the allocation of certain roles and responsibilities to specific personnel. Project plans are reusable artifacts in that the mature organization will have in place schedule and staffing templates that can be adapted to each new project.

Because the organization had no experience with an object-oriented project before, the development manager conducted a number of exercises to calibrate the capability of his team. CRC card sessions, walkthroughs of other well-structured frameworks, and the rapid production of a few small prototypes provided enough real experience to gather data on each team member. From this experience, the development manager wrote up a staffing plan that matched skills with different roles. In some cases, it was clear that the current team members did not have all the skills necessary to be successful (especially with regard to architectural design), so outside mentors were hired to grow these skills in the group.

Whereas project planning addresses scheduling and staffing, test planning addresses quality and correctness. In the most chaotic projects, testing consists of little more than making certain that the application doesn't crash at the most embarrassing moments. In more mature object-oriented projects, testing involves the more deliberate testing of individual classes, collaborations of classes, and system-wide scenarios. Test plans are reusable artifacts in the sense that the mature organization will use the same test artifacts for each new incremental release of a project, as well as adapt these plans for new variations of some original framework.

Early in the life cycle, this MIS organization established a core development team consisting of an architect, one other senior developer, an end user, an analyst, the documentation manager, and the test team manager. The test team manager participated in requirements analysis, during which time scenarios were developed that captured the system's desired behavior. In parallel with development, the test team used these scenarios to build test scripts, which were ready for use as early as the first architectural release. Early involvement by the testing team proved to be an important factor in the high quality of the delivered product.

Documentation is the final reusable artifact of interest to the management team. For the most part, what documents are produced by a team depends upon the level of formality required by the project either to mitigate risk or to provide a legacy sufficient for developers who must maintain or evolve the application long after the original development team breaks up. In the most mature projects, documentation is simple, direct, and never excessive.

In this modest-sized and successful object-oriented application involving an embedded controller, only a handful of formal documents were developed: a requirements document (consisting of several fully developed scenarios), an architecture document, an interface control document, and a development and testing plan.

For all of these artifacts, I have distinguished between an intangible form and a more tangible one. In the most abstract and intangible sense, all such artifacts may exist only in a developer's mind. However, beware: this practice is acceptably only for the most trivial projects, wherein the cost of producing tangible artifacts far exceeds their benefits and overwhelms the cost of producing the software itself.[*] In the most tangible sense, which is the inclination of the more mature and successful projects, all such artifacts may exist as a piece of code, a prototype, or a document. Because it is impossible to suggest the right balance of informality/formality for every project, I can only offer the following recommendation:

P 22

In deciding what tangible artifacts to develop beyond the software itself, the successful project must consider all those elements that contribute to reducing risk, provide points of control for management, and help to ensure conceptual integrity in the architecture.

Consider each of the three criteria. Tangible artifacts can help reduce risk by forcing strategic and tactical decisions out in the open. For example, prototyping human interfaces early in the life cycle stimulates the dialog between end users and developers and leads to a better and earlier understanding as to the

---

[*] Unfortunately, many projects grossly overestimate the cost of producing tangible artifacts and irrationally underestimate their value. This is false economy, because the organization usually pays the cost (and then some) over the lifetime of the software.

real priorities of certain features. Tangible artifacts can provide points of control for management by making such decisions explicit. For example, as I discuss further in the next chapter, scenarios developed during requirements capture drive the rhythm of incremental architectural releases, and provide a focus for the testing team. Finally, tangible artifacts help ensure conceptual integrity by capturing the vision of the developer, and propagating that vision to the rest of the team. In particular, architecture documents express the system's strategic decisions, and style guides express standards for many of the system's tactical decisions. Together, such artifacts help unify disparate parts of a complex system.

It is important to realize that few such software development artifacts, especially documentation, can be treated as inerrent and unchangeable over their lifetime. Rather, just like the craftsman who creates templates and erects temporary scaffolding, most successful software projects view all software artifacts as things that by necessity must evolve during development. Of course, too much change leads to instability, and so it is the very important responsibility of software management to drive certain artifacts to closure at the appropriate times.

What is it about the nature of all the reusable artifacts of a software project that require them to be somewhat fluid? The answer lies in the cycles of discovery, invention, and implementation found in all successful projects.

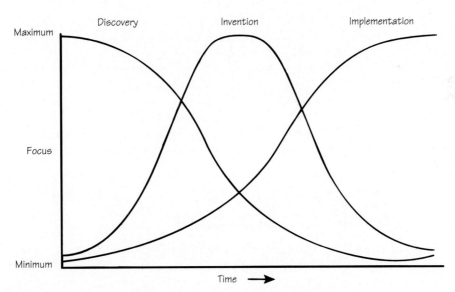

Figure 2-2   Discovery, Invention, and Implementation in the Life Cycle*

---

* Adapted from Bran Selic, who sketched this diagram for Philippe Krutchen during lunch at OOPSLA '93.

Discovery is the activity of investigation that leads to an understanding of a system's desired behavior. Raw discovery peaks during the analysis of a system, but never disappears entirely. Indeed, it is impossible to know all things about the desired behavior of a system, largely because the mere presence of early releases allows users and developers to understand the implications of their earlier discoveries. Note that discovery often starts rising again at the end of a life cycle: the presence of a new software system can change the problem space itself, leading users to discover yet new requirements that they simply could not have known *a priori*.

Invention is the activity of creation that leads to a system's architecture. Invention peaks during design, at which time an application's major strategic and tactical decisions are conceived, validated, and then put into place, thus shaping all that is to come. Invention can start early in the life cycle (as experimentation with new technology and new paradigms begins) and continues during a system's evolution (because there are always a myriad of details that must still be worked out and tuned as development proceeds).

Implementation is the activity of programming, testing, and integration that leads to a deliverable application satisfying a system's desired behavior and performance. Implementation peaks during a system's evolution, as the details of design are worked out and substance added to the system's architectural skeleton. Implementation can start early in the life cycle, during which time tools are honed, management and testing scaffolding is erected, and frameworks are built as componentware for use later during development.

In all successful object-oriented projects, discovery, invention, and implementation tend to follow one another in overlapping waves as Figure 2-2 illustrates. Thus, all the different artifacts of such a project tend to evolve incrementally and iteratively along these cycles. Furthermore, certain of these artifacts become stable at the appropriate time, late enough that they are sufficiently mature, but early enough such that they can have an impact on risk reduction, management control, and conceptual integrity.

There is a rule of thumb that derives from these waves of discovery, invention, and implementation, that affects the life cycle I discuss in the following two chapters:

R 13

70% of the classes in a system are relatively easy to discover. 25% of the classes emerge during design and implementation. The remaining 5% are often not found until maintenance.[*]

There is a corollary to this rule that relates to the reusable artifacts of a project:

---

[*] Ward Cunningham first described this rule to me in far less precise terms; the percentages are my own interpretation. Please remember that this is just a general rule and it is not intended to be taken literally.

In most projects, there are typically only about 3-5 tangible artifacts beyond the software itself that are truly central to risk reduction, management control, and conceptual integrity. Most of these artifacts begin to show up fairly early in the life cycle.

R 14

Every one of the artifacts Jones describes is important, but in my experience, the ones most important to the success of a project include:

- Requirements
- Architecture
- Code
- Project plan
- Test plan

Clearly, the complexity inherent in some projects requires many more artifacts than just these few, but the point is that the greatest management leverage typically comes from just a handful of key products.

ESTABLISHING A RATIONAL DESIGN PROCESS

Knowing what artifacts a project needs to generate is not enough: we need a well-defined process that tells us how and when to generate them. Indeed, given the overlapping cycles of discovery, invention, and implementation found in ever successful project, the key management activity involves choosing the right artifacts and driving them to closure at the appropriate times.

From the perspective of the individual project, it is this activity that fuels the development life cycle. From the perspective of the company as a whole, it is important that these activities and the resulting products be carried out in the context of a mature, repeatable process. By so doing, we help to optimize the use of the entire organization's scarce development resources across all its projects.

However, there is a large gulf between simply pounding out a pile of code and constructing a family of programs that serve as an organization's capital asset, all accomplished in the face of changing technology and changing business needs. Indeed, this is exactly what Parnas meant by faking it: there is no escaping the fact that industrial-strength software development is hard, because it is inherently iterative and incremental. It is iterative in the sense that discovery, invention, and implementation come in cycles. It is incremental in the sense that all artifacts must build upon earlier ones, each moving closer to the delivery of a final, supportable application.

This is why we have software development methods:

> A method encompasses:
> - A notation, whose purpose is to provide a common means of expressing strategic and tactical decisions, ultimately manifesting themselves in a variety of artifacts.
> - A process, responsible for specifying how and when certain artifacts should be developed.

Object-oriented methods are a special brand of software development method, focusing upon the construction of systems for which the class is the fundamental unit of architectural abstraction. Every useful notation has three roles:

- Serve as the language for communicating decisions that are not obvious or cannot be inferred from the code itself.

- Provide rich enough semantics sufficient to capture all important strategic and tactical decisions.

- Offer a form concrete enough for humans to reason about and for tools to manipulate.

A wealth of notations is possible, ranging from informal scratches on the back of a napkin, to formal languages backed up with a lot of hairy mathematics.[*] For object-oriented systems in particular, a handful of notations have proven to be particularly useful:

- Class diagrams, used to show the static existence of classes, class categories, and their relationships.

- Scenario diagrams, used to show the dynamics of scenarios and mechanisms, both involving the collaboration of several classes or objects.

- State machines diagrams, used to show the dynamics of individual classes.

Notice that, collectively, these three diagrams provide coverage for all the important logical elements of an object-oriented architecture.

As examples in the next chapter will illustrate, there is nothing particularly complicated about any of these three diagrams. Often, these diagrams are sup-

---

[*] Do not discount either end of this notational spectrum. Many a successful system has been launched from a quick sketch on the back of a wet cocktail napkin. Furthermore, when I interact with a software-intensive system that my life happens to depend upon (such as when I'm a passenger in a fly-by-wire commercial aircraft), I feel much better knowing that it was developed with some mathematical rigor. The last announcement I want to hear from a pilot when I am flying is this: "Is there a programmer on board?"

plemented with others as necessary to express the meaning of decisions regarding the deep, dark corners of a system's behavior or structure.*

Every well-defined process has four roles:

- Provide guidance as to the order of a team's activities.
- Specify what artifacts should be developed.
- Direct the tasks of individual developers and the team as a whole.
- Offer criteria for monitoring and measuring the project's products and activities.

These four roles define the purpose, products, activities, and measures of goodness for each step in the object-oriented software development life cycle.

Every organization can be classified according to the maturity of its process.‡

> There are five distinct levels of process maturity for a software development organization:
> - Initial
> - Repeatable
> - Defined
> - Managed
> - Optimizing

Figure 2-3 illustrates the differences in these levels by measuring performance (cost, schedule, and quality) against successive projects.

Be careful how you apply these levels; they are *descriptive*, not *proscriptive*. In particular, successful development organizations will tend to rate high on this scale. However, organizations that rate high in a process assessment are not necessarily successful.

For organizations at the initial level, the development process is *ad hoc* and often chaotic, with success relying upon the heroic efforts of a few dedicated individual contributors. An organization can progress by introducing basic project controls. Organizations at the repeatable level have reasonable control over its plans and commitments. Organizations can progress by institutionalizing a well-defined process. In organizations at the defined level, the development process is reasonably well-defined, understood, and practiced. Such a process serves as a stable foundation for calibrating the team and predicting

---

* For detailed information, with examples, about the notation of the Booch method, see *Object-Oriented Analysis and Design with Applications*. This particular work provides a unification of methods, drawing upon my earlier work, with important influences from OMT, Jacobson, and others.
‡ For more detail on organizational maturity, see Humphrey's *Managing the Software Process*.

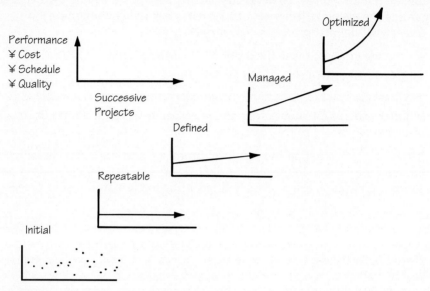

Figure 2-3   Process Maturity Implications*

progress. Organizations can progress by instrumenting their development practices.

Organizations at the managed level have quantitative measures of its process. Organizations can further progress by lowering the cost of gathering this data, and instituting practices that permit this data to influence the process. At the highest level of maturity, optimizing organizations have in place a well-tuned process that consistently yields products of high quality in a predictable, timely, and cost-effective manner.‡

Sadly, too many of the organizations that I encounter are at the initial level; some make it up to level two, and a handful manage to achieve the defined or even the managed level. This is actually not so bad: organizations at this level of sophistication still tend to be fairly successful at regularly building quality products. There is not so much rigor that it stifles creativity, but there is not so much chaos that its developers are constantly in crisis.

This mention of creativity and chaos raises a significant point:

---

* Adapted from Walker Royce.
‡ Perhaps I don't get out enough, but I personally have never encountered an entire company at this highest level of maturity. I have seen several organizations reach the defined level, and a few teams reach the managed level. Such hyperproductive teams truly stand out from the crowd, exuding a chemistry that is almost magical. Not only are such teams highly productive, they also tend to be really fun places to work.

> How does a project reconcile the creative needs of its individual programmers with management's needs for stability and predictability?

Indeed, this is the crux of the problem that ever mature process must address. Creativity is essential to the crafting of all well structured object-oriented architectures, but developers allowed completely unrestrained creativity tend to never reach closure. Similarly, discipline is required when organizing the efforts of a team of developers, but too much discipline gives birth to an ugly bureaucracy that kills all attempts at innovation.

For object-oriented systems, the answer to resolving this tension appears to lie in distinguishing the macro and micro elements of the development process. The macro process is closely related to the traditional waterfall life cycle, and serves as the controlling framework for the micro process. The macro process is the primary concern of the software management team, whose time horizon is typically measured in weeks, months, and—for truly massive undertakings—years. The micro process is more closely related to the spiral model of development, and serves as the framework for an iterative and incremental approach to development. The micro process is the primary concern of the individual developer or a small group of developers, whose time horizon is typically measured in weeks, days, and—for really rapid development efforts—hours.

This suggests the following recommendation:

> Institute a process that reconciles the macro and micro life cycle. This approach allows an organization to "fake" a fully rational development process and provides a foundation for at least the defined level of software process maturity.

P 23

Chapter 3 examines the macro process in detail; Chapter 4 does the same for the micro process.

The Macro Process

The Macro Process

Make it so.
JEAN LUC PICARD

Every healthy software project I have encountered has a natural rhythm whose beat is sounded by a steady and deliberate forward motion toward the delivery of a meaningful product at a reasonably-defined point in time. Even in the presence of a crisis, such as the discovery of an unexpected requirement or the failure of some technology, the healthy team does not panic. Rather, it is this steady rhythm that helps keep the project focused on its ultimate goal and gives the team its resilience to roll with the punches.

Not surprisingly, different projects march to different beats, and so they have different time horizons. I have seen successful object-oriented efforts whose life cycles vary from several weeks to several years. Consider the following spectrum of life cycles, measured from project inception to delivery:

- A few days
  Sometimes found in the frantic world of financial services, where missing a trading window can mean millions of dollars in lost revenue.

- A few weeks
  Typical of exploratory development, such as when prototyping a larger effort or running experiments against a shifting source of data.

- A few months
  Often found in the steady state of a hyperproductive organization that is able to spawn new releases quickly from the base of a mature framework and that's driven by the desire to seize a window of opportunity in the market place. This time horizon is also common to some applications in the telephony business and in the entertainment industry, whose schedules are dictated by fickle consumer demand.

- About one year
  Perhaps the median duration for most object-oriented projects representing a fair capital investment.

- A few years
  Present in projects that affect an organization's entire line of business, and common in domains where hardware and software development must proceed in parallel. Projects of 5 to 10 years exist, although I have seen very few of them succeed, at least as measured against the initial scope of the project. In any case, geopolitical issues—not technical ones—tend to dominate, mainly because so much is at stake.

There are two time horizons of particular interest to me: projects lasting about a year (because this schedule is common to projects across a variety of problem domains) and projects lasting only a few months (because this is typically the rhythm of a project successful at generating a family of programs from a stable set of application-specific frameworks). In this chapter, I will focus on the rhythm of both such kinds of projects, although it is possible to scale these lessons up and down to longer or shorter time horizons.

I have seen my share of unhealthy projects, and they tend to lack rhythm. The slightest crisis throws such a project out of whack. The mere mention of risks incites panic, manifested by its managers focusing on political games, its analysts paralyzed by details, and its developers burying themselves in their technology instead of focusing themselves on finding constructive solutions.* To use an analogy, if the healthy software project is like a well-oiled, smoothly running machine, then the unhealthy one is like a broken-down engine, running in fits and starts on one cylinder, and belching out a lot of smoke and leaving spots and parts on the road as it clanks along the way.

As I explain in the first chapter, one important habit that distinguishes healthy projects from these unhealthy ones is the use of an iterative and incremental software development life cycle. An *iterative* process is one that involves the successive refinement of a system's architecture, from which we apply the experience and results of each major release to the next iteration of analysis and design. Each iteration of analysis/design/implementation is repeated several times over the object-oriented architecture. The process is *incremental* in the sense that each pass through an analysis/design/implementation cycle leads us to gradually refine our strategic and tactical decisions, extend our scope from an initially skeletal architecture, and ultimately lead to the final, deliverable software product. The work of preceding iterations is not discarded or redone, but rather is corrected and augmented. The process is also incremental at a finer level of granularity, that is, in the way each iteration is internally organized, as in a succession of builds.

This iterative and incremental process is also one that is risk driven, meaning that for each evolutionary cycle, management directs the project's resources in such as way as to mitigate the project's highest risks, thus driving each evolution closer to a final, meaningful solution.

This is indeed the rhythm of all successful object-oriented projects. This is also the focus of the macro process, the time horizon of which spans the entire software development life cycle, and the activities of which serve as the central focus of management's attention and control. The rhythm of the macro process can be summarized in the following two practices:

> The macro process of the object-oriented project should comprise the successive refinement of the system's architecture.

P 24

> The activities leading up to every evolutionary release in the macro process should be risk-driven: first assess the project's highest risks, and then direct the project's resources in such as way as to mitigate those risks.

P 25

---

* The healthy project does not fear risk, but rather, views it as an opportunity: If you can triumph over a risky situation that others may have simply ignored, then you've achieved a competitive advantage.

In the remainder of this chapter, I'll concentrate upon the rhythm of the macro process.

THE ONE-MINUTE METHODOLOGY

I am always careful when explaining the macro process of object-oriented development. Once they understand its phases and activities, some naive organizations will then conclude that "if I do x first, and then y, and then z, just as Grady told me, then I'll consistently deliver my perfectly maintainable and adaptable products on time and on schedule." Nothing could be further from the truth. Reality is, successful software development is hard work, and no amount of ceremony will make that problem go away.

> A large MIS organization decided to embrace object-oriented stuff in a big way, and so it formed a group to decide upon the method the organization would use. Being big on process, the group focused on defining their software development life cycle in great detail. They borrowed from a variety of object-oriented methods and adopted practices from their own culture. Along the way, as they added activities and deliverables to address a variety of problems they'd encountered in earlier systems, their process grew more and more meticulous. Everyone the group was proud of their final results, and confident that they'd considered every possible contingency. However, once they began to roll this work out to their field, real projects actively rejected their effort, because the resulting life cycle was so rigid and so full of ceremony that it actually added risk and extended schedules.

At the other end of the spectrum are those organizations that reject any hint of ceremony, and so seek object nirvana from the perfect tool, the perfect language, or the most light-weight process. This leads to the magical software development life cycle wonderfully satirized by Orr and called the One Minute Methodology. As Orr wryly observes, the secret of the One Minute Methodology is simply that "it's not important that you have real information, it's just important that you feel like you do."[*]

Orr rightfully goes on to say that "the truth is, building systems that are able to respond quickly to management needs takes a long time. Nobody wants to hear that . . . . You can build good systems, and you can build them quickly. but you can't build them without skillful planning and solid requirements defini-

---

[*] Orr, K. 1984. *The One Minute Methodology.* Topeka, Kansas: Ken Orr and Associates, p. 35.

tion."* Skillful planning is what the macro process is all about. If there is a secret to this process, it's best summarized by the following recommended practice:

> In the context of continuously integrating a system's architecture, establish a project's rhythm by driving to closure certain artifacts at regular intervals; these deliverables serve as tangible milestones through which management can measure the project and then meaningfully exert its control.

P 26

There are three important elements to this practice:

- The macro process of object-oriented development is one of *continuous integration.*

Rather than setting aside a single period of formal system integration toward the end of the life cycle, the object-oriented life cycle tends to integrate the parts of its software (and possibly hardware) at more regular intervals. This practice thus spreads the integration risk more evenly throughout the life cycle rather than back-loading the development process, where there is less room to maneuver if things go wrong.

- At regular intervals, the process of continuous integration yields executable releases that grow in functionality at every release.

The delivery of these and other artifacts (namely, the ones identified by Jones and described in the previous chapter), serve as milestones in the macro process. As I will discuss in more detail later in this chapter, the most important such concrete deliverables include initial proof of concept prototypes, scenarios, the system's architecture, various incremental releases, and a punch list.

Notice, by the way, that the refinement of a system's object-oriented architecture weaves a common thread through the macro process. This is why I gave so much attention to the importance and meaning of architecture in the previous chapter.

Finally,

- It is through these milestones that management can measure progress and quality, and hence anticipate, identify, and then actively attack risks on an ongoing basis.

Management cannot control those things it cannot see. If risks are to be mitigated, then they must be explicitly sought out and identified. Constantly reacting to risks as they reveal themselves is a recipe for disaster, because it destroys the rhythm of a project.

---

* Orr, pp. 51–53.

Before I can continue, there is a critical issue to consider :

Why is the rhythm of the macro process so important? There are three key reasons:
- Iterative and incremental releases serve as a forcing function that drives the development team to closure at regular intervals.
- As problems arise—and they will—management can better schedule a suitable response and fold these activities into future iterations, rather than completely disrupt ongoing production.
- A rhythmic development process allows a project's supporting elements (including, testers, writers, toolsmiths, and domain experts) to better schedule their work.

This is what a mature development process is all about. The first step toward process maturity is to define a project's rhythm. Once this rhythm is established, then and only then can the project work to keep improving the beat. If you happen to be thinking, "but this is all just common-sense project management," you are partially correct. There is nothing radically new here. However, in the presence of object-oriented technology, there is one very different thing: rather than discretely analyzing, then designing, then implementing a system from the top-down, the object-oriented process tends to spiral from the primitives out. In other words, we start with what we know, devise a skeletal object-oriented architecture, study the problem some more, improve upon our architecture, and so on, until we expand to a solution that satisfies our project's essential minimal characteristics.

Thus, what Parnas observes is so true: no real project of any substance flows top-down from a statement of requirements to a perfectly wonderful implementation. Rather, all real processes are both cyclic and opportunistic: cyclic in the sense that they require iteration, and opportunistic in the sense that it is impossible to know a priori everything there is to know. Hence, projects must react to things that they discover along the way. However, as I discuss in the first chapter, Parnas also observes that it is important that the development process appears as if it is top-down—and that is the role of the macro process of object-oriented development.

In my discussion about architecture-driven projects in Chapter 1, I explain the typical process used by projects in this culture. Using this process as a foundation, let me expand upon it and explain the flow of activities found in successful object-oriented projects:

The major phases of the object-oriented macro process include:
- Conceptualization   Establish core requirements.
- Analysis   Develop a model of the system's desired behavior.
- Design   Create an architecture for the implementation.
- Evolution   Evolve and deploy the implementation through successive refinement.
- Maintenance   Manage postdelivery evolution.

Figure 3-1 provides an illustration of this process.

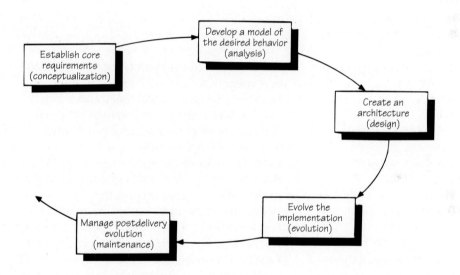

Figure 3-1 The Macro Development Process

Although there are some similarities, realize that the macro process is not at all like the strict, traditional waterfall approach to development. Rather, the macro process is explicitly iterative and incremental, and so is somewhat closer to Barry Boehm's seminal work on the spiral model.* Specifically, each of the

---

* Boehm, B. August 1986. A Spiral Model of Software Development and Enhancement. *Software Engineering Notes,* vol. 11(4). In Boehm's work, he combines my phases of conceptualization and analysis into one.

phases of the macro process (conceptualization, analysis, design, evolution, and maintenance) encompass a set of iterations united by a common economic objective. Each of these iterations, then, serves as a product baseline, carried out through the opportunistic process of the micro process. During conceptualization and analysis, constituting the inception of a project, we find iterations that form the project's vision and its business case. During design, we find iterations focused on elaborating and then stabilizing the system's architecture. Evolution is then the construction of the rest of the system upon this architectural foundation, and so is composed of a number of release iterations. Finally, maintenance is a period of transition, during which time there may be iterations of maintenance releases, delivered back to the deployed base of end users.

To further help you build a conceptual model of the macro process, let me describe it in broad strokes in another way, namely, in terms of the major activities in each phase:

The major activities in each phase of the macro process include:

- Conceptualization   Bracket the project's risks by building a proof of concept.
- Analysis   Develop a common vocabulary and a common understanding of the system's desired behavior by exploring scenarios with end users and domain experts.
- Design   Establish a skeleton for the solution and lay down tactical policies for implementation by drafting the system's architecture.
- Evolution   Refine the architecture and package releases for deployment; this phase typically requires further analysis, design, and implementation.
- Maintenance   Continue the system's evolution in the face of newly-defined requirements.

One final way to think about the macro process is in terms of how its products unfold over time. In Figure 3-2, I have taken the five most important reusable artifacts as described in the previous chapter, and plotted their development against the major phases of the macro process. The darker the band, the more focus being spent on that artifact.[*]

---

[*] Please note that the time axis in this figure is not to scale. As I describe later in this chapter, each of the phases of the macro process really take up a different amount of time, with evolution typically the longest phase.

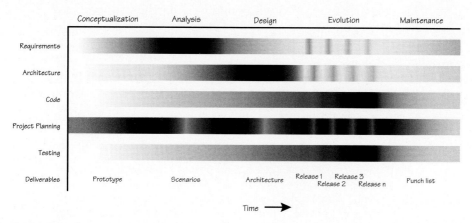

Figure 3-2 The Rhythm of the Macro Process

This figure clearly illustrates the rhythm of the macro process. Thus, we see that an understanding of a system's requirements evolves during analysis, and this understanding is revisited at each iteration. Similarly, a system's architecture begins to be formulated during the later phases of analysis, is made reasonably stable during design, and then is also refined in each iteration. Code artifacts grow steadily over the life cycle, with discrete jumps in code completeness at each iteration. Not surprisingly, testing tracks these code artifacts fairly closely. Finally, project planning hardly ever gets a break, for it must lead every other activity.

I must emphasize that every project is unique, and hence management must establish the right level of formality in its use of the macro process. For exploratory applications developed by a tightly knit team of highly experienced developers, too much formality will stifle innovation; for very complex projects developed by a large team of developers who are not co-located, too little formality will lead to chaos.

This organization, tasked with building a very innovative system for semiconductor wafer fabrication, was staffed with fairly experienced developers. The project—which was ultimately quite successful—required only a modest amount of project planning ceremony. One obvious sign of this project's informality was the lack of physical boundaries among developers. Most of the team's programmers were housed in the same open room. Each had a partitioned workspace, arranged in a large circle centered around and open to a common area containing a large table and chairs, where random groups of developers could meet and discuss issues with their peers as the need arose.

This organization, tasked with building a decision support system for the entire company, had subprojects scattered across the United States and Europe. Because there were so many players, the project had a great deal of inertia. To help synchronize the activities of this dispersed group, the project held a major architectural review every three months at a central location.

There is a rule of thumb I use to find the right balance between informality and formality:

R 15

If there is not a single organization chart posted around your office, your software project likely needs to be nudged in the direction of more formality; if your programmer's desk drawers have several such charts, your software project likely needs to be nudged in the opposite direction, toward more informality.

In the remainder of this chapter, I explain each phase of the macro process in detail. As usual, I include examples, recommended practices, and rules.

To reach a higher level of process maturity, each phase of a software development process must be described in terms of its:
- Purpose
- Products
- Activities
- Agents
- Milestones and measures

CONCEPTUALIZATION

Purpose

The purpose of conceptualization is to establish the core requirements for a new system or for the major overhaul of an existing one.

Not every project requires this phase. Indeed, my recommendation is as follows:

P 27

Enter into conceptualization only when the project's risks are relatively high or when it is necessary to forge an initial bond between the customer and development organization; otherwise, press forward directly into analysis.

A project's risks may be unusually high under a number of circumstances, such as when entering into a new line of business or when trying out some new technology (be it a new platform, new languages, new tools, or even new processes). A project's risks are also especially high when there exist certain extraordinary conditions, such as demanding performance or capacity requirements, that represent a major constraint upon the system's behavior.

Forging the customer/developer bond is another reason why the conceptualization phase can be important. Projects of modest size or larger will at the very least represent an opportunity cost for either the customer and the development organization, and at the very most will represent a major capital investment for both Rather than work out the relationship between the two in the context of production development where the stakes are much higher, a period of conceptualization permits both parties to learn how the other works, their limits, and their real needs and concerns.

There's a rule associated with these practices:

> A project's risk starts reaching critical proportions once you begin to change more than two factors relative to existing practices (such as the team, the technology base, the platform, the method, the tools, the development language, and system's requirements).

R 16

Ultimately, conceptualization serves as a proof of concept for the project as a whole. When complete, management should be able to answer the following two questions:

- What are the major risks ahead for this project?
- Are these risks sufficiently manageable so as to warrant committing further resources to the project, or are they so intractable as to require further investigation (perhaps including, in extreme cases, the decision to cut ones losses and abandon all future effort)?

Conceptualization thus allows an organization to better assess its odds when betting the future of a project or perhaps even the whole company.

For any truly new piece of software or even for the novel adaptation of an existing system, there exists some moment in time where, in the mind of the developer, the architect, the analyst, or the end user, there springs forth an idea for some application. This idea may represent a new business venture, a new complementary product in an existing product line, or perhaps a new set of features for an existing software system. It is not the purpose of conceptualization to completely define these ideas. Rather, the role of conceptualization is to establish the vision for the idea and validate its assumptions.

Products

During conceptualization, three artifacts are generated. In order of importance, they include:

- An executable prototype
- A risk assessment
- A general vision of the project's requirements

An executable prototype is the most important product of conceptualization, because it serves as a tangible proof of concept. Such a prototype makes it possible to determine early in the development life cycle whether or not the project's assumptions of functionality, performance, size, or complexity are correct, rather than later in the life cycle where abandoning the current development path would generally prove to be financially or socially disastrous.

It is important that such prototypes be *executable*, because this forces the project's visionaries to concentrate only upon those things that are practically implementable within their lifetimes. It is also important that such prototypes be *broad* and *shallow*. By building broad prototypes—meaning that a range of the systems' functionality is considered—the project is forced to think about the breadth of the systems' desired behavior. By building shallow prototypes—meaning that the prototype is knowingly incomplete and thus void of most detail—the project is not allowed to get wrapped up in lots of tactical implementation details. Finally, it is also important that such a prototype be *discarded* or at least *cannibalized* because it is not the intent of this phase to produce production quality code.[*] Besides, as Brooks wisely suggests, "plan to throw one away; you will, anyhow."[‡] This is the one to throw away, because throwing away later release is so much more costly.

Thus, a recommendation for the successful object-oriented project:

P 28

> During conceptualization, focus upon establishing the project's vision by quickly developing a fairly broad yet shallow executable prototype. At the end of this phase, throw the prototype away, but retain the vision. This process will leave the project with a better understanding of the risks ahead.

A risk assessment is the next most important artifact. This need not be anything fancy: simply enumerating the technical and non-technical risks uncovered during conceptualization is sufficient to set expectations for management and for the development team as to the challenges ahead. Technical risks might

---

[*] By *cannibalize*, I mean that one takes the essence (and perhaps even the substance) of the prototype and injects it into the production system.
[‡] Brooks, p. 116.

include issues such as "we are worried about performance bottlenecks in shoving persistent data across our network," "we are uncertain as to the right look and feel for this product," and "is C++ (or Smalltalk or Ada or some 4GL) the right language to use?"* Nontechnical risks might include issues such as "can we find the people with the right skills at the right time to staff our development team?" and "the timing of Microsoft's (or Apple's or IBM's or Sun's) next release of their operating system may destabilize our development activity." Being up front about such risks early in the life cycle enables management to begin to formulate plans to actively attack those risks.

A general vision of the project's requirements is the final important artifact of this phase. Again, this need not be anything fancy: a brief, written project report is sufficient for most projects. For the most informal and hyperproductive teams, this vision may simply be locked up in the architect's head, to be refined and revealed during the more formal phase of analysis.

Activities

The primary activity of conceptualization is the building of a proof of concept that serves to bracket a project's risks.

> An organization decided to embark upon the development of tools for an entirely new market. Not only was the market new, but so was the platform (they had traditionally been workstation vendors, and were migrating to personal computer products) as was the language (they had never launched a serious project using an object-oriented programming language). To better assess the projects' risks, their architect, together with two other colleagues, armed themselves with portable computers loaded with Smalltalk, and hid themselves away for a short while to create. At the end of a month, the group returned with a proof-of-concept executable prototype that it could show to management as well as to potential customers. Although there were still risks, there was a sufficient understanding of those risks to commit to a full-scale development effort.

It is hard to say precisely when conceptualization begins. New ideas can spring from virtually any source: end users, user groups, developers, analysts, the marketing team, and so on. It is wise for management to maintain a record of such new ideas, so that they can be prioritized and scarce resources intelli-

---

* Purists criticize me for worrying about language issues this early in the life cycle. However, I'm intensely pragmatic. Selecting a suitable implementation technology is a critical factor, because it affects staffing, tool selection, and yes, to some degree, even a system's architecture.

gently allocated to explore the more promising ones. Indeed, some of the most interesting new classes of applications arise not necessarily because they were planned, but because they were born from the unrestrained creativity that exists during conceptualization.

Once a particular avenue has been selected for exploration, building a proof of concept typically tracks the following order of events. First:

- Establish a set of goals for the prototype together with an end date.

When setting the prototype's goals, it is important to explicitly enumerate what it *will* do, as well as what it will *not* do, and at what costs. In this manner, the project can begin to set management's and end users' expectations for the scope of the overall effort.

It is equally important to set an explicit end date. Conceptualization is by its very nature an intensely creative activity, which, frankly, most developers find to be a lot of fun. Being unfettered by rigid development roles is also a hoot, and it is difficult to stop doing once you have started. If your entire software development life cycle looks like the activity of conceptualization, then your project is clearly out of control, for this is neither a sustainable nor a very mature process. This is why management must be very firm about schedules at this stage, lest bad habits begin to grow.

With regard to schedules, I typically apply the following rule of thumb:

R 17

> For projects of modest complexity whose full life cycle is about one year, the conceptualization phase typically lasts about one month.

Obviously, for especially large and complex applications, the prototyping effort itself may demand a large undertaking, equivalent to the work required for an entire moderately complex project. There is nothing wrong with extending the duration of conceptualization, except that, the longer it continues, the more formality it demands. At the limit, proofs of concept lasting a year or so typically take on the shape of the complete macro process.

The next step in this activity is as follows:

- Assemble an appropriate team to develop the prototype, and let them proceed, constrained only by the prototype's goals and schedule.

There is an important practice implicit in this step that many successful object-oriented projects seem to follow:

P 29

> After establishing the goals and a firm schedule for the delivery of a prototype, the best things management can do during conceptualization is to get out of the way.

Please understand: I do not mean to incite anarchy. Rather, I mean that, during conceptualization, the development team should not be fettered by rigid development rules. Conceptualization requires relatively unrestrained creativity, and the one thing that will absolutely crush such creativity is a lot of ceremony.

What is perhaps most important is for the development organization to set in place a structure that provides sufficient resources for new ideas to be explored. There is nothing inherently object-oriented about conceptualization. Any and all programming paradigms should be allowed to develop proofs of concept. However, it is often the case that, in the presence of a reasonably rich object-oriented application framework, developing prototypes is often faster than any alternative. This is why it is not unusual to see proofs of concept developed in one language (such as Smalltalk, various 4GLs, or even Visual Basic) and product development to proceed in another (such as C++, Ada, or even Object-Oriented COBOL).

The final step in this activity addresses the issue of risk management:

- Evaluate the resulting prototype, and make an explicit decision for product development or further exploration. A decision to develop a product should be made with a reasonable assessment of the potential risks, which the proof of concept should uncover.

Evaluating the prototype means showing it to domain experts and potential end users. and gauging their reaction. Even negative feedback is useful at this stage, because it helps point out potentially futile paths.

Obviously, the resulting prototype should be thrown away or cannibalized, once it has served its purpose. Trying to dress up ragged prototypes and drag them into production is usually a terrible decision, because they are rarely adaptable or maintainable, nor do they typically conform to the final production architecture.

If an evaluation of the project's risks at this point seems tolerable, then the most prudent next action is to formalize the production process, and make explicit the leap from concept to product.

Agents

I use the following practice when staffing a project's conceptualization activity:

> The most effective prototypes generated during conceptualization are those built by a small team, consisting of the system's architect and perhaps one or two other developers who collectively continue their engagement through analysis and design.

P 30

Small projects can get by with a team of one, consisting of an architect who is usually the original visionary. For modest sized projects, the architect is typically supported by one or two other developers, often including an abstractionist and a toolsmith. Only in larger projects will the team size exceed three or four developers, sometimes growing to ten or so. In any case, note that the architect should always be a *builder* and not just *draftsman* of plans.

Note that I recommend this early staff continues with the project well into later stages of the development life cycle. This is because there are many lessons learned during conceptualization that cannot easily be written down, and so become a part of the invisible corporate memory.

Milestones and Measures

The most important milestone in this phase is the delivery of the executable prototype. Management can use this milestone as a way of measuring the project's health—if the team really blows the schedule at this phase of development, then it is clear that a lot of hard work remains, and steps must be taken to mitigate the future schedule risk. Often this means relaxing certain constraints (in particular, schedule or functionality) or exploring radically different alternatives.

The most important measure in this phase is an evaluation of the completeness of the prototype. Consider the prototype's goals established in the first step. Failure to complete some things the prototype was supposed to do is a warning sign that there is high technical risk. Completion of more than what the prototype was supposed to do is an encouraging sign. However, do not be naively optimistic: it is easy to develop flashy behavior quickly, when you do not have to worry about anything else.

ANALYSIS

Purpose

The purpose of analysis is to develop a model of the system's desired behavior.

Every project requires this phase. If you ignore it or rush through it, then abandon all hope, for your project will surely fail to build the right thing. Some projects—especially those who are not big on ceremony—loathe this phase because they think it keeps them away from their code. You can mitigate this attitude by conducting a conceptualization phase first, which permits controlled experimentation with new technology.

Analysis focuses upon behavior, not form. It is largely inappropriate to pursue issues of detailed class design, representation, or other tactical details during this phase. Rather, analysis must yield a statement of what the system does, not how it does it. Any intentional statements of "how" during analysis should be viewed as useful only for the purpose of exposing the behavior of the system, and not as testable requirements of the design.

When reasonably complete, management should be able to answer the following six questions:

- What are the system's major functions?
- With respect to these functions, what are the primary behaviors that the system exhibits?
- For each of these primary behaviors, what variant behaviors may arise?
- What are the roles and the responsibilities of the key classes and objects that contribute to these behaviors?
- How must the system relate to other systems?
- Are there any new or revised areas of risk that have been uncovered during the discovery process?

The process of finding answers to these questions serves as a forcing function that causes a system's users to better articulate what they really want. The first five questions in particular serve to establish a common vocabulary between the system's domain experts and end users and its developers. The last question serves to continue the momentum of risk-driven development as begun during conceptualization.

By focusing upon behavior, we are able to identify the function points of a system. Function points denote the outwardly observable and testable behaviors of a system. From the perspective of the end user, a function point represents some primary activity of a system in response to some event. Function points often (but do not always) denote the mapping of inputs to outputs, and so represent the transformations that the system makes to its environment. From the perspective of the analyst, a function point represents a distinct quantum of behavior. Indeed, function points provide a measure of complexity: the greater the number of function points, the more complex the system. During analysis, we capture the semantics of a system's function points through scenarios.*

Analysis never stands alone. During this phase, we do not expect to complete an exhaustive understanding of the system's behavior. Carrying out a complete analysis before allowing design to commence is neither possible nor desirable, because the very act of building a system raises questions of behavior that no reasonable amount of analysis can uncover efficiently. It is sufficient that we accomplish an analysis of most of the primary behaviors of the system, with a sprinkling of secondary behaviors considered as well to ensure that no essential patterns of behavior are missed.

---

* To be clear, a single function point equates to one scenario.

A reasonably complete and formal analysis is also essential to serve the needs of traceability. Traceability is largely a problem of accountability, through which we ensure that no function points are neglected. Traceabilty is also essential to risk management. As development proceeds in any nontrivial system, management will have to make difficult trade-offs in allocating resources or in resolving some unpleasant tactical issue. By having traceability from function points to the implementation via scenarios, it is far easier to assess the impact of disturbing a system's architecture when such knotty problems arise.

Products

During analysis, four artifacts are generated, each of almost equal importance:

- A description of the system's context
- A collection of scenarios that define the behavior of the system
- A domain model
- A revised risk assessment

Executable prototypes are also a common product of analysis, but these are all of secondary consideration because they are usually generated in support of producing these four primary artifacts and then eventually thrown away.

The description of a system's context establishes the boundaries of the project and distinguishes between those elements that are inside and those that are outside. In the most informal projects, a system's context may be specified simply by knowing or explicitly enumerating the hardware and software components that sit at the fringe of the system. In slightly more formal projects, such boundaries may be specified in a context diagram that shows those agents that live at the system's edge.* In more formal or more complex projects, establishing a system's boundary may include specifying the protocol of services and the layout of data provided by all such agents.‡

In the object-oriented community, a practice has emerged that serves as a very pragmatic means of discovering, capturing, documenting, and then communicating a system's requirements. This is the practice of use cases, first proposed by Ivar Jacobson. Use cases are fundamentally a simple concept, and beyond the rhetoric, what's most important is that they work

---

* Notationally, an object message diagram can serve as a context diagram. In such a diagram, one object denotes the system as a whole. This central object is surrounded by other objects that represent external hardware or software agents at the fringe of the system and with which the system interacts.

‡ In these more complex projects, the stability of such services and data is critical. Since this represents a high risk factor, sometimes it is useful to capture these services and data in the form of an interface control document that undergoes formal review and change control. Just like other artifacts, however, expect the details of these protocols and layouts to evolve.

Specifically, a use case specifies some region of a system's behavior. For example, "book a shipment" might be a use case in a transportation system. Whereas a use case is a more general thing, associated with each use case is a set of scenarios. A scenario is an instance of a use case, and thus represents a single path through that use case. For example, "book a shipment of tennis shoes from Hong Kong for delivery to Long Beach on the ship H.M.S. Bilgewater and then on to Chicago by rail starting next Friday" is one scenario that might be associated with the earlier use case. During analysis, the collective desired behavior of a system may be expressed as a web of such scenarios. We apply use cases largely to organize this web of scenarios.*

To explain the significance of scenarios, let me use an analogy from the movie making industry. In very simple terms, the process of producing a movie begins with some statement of the picture's story, characters, and scenes. Once the basic shape of the movie is agreed upon (in a sense, when the context and requirements of the movie are established by the production company), then planning continues with the creation of a script.

Because the flow of a movie is so important, storyboards are commonly used to elaborate upon the picture's action. Storyboarding, actually a part of movie-making since its beginnings, emerged as a fundamental practice through the efforts of Walt Disney and other animators during the 1930s. Today, the use of storyboarding is pervasive, and has received a boost through the presence of a number of tools that help automate the storyboarding process.

Specifically, a storyboard "provides the continuity of the action, which is worked out scene by scene simultaneously with the . . . script. In the story-board, the story is told and to some extent graphically styled in a succession of key sketches with captions and fragments of dialogue."‡ A storyboard thus represents a path through the flow of the movie, together with a specification of the actors responsible for carrying out this action.

Storyboards serve three purposes. First, they provide a means of capturing decisions about the action in the movie. Depending upon the nature of a particular scene, a storyboard might be very detailed (in other words, high-fidelity, perhaps even showing camera angles and background action) or it might be very coarse (that is, low-fidelity, showing only the placement of a few key characters). Second, they provide a vehicle for communicating these decisions to all the various parties in the production company, and letting them discuss and reason about the meaning or the details of a particular scene. Finally, they serve as instructions to the director, who is responsible for taking a script and its associated storyboards and implementing it through concrete camera work.

---

* Thus, a use case names a collection of related scenarios, each of which represents a prototypical thread through that use case.

‡ Motion Pictures. 1985. *Britannica*, 15th ed., vol. 24, p. 438.

Object-oriented analysis is similar. A scenario provides an outline of activities that signifies some system behavior. Scenarios document decisions about requirements or designs, provide a focus for communication about a system's semantics, and can serve as a blueprint for detailed implementation.

For example, consider a decision support system for managing consumer loans. In the context of the single use case "manage a loan," end users probably have a number of scenarios that they view as central to this business domain, such as the following:

- Applying for a loan
- Making a payment on a loan
- Paying off a loan
- Checking the history of payments on a loan
- Selling the loan to another financial institution
- Handling a late or a missed loan payment

I have a rule about the number of use cases and scenarios typically found in object-oriented systems:

R 18

> For projects of modest complexity, expect to find a few dozen use cases, an order of magnitude more primary scenarios, and an order of magnitude more secondary ones.

A primary scenario represents some fundamental system function; secondary scenarios represent variations on the theme of a primary scenario, often reflecting exceptional conditions. For example, one primary scenario in a telephone system would involve making a simple connection from one telephone to another (an activity called POTS for "plain old telephone service"). In an air traffic control system, the scenario of an aircraft entering a controlled airspace would represent a primary behavior.

Of course, even the smallest system involves a multitude of possible exceptional conditions and alternative paths. These behaviors are best expressed as secondary scenarios, not because they are of secondary importance, but mainly because each secondary scenario typically represents a variation on the theme of some primary scenario.* For example, a secondary scenario in a telephony system might deal with the unexpected disconnection of service during a phone call. In an air traffic control system, a secondary scenario might involve the behavior of the system when an aircraft without transponder identification enters an airspace. Thus, primary and secondary scenarios often form a hierarchy: a secondary scenario is often "a kind of" a primary scenario, with variations.

---

* In fact, secondary scenarios often introduce the most challenging design problems.

Primary and secondary scenarios may be connected in another way: a secondary scenario can extend the behavior of a primary one. For example, in a system for managing consumer loans, making a payment on a loan and paying off a loan will both involve handling certain business rules regarding the handling of taxes and interest. Rather than having each primary scenario repeat this behavior, we might express this common behavior in a secondary scenario that elaborates upon some behavior expressed more abstractly in the two primary scenarios.

As viewed from the outside by its end users and domain experts, much of the interesting desired behavior of a system can thus be captured through a web of scenarios. This is a practice often found in successful object-oriented analysis:

> During analysis, focus upon developing a model of the system's desired behavior by examining various scenarios that represent threads of activity typically cutting across different parts of the system.

P 31

However, do not be overzealous in the use of scenarios during analysis:

> A team was given a small set of textual requirements which were refreshingly fairly complete and self-consistent. The analysis team took these as their direction and proceeded with a scenario-based approach to requirements analysis. Unfortunately, the team quickly got bogged down in details. The project ground to a halt by the time the group had examined around 600 different scenarios written for a requirements document that was only a few dozen pages. The project was never completed.

This web of scenarios in the analysis of a software system serves much the same purpose as do storyboards in making a movie. However, the analogy breaks down because of the mention of the word *web*. Movies (at least, with today's technology) have only one path of action through them, and so they can generally be represented by one long, continuous storyboard with several supplemental storyboards that extend or provide more detail for certain scenes. However, all interesting software applications rarely have a single path of behavior. Rather, the behavior of most complex systems, especially those driven by external events including user interaction, are best characterized as a set of nearly-independent scenarios. Within this web will be found a number of different clusters of scenarios, with each group formed by scenarios that are all closely related to some major system function; these groups we organize as use cases.

Scenarios are *nearly-independent* in the sense that they can be studied in isolation, although in reality each one has some semantic connection to other scenarios. For example, a scenario exposing the activity of a loan payment can be discussed with end users and developers in isolation. This scenario likely involves the action of checking the loan's history (since payment is an important historical event in the lifetime of a loan), and this action itself might be elaborated upon in a separate scenario. Similarly, the late payment scenario interacts with normal loan payment scenario, since the record of past payments has a bearing on the course of action: one missed payment by a valued customer might result in sending a polite letter, whereas a late payment by an habitually-late customer might result in a more personal visit.

In this context of an object-oriented system, scenarios thus provide a means of expressing the behavior that results from the collaboration of several classes or objects. Just as scenarios rarely stand alone, classes and objects rarely stand alone in a complex system. In a complex system, classes and object collaborate among themselves. For example, plain old telephone service in a switching system involves at a minimum the collaboration of four agents: two terminals (representing the two telephones), a path (denoting a physical path through the network) and a conversation (conversations are a central abstraction because each one is a conceptual object that represents something for which the telephone company can bill customers). These same agents are likely to participate in other scenarios and may even collaborate with different agents. For this reason, it is fair to say that most interesting scenarios cut across large parts of a system's architecture and each one touches a different set of collaborating classes and objects. Furthermore, the most interesting abstractions are those that appear in multiple scenarios.

What good are scenarios in object-oriented software development?
- They serve as an essential part of capturing the requirements about a system.
- They provide a vehicle for communication.
- They provide instructions to individual developers as well as to the testing team.
- They form an essential basis to the scheduling of iterations during design and evolution.

Scenarios speak the language of the end user and the domain expert, and therefore scenarios provide a means for end users to state their expectations about the desired behavior of a system to its developers. Scenarios can be either low-fidelity or high-fidelity, depending upon the relative importance of the details to its end users. For example, in the early stages of analysis of an inventory control system, it might be sufficient to explain the scenario of taking an item out of a warehouse in just a few free-form sentences. On the other hand, in a human-critical system such as a flight control system, it might be necessary to spell out details of timing and presentation.

By focusing end users and domain experts upon scenarios at the level of the problem domain, it helps them avoid the temptation of diving into solution-oriented abstractions. By focusing developers upon scenarios, it forces them to be grounded in the language of the problem domain, and also it forces them to consider an intelligent distribution of responsibilities throughout the system. Scenarios, no matter what representation they might take, also address the social aspect of joint development by providing a common artifact which end users and developers can talk about, cast stones at, argue about, and ultimately converge on.

For the developer, each scenario provides a reasonably unambiguous statement of the system's desired behavior which must be satisfied by the set of classes and objects presently under development. For the testing team, a scenario provides a reasonably unambiguous statement of testable behavior, first established as a system requirement and ultimately realized by the products of the developer. In this manner, there is an obvious kind of traceability possible, from the scenarios that capture system requirements, through the classes and objects that collaborate to provide this behavior, to the system tests that serve to verity that the system properly carries out this behavior.

What are scenarios not good for? In practice, scenarios turn out to be a marvelous way to characterize and then validate the resulting object-oriented architecture invented during design, the next phase of the macro process. However, it is important to realize that scenarios do not by themselves *define* an architecture. Scenarios can only illustrate or animate the dynamic interactions that occur in the context of a given architecture.

The concrete products of scenario-based analysis may take on any one of three different forms. First, CRC cards prove to be a delightful way to brainstorm about and visualize scenarios.* CRC cards are sort of a poor man's CASE tool, requiring a trivial investment of a few dozen index cards and some pencils with really good erasers. Their major attractions as a serious development technique are that they are totally free-form, they encourage the active interaction of the development team and domain experts, and they force the team to consider the intelligent distribution of responsibilities throughout the architecture. In practice, I have found CRC cards to be useful during analysis as well as during the later stages of design and evolution, particularly when further analyzing the dark corners of some aspect of the system's behavior. Elaborating upon a scenario with CRC cards also turns out to be a good way to identify the abstractionists on your team: they are the people who tend to end up in the center of a CRC card exercise.

---

* CRC stands for Class, Responsibilities, Collaborators. CRC cards were invented by Kent Beck and Ward Cunningham and popularized by others, most notably Rebecca Wirfs-Brock.

However, CRC cards do suffer from one major limitation: after elaborating upon a scenario, the developer cannot simply wrap a rubber band around the pack of cards, hand them to the customer as documentation of the analysis phase, and declare victory. CRC cards are by their very nature dynamic beasts, and left by themselves, they do not communicate the temporal or spatial aspects of a scenario.

Scenario diagrams mitigate the limitations of CRC cards and provide the second and third means of representing the semantics of a scenario. Scenario diagrams include message trace diagrams, which emphasize the flow of messages over time, and object message diagrams, which focus on messages dispatched among collaborating objects. In practice, starting with CRC cards is useful for brainstorming and then, as the semantics of the scenario become more concrete, the flow of the scenario may be captured in one of the two different kinds of scenario diagrams.

Figure 3-3 provides an example of a message trace diagram illustrating the scenario of paying off a loan. The major attraction of this kind of scenario diagram is that it clearly shows the flow of activity over time, starting at the top of the script (on the left hand side) and running down the diagram. Across the horizontal axis, message trace diagrams also show the classes and objects that collaborate in a given scenario. In this manner, each such scenario diagram (which expresses some temporal behavior of the system) achieves a tight coupling with the system's domain model (shown in class diagrams that collectively express some atemporal aspect of the analysis).

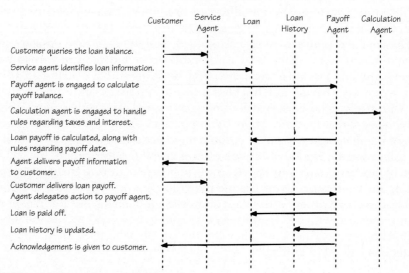

Figure 3-3 A Message Trace Diagram

Scenario diagrams, especially message trace diagrams, are well-suited for communicating business processes because at a high level, they speak the language of end users and domain experts. Early during analysis, we write scenario diagrams that contain message flows written as free-form text. As the team continues with the analysis, and even later, the architecture evolves by establishing its details, we might show the same diagram but now with concrete operations written for each message flow. This is part of the way in which scenario diagrams aid in the traceability of requirements: the same scenario may be expressed by different scenario diagrams, each at different levels of abstraction.

Message trace diagrams have one limitation: they can only show collaborative activity that is relatively sequential in nature. Message trace diagrams cannot by themselves show concurrent messaging, timing considerations, or more spatial issues such as the fact that one object in the collaboration is actually a part of another.

This leads to a third common representation for scenarios during analysis, namely object message diagrams, which mitigate the limitation of message trace diagrams.* Message trace diagrams and object message diagrams are both kinds of scenario diagrams, and to a large degree, they are isomorphic, meaning that it is possible to transform a message trace diagram into an object message diagram and vice versa. Thus, message trace diagrams and object message diagrams can be viewed as alternative representations of the same scenario. However, object message diagrams are valuable because they can show additional information, such as parallel threads of control and aggregation relationships.

In the more casual projects, this product of analysis is simply an informal collection of scenarios provided in any or all of these three representations and managed on paper or in the context of an analysis tool. In more formal projects, these scenarios are typically assembled into a requirements analysis document that is reviewed and whose change is controlled. This more tangible product thereby gives management an artifact that can be used to gain consensus on the desired behavior of the system and that can serve as the basis of system testing. Such a document typically states all of the system's behavioral requirements as illustrated in scenarios, together with a statement of all the non-behavioral aspects of the system, such as efficiency, reliability, security, and portability. This kind of document is discussed in more detail in Chapter 6.

Another important product of analysis is a domain model, the purpose of which is to visualize all of the central classes responsible for the essential behavior of the system. In the more informal projects, this model is expressed

---

* In the section on design that follows, Figure 3-5 provides an example of an object message diagram. Message trace diagrams are typically used more during analysis and less so during design, whereas object message diagrams are commonly used more during design and less during analysis. The good news is that both notations are semantically equivalent, and both span the activities of analysis and design.

simply as a dictionary of all the interesting classes that participate in the various scenarios discovered during analysis. In all other cases, a system's domain model typically is manifest in one or more class diagrams that include these key classes and their relationships. Figure 3-4 provides an example of such a diagram, drawn from the domain of a system that manages consumer loans.

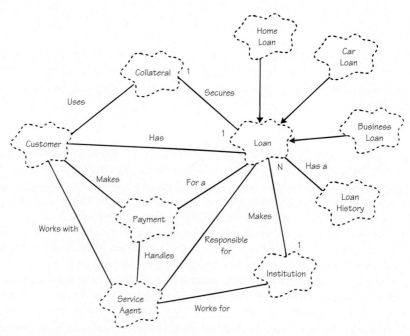

Figure 3-4   A Class Diagram

A domain model is not merely a product of invention; rather, it is largely a product of discovery. The classes found in such diagrams are drawn directly from the vocabulary of the problem space, and so they represent the central things in the world that the end user and domain expert see. In fact, the classes and objects that appear in scenario diagrams are typically the only ones that show up in a domain model. As I discuss in the next section, the activities that lead to creating such diagrams require the analyst to understand the problem domain in reasonable detail, identify these key classes, and then draw their boundaries.

I have a rule of thumb about the size of a typical domain model:

For projects of modest complexity, expect to discover about 50 to 100 classes in the domain model of a system which represents only those key abstractions that define the vocabulary of the problem space.

R 19

Applying the following recommended practice helps achieve this measure:

In the creation of a domain model during analysis, focus only upon those classes that make up the central vocabulary of the problem domain. If the removal of any one particular class does not make the model collapse, remove it, because it is not important to the analysis.

P 32

For all but the most simple applications, it is best to represent a system's domain model in more than one class diagram. Collectively, these diagrams cover the entire model with each diagram focusing upon some interesting cluster of classes. There is another recommended practice that helps keep a system's domain model manageable as analysis proceeds:

When creating a domain model, focus mainly upon the associations among its classes, and identify their meaning and (where appropriate) their cardinality. Rarely worry about identifying inheritance relationships this early in the life cycle, unless it is really central to the problem domain.

P 33

Applying these two practices yields a domain model that is quite similar to entity-relationship (ER) modeling, except for one thing. Whereas both object-oriented domain modeling and ER modeling focus upon a system's fundamental entities and their relationships during analysis, domain modeling adds the dimension of behavior.

Specifically, in addition to visualizing the classes that form a problem's vocabulary, a domain model serves as the product whereby analysts record their discovery of the distribution of roles and responsibilities in the system. As the previous chapter explains, a responsibility is some behavior for which an object is held accountable. For example, the responsibilities of a loan in the consumer lending problem might include the following:

- Keep track of essential loan information, including the loan's current principle, interest, and taxes.
- Manage the business rules regarding the loan's payment schedule.
- Handle the business rules regarding rights of transfer and distribution of funds.

Note that these responsibilities involve far more than merely breaking out the individual data elements that are a part of each abstraction. Rather, the more important responsibilities specify some action or reaction on the part of the class of objects under consideration.

What an object is and is not responsible for is an essential part of under-standing the meaning of the things in the vocabulary of the problem space. Thus, a key part of object-oriented analysis is discovering the distribution of responsibilities throughout the system because the very act of creating this product forces end users and developers to come to agreement about the boundary of each abstraction. Note that in the best-formed domain models, a domain model does not serve to identify the precise operations associated with each class. Identifying responsibilities is largely an activity of discovery; identi-fying operations that carry out these responsibilities is primarily an activity of invention.

In addition to specifying each abstraction's responsibilities, a domain model may also include the identification of the roles played by each. A *role* is the face that an object or a class presents to the world. The same object may play differ-ent roles at different times and so logically present a different face each time. Collectively, the roles of an object form the object's protocol.

During the analysis of a trading system, domain experts identi-fied financial instruments as a key abstraction. Further analysis revealed that such instruments played many different roles in different parts of the system. For example, at any given time, an instrument might take on the role of a contractual obligation, a kind of collateral for securing other instruments, or a tangible ele-ment of some tradable value. By studying these different roles, the team was able to understand this very complex abstraction from a number of orthogonal angles, and yet achieve simplicity because all of these roles were unified in a common class.

Thus, a domain model serves as an important product of analysis because it is the one place where the behavior that is manifested in the system's scenarios comes together in the form of the classes that carry out this common behavior. This is why typically the domain model of a system is expressed tangibly as a set of class diagrams together with a specification of the roles and responsibili-ties of each class.

In some cases, this tangible product is extended by providing a specification of the lifetime of certain classes. For example, the lifetime of a loan commences at its creation, continues through its payment periods and encompasses its payoff, and eventually ends some time later, according to the rules of how long loan information must be archived. Typically, this lifeline of an abstraction is illustrated in a scenario. For more complex objects that are driven by well-defined events, this lifeline is better illustrated as a state machine diagram, such as the one illustrated in Figure 3-5.

The final product of analysis is a risk assessment that identifies the known areas of technical and non-technical risk that may impact the design process. If

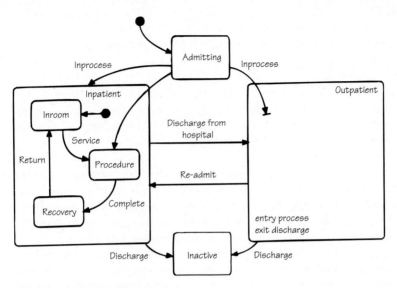

Figure 3-5   A State Machine Diagram

there were an earlier conceptualization phase, then this risk assessment is just an evolution of the earlier one in light of what has been learned during analysis. The most important part of this risk assessment is the identification of the scenarios that are most critical to the project's success in the context of its essential minimal characteristics. As I discuss in a later section, identifying these high-risk scenarios early is important because they are used to drive the process of evolution.

At this stage of development, other areas of risk should also be characterized. This may include risks of the unknown, specifying what areas of system behavior the project's analysts have not studied thoroughly or that the end user is still ambiguous about. This may also include technological risks uncovered during the creation of scenarios, such as concerns about capacity, performance, or even human factors issues of the system's look and feel. No matter what risks are uncovered, it is important that this product of analysis focuses upon the nature of the risks and not upon their solution, an activity that is best left to the next phase of development. Indeed, facing up to the presence of these risks early in the development process makes it far easier to make pragmatic architectural trade-offs later in the development process.

Activities

There are two primary activities associated with analysis:

- Scenario planning
- Domain analysis

The purpose of these two activities is to develop a common vocabulary and a common understanding of the system's desired behavior by exploring scenarios with end users and domain experts.

> An organization had grown over the last decade—largely through the acquisition of a number of other smaller companies. Not surprisingly, the company's information systems were in a shambles. As a part of a business process reengineering effort, the company's analysts sat down with end users and the people conducting the reengineering effort to understand the processes fundamental to the conduct of the company's business. The resulting product consisted of a set of scenarios that modeled the entire business. These scenarios were then used as the basis of requirements for the company's next generation information management system, expected to have a lifetime of 7 to 10 years.

With regard to scheduling this phase, I typically apply the following rule of thumb:

> For projects of modest complexity whose full life cycle is about one year, the analysis phase typically lasts about one to two months.*

R 20   Scenario planning is the central activity of analysis. During this activity, individual scenarios are investigated, and the system's domain model is constructed. Although every project should adapt a process suitable to its culture, most successful object-oriented projects typically track the following order of events during scenario planning. First,

- Enumerate all of the primary system functions and, where possible, organize them into use cases denoting clusters of functionally related-behaviors.

Why do I mention the "f" word (*function*) here in the context of this object-oriented process? The reason is that at the highest level of abstraction, all sys-

---

* Note that this rule does not scale linearly. For projects specified by several hundreds or even a thousand or more scenarios, analysis may take as long as a year. In projects of such scale, it is important that architectural design not be delayed, but rather, should proceed in parallel with all but the earliest stages of analysis.

tems are just bundles of behavior or services. Starting with a functional orientation during analysis helps the system's developers bound the scope of the system.[*]

The next step in scenario planning is as follows:

- Specify the system's context.

This step involves creating a context diagram showing what things are inside the system versus those things that are outside.

Next:

- Enumerate a list of primary scenarios that describe each system function.

The very act of building this list forces end users and domain experts to arrive at some consensus about those behaviors that are most important to the project's essential minimal characteristics and how the various behaviors of the system can be distinguished from one another. In even the most complex system, naming its principle scenarios is an important step because it provokes discussion between a system's customers and its developers.[‡]

Closely following this step, we have:

- For each interesting set of system functions, storyboard its primary scenarios.

As I have already suggested, CRC card techniques can be quite effective in brainstorming about each scenario. As the semantics of each scenario become clearer, these scenarios can then be documented through some combination of message trace diagrams or object message diagrams that illustrate the classes and objects that are initiators of or contributors to behavior, and that collaborate to carry out the activities in the scenario. Another important part of this step is the creation of a script for each scenario that shows the events that trigger the scenario and the resulting ordering of activities. In addition to the exposition of this strictly functional behavior, it is also important in some cases to document the assumptions, constraints, pre- and post-conditions, and performance issues of certain scenarios.

The next step is so critical to successful object-oriented analysis that it warrants a mention as an important practice:

> Interview domain experts and end users to establish the vocabulary of the problem space. First through techniques such as CRC cards, and

P 34

---

[*] One of the largest successful object-oriented applications I have encountered had nearly one thousand system functions. Most projects have far fewer, as my earlier rule of thumb suggests.

[‡] The idea of bashing users and programmers together during development is not a new one, and is, in fact, a central tenet of JAD (Joint Application Development) techniques. JAD is a high-ceremony approach whose basic principles can be reduced to the one sound bite "Hey . . . let's talk to real users about what they want!" As a decidedly low-ceremony kind of developer, I prefer this reductionist view.

then more formally through scenario diagrams, capture their understanding of the scenarios that define the system's behavior.

For the most trivial systems, a large white board is usually a sufficient tool for this step. As the complexity of a project grows, however, more automated solutions should be employed to capture these analysis decisions and provide a lasting legacy necessary for validating the system's architecture during design and for system testing during evolution.

Quite often during this step, analysis paralysis can set in. Users get bogged down in the details of individual scenarios, and developers become seriously discouraged over their ability to manage this growing complexity. The good news is that this condition can often be treated by conducting a broad CRC card exercise. Led by an outside mentor, such an activity brings together possibly hostile users and developers and forces them to reason about the system in a very concrete way.

In a project at a bank's MIS shop, end users were skeptical, and in fact they were openly opposed with the plans to apply object-oriented technology to their project. From past experiences, they were quite happy with data flow diagrams or even just free text for expressing requirements (even though the resulting projects were rarely on time). Ultimately, end users just did not want to talk to these upstart object-oriented developers, and developers were quickly becoming overwhelmed with trying to figure out the nature of the problem on their own. To mitigate this problem, the development team brought in a mentor that used CRC cards as a non-threatening way to get the end users to just talk about their needs in object-oriented ways. By the end of the first day, one wall was covered with CRC cards, the end users were engaged in focused and energetic discussions with one another over the resulting domain model they had developed, and the developers left with a far better model of the real requirements of the system.

This suggests another practice:

P 35

If you find your project getting bogged down in analysis, bring in an outside mentor to conduct a CRC card exercise that forces users and developers to talk to one another again about important scenarios. Hide this group away from the rest of the organization, and do not release them until progress is made in breaking this mental logjam.

In some projects, you may find end users that are forever in crisis mode such that no amount of human effort will break them free to help during analysis.

Projects facing this problem have two choices: either ignore these users and hope that your analysts will make the right guesses (not very likely), or turn your analysts into domain experts.

> Traders at a financial institution were in desperate need of new automated support, but they were so busy making trades that they had less than zero time to talk with developers. To mitigate this problem, the project sent several of its analysts to live with the traders over a period of several days, observing what they did on the trading floor. Armed with this knowledge, the team was then able to continue a more formal object-oriented analysis with more confidence. As prototypes were developed, these were brought up on the trading floor, and these were used under controlled circumstances by the traders themselves.

Overlapping with this exposition of primary scenarios is another step:

- As needed, generate secondary scenarios that illustrate common behavior or behavior under exceptional conditions.

Again, these secondary scenarios are not necessarily of secondary importance. Some such scenarios represent common behavior that extends a number of other primary scenarios (for example, checking a transaction on a loan for indications of fraud). Other such scenarios represent variations on the theme of primary ones (for example, manipulating a control surface in a fly-by-wire aircraft in the presence of high G-forces). As such, certain secondary scenarios may represent behaviors that are high risk and so should be given sufficient attention commensurate with that risk. Another reason for separating the analysis of primary and secondary scenarios is that a failure to do so will cause the system's analysts to get bogged down in the consideration of exceptional conditions, at the expense of understanding the larger problem.

For more complex systems, this distinction is important in managing the complexity of a system's many behaviors.

> Organize the web of scenarios that defines a system along two dimensions: first clump them in use cases according to major system functions, and then distinguish between primary scenarios (that represent a fundamental kind of behavior) and secondary ones (that represent variations on the theme of primary ones, often reflecting exceptional conditions).

P 36

The next step in scenario planning takes the knowledge learned in the exposition of each scenario and uses it to populate the system's domain model with the classes and objects that carry out these behaviors. As scenario planning continues, the details of each abstraction's role and responsibilities may be recorded as they are discovered.

- Update the evolving domain model to include the new classes and objects identified in each scenario, along with their roles and responsibilities.

The next two steps in scenario planning take another cut at analysis by using this domain model as a foundation.

- Where the life cycle of certain objects is significant or essential to the behavior of the system, develop a scenario or a state machine diagram for this class of objects.

- In those cases when external events tend to drive the system's behavior, enumerate all such events and analyze their impact upon the system by tracing these events through the domain model. Event tracing involves discovering which classes are responsible for detecting each event, which classes are responsible for handling each event, and which classes are responsible for reacting to each event.[*]

Object-oriented analysis involves far more than just idly looking at the world and modeling reality as we see it. These previous two steps serve to build domain models that are much more than passive clumps of data, and instead they are full of action and behavior.

The final step of scenario planning exists to encourage the creation of simple analysis models:

- Scavenge for patterns among scenarios and the domain model, and express these patterns in terms of more abstract, generalized scenarios or in terms of classes that embody common structure or common behavior.

Although I have described scenario planning as a very linear activity, in practice it is rarely so orderly. In practice, analysts will commonly bounce back and forth among these steps. As some scenarios are examined, others will be exposed that could not have been known *a priori*. Understanding the life time of an object may become an important issue in the middle of studying a larger scenario. Pattern scavenging is always opportunistic and may happen at just about the time common things are discovered. No matter what the precise order of activities a particular project may follow, the important thing to understand is that these steps all represent critical activities in the conduct of a successful object-oriented project, and their partial ordering as described above is the most common flow of events, although not the only possible and useful one.

What really prevents scenario planning from being a totally linear process is the simple fact that discovery cannot be scheduled. To mitigate the risks associated with this uncertainty, successful object-oriented projects must be proactive when dealing with discovery and thus will often employ a second activity during analysis, namely, domain analysis.

---

[*] See Chapter 7 for more information about modeling reactive systems.

Domain analysis seeks to explicitly uncover risk and to identify the classes and objects that are common to a particular problem. Domain analysis is typically an opportunistic activity, meaning that it is scheduled as the need arises. This activity has two semi-independent steps. First:

- Study existing systems that are similar to the one under development.

Before setting out to implement a new system, it is often wise to study existing ones. In this way, the project benefits from the experience of other teams that had to make similar development decisions. In the best of all worlds, the results of a domain analysis may lead the team to discover that it does not need to develop much if any new software, but rather can reuse or adapt existing frameworks.

Second:

- For those areas of great uncertainty, develop a prototype to be used by the development team to validate its assumptions about the desired behavior of the system, or to serve as a basis of communication with end users.

As with all such prototypes, once their purpose has been served, resist the urge to drag their implementation directly into production development. Instead, throw them away or cannibalize them, but retain what you have learned from the experience.[*]

Develop executable prototypes during analysis only for noble reasons, not as an excuse to accelerate coding. Noble reasons include exploring areas of human interaction (such as for experimenting with the application's look and feel) or investigating novel abstractions and algorithms (such as studying the dynamics of a control system).

P 37

Domain analysis plays an important role in creating a risk assessment during analysis by providing a means for management to explore areas of risk without disturbing the rhythm of scenario planning.

Agents

I use the following practice when staffing a project's analysis activity:

Analysis is best conducted by a small team, ideally made up of a core group consisting of only 4 to 6 people including the system's architect,

P 38

---

[*] Some such prototypes may have a relatively long lifetime, because they serve as an operational model of the system's desired behavior. This is particularly true of prototypes that model an application's look and feel, including the representation of its screens and reports. It is important to note that these prototypes are just models and generally should not be directly transmogrified into a production system.

one or two analysts/senior developers, one or two domain experts or end users, and a member of the quality assurance/testing team.

Small projects can get by with a team of one or two, consisting of at least the architect and perhaps one domain expert. For larger projects, this core team is typically supported by other small groups of analysts, developers, and domain experts who focus upon investigating particular functional areas of the system. It is important that these groups work with and report back to the core group, which is responsible for driving and preserving the conceptual integrity of the analysis phase.

Indeed, the role of the architect on the core team is to provide this sense of conceptual integrity. All too often, projects that are staffed by a random group of analysts fail to discover the specifics of a system's desired behavior at the same level of detail or coverage, leading to blind spots in the team's understanding of the project at hand.

Scenario planning is carried out by the one or two analysts or senior developers (or groups of them for larger projects) in conjunction with the domain experts and end users. I am deliberately vague as to whether or not a project should be staffed with dedicated analysts or developers. Analysts who know nothing about building real systems are never a good choice because they will tend to specify requirements that are unattainable at any reasonable development cost. Similarly, developers who know nothing about the problem domain are a terrible choice, because they will be driven by the technology, not the needs of the system's users. This is one case where individual personalities really make a difference. Thus, the core team must be staffed with the right balance of skills between its pure analysts and pure developers.

The teams who carry out domain analysis are staffed as needed and then dispersed once their tasks are completed. Such groups—sometimes called tiger teams or SWAT teams—are usually drawn from individuals in the core team and supplemented by other analysts and developers, most of whom will be engaged on the project in later phases of development. Involving other development team members like this during analysis is also an effective way to get them invested in the development process, and to foster their understanding of the system's vision.

Typically, I like to engage at least one member of the quality assurance/testing team during in scenario planning, since scenarios represent behaviors that can be tested. Involving quality-assurance personnel early in the process helps to institutionalize a commitment to quality.

In more than a few organizations, it is common to almost fully staff a project during analysis. The question then arises, what to do with all of the people who are not directly involved in the activities of analysis? The wrong thing to do is put all of these people on the tasks of scenarios planning and domain analysis. The right thing to do is to use the remaining "unemployed" staff to pursue some risk mitigating prototyping, especially ones that will lead to a better understanding of the system's sizing (volumetrics) and performance

Milestones and Measures

There are three major milestones in this phase:

- Specification of the system's context, functions, and scenarios
- Elaboration of the system's scenarios
- Completion of the system's domain model

Specification of the system's context, functions, and scenarios occurs relatively early during analysis, and marks the point in time when the scope of the problem has been reasonably bounded. Elaboration of the system's scenarios and domain model are not quite so discrete, but instead are milestones that unfold during analysis. Practically, this means that management should not proscribe one big-bang milestone at the end of analysis, but rather should establish intermediate milestones for the discovery of behavior relative to functional groupings of scenarios and parts of the domain model.

Analysis never really finishes until a system is delivered, but we can declare closure with a formal analysis phase when the team has elaborated and *signed off* on scenarios for all fundamental system behaviors. By signed off I mean that the resulting analysis products have been validated by the core team and the project's customers; by *fundamental* I refer to behaviors that are central to the application's purpose. Again, I neither expect nor desire a complete analysis. It is sufficient that only primary and some secondary behaviors be considered. This leads to the next rule:

> The analysis phase should be drawn to a close once the team has elaborated approximately 80% of a system's primary scenarios along with a representative selection of the secondary ones. Elaborate upon any more, and your analysis will likely reach diminishing returns; elaborate upon any fewer, and you will not have a sufficient understanding of the desired behavior of the system to properly understand the risks.

R 21

Secondary milestones that can be managed during analysis include the completion of studies or prototypes by the groups doing domain analysis.

The measures of goodness to look for during analysis include completeness, stability, and simplicity. A good analysis will cover most primary scenarios and a statistically interesting set of secondary ones. This set of scenarios should specify only the system's external behavior, any constraints upon the system, and the system's response to expected as well as undesirable events. A good analysis will also carry out walkthroughs of all strategically important scenarios, so as to help to communicate a vision of the system to the entire development team. If you find a lack of consensus during these walkthroughs, or if you find the domain model changing erratically, these are signs of instability in the analysis process. Where massive instability exists, delegate a "tiger team" to attack the problem and drive it to closure. Lastly, a good analysis will also yield the discovery of patterns of behavior, resulting in a simple domain model that exploits all that is common among different scenarios. Analysis models that are clumsy or bloated are an indication that the team does not really understand the underlying problem.

DESIGN

Purpose

The purpose of design is to create an architecture for the evolving implementation.

Once analysis is done, there is the tendency in immature projects to consider the domain model resulting from analysis as ready to code in C++,[*] thus skipping any further design. Healthy projects recognize that there is still quite some work to do, involving issues such as concurrency, serialization, safety, distribution, and so on, and that the design model may end up looking quite different in a number of subtle ways.

Thus, every project requires this phase. As I describe in the previous two chapters, establishing a sound architectural foundation is absolutely essential to the success of an object-oriented project. Some teams try to ignore this phase, either because they are in such a rush to get a product out quickly they feel they do not have time to architect, or because they do not believe that architecting provides them any real value. Either way, the resulting head-long rush to code is always disastrous: fail to carry out this step properly, and your project will be likely to experience software meltdown. Your project may still develop a few reasonably good classes, but without an architecture in place to provide some much-needed conceptual integrity, those classes will never hang together well, resulting in a system that is brittle, hard to understand, and far more complex that it really needs to be.

Architectural design can only begin once the team has in place a reasonable understanding of the system's requirements. It is important to avoid premature designs, wherein development begins before analysis reaches closure. It is equally important to avoid delayed designing, wherein the organization

---

[*] Or in whatever is the project's language of choice.

thrashes while trying to complete a perfect and hence unachievable analysis model.

Design, just like analysis, never really stops until the final system is delivered. During this phase, we reach some degree of closure by putting in place most of the system's strategic design decisions and then establishing policies for various tactical issues. The successful object-oriented project tries to defer the myriad of other tactical design details (such as the interfaces and implementation of many implementation-specific classes) to the later phase of evolution, at which time there is more information to make intelligent decisions.

Design focuses upon structure, both static and dynamic. Further analysis may occur during the design phase, mainly to explore areas of uncertainty regarding the system's desired behavior, but design mainly serves to create the system's concrete skeleton upon which all the rest of its implementation hangs. At the end of the formal phase of design, management should be able to answer the following five questions:

- What is the basic structure of the system under development?
- What patterns shape this structure and offer it simplicity?
- What parts of the system can be reused or adapted from other sources?
- What is the plan to evolve the resulting architecture into a production system?
- Are there any new or revised areas of risk that have been uncovered during this process of invention?

Finding answers to these questions is what drives the process of design. The first two questions address the form of the resulting architecture. The third question concerns finding ways to solve the problem at hand by adapting existing frameworks, using various application generator tools, and exploiting legacy systems. The remaining two questions deal with establishing the plan for evolving this architecture during its next phase of development.

Products

During design, five artifacts are generated:

- An executable and baselined architecture
- The specification of all important architectural patterns
- A release plan
- Test criteria
- A revised risk assessment

The first two of these artifacts establish the system's structure, and the remaining three of these artifacts support the process of risk-based develop-

ment for evolving this structure. An executable architecture is the most important product of this phase of development.

Why is an executable architecture the essential product of design? Because it:
- Serves as a tangible manifestation of many strategic decisions
- Provides a platform for validating a number of important analysis and design assumptions
- Offers a stable intermediate form that can be more easily evolved as further details of the problem are discovered and new structures are invented

---

Building so tangible an artifact at this relatively early stage of development makes a difference:

This organization was tasked with replacing an absolutely aging financial system, originally written in COBOL. Responding to new requirements was terribly painful, owing to the fact that the system had mutated over the years as new features were slapped on without regard for their impact upon other features. Maintenance was also more than slightly inconvenienced by the fact that the customer had lost some of the original source code. With some real opposition, the team eventually succeeded in building an executable architecture that forced it to touch a number of key interfaces. This was basically a transaction processing system, and requirements for the complete system had identified about 400 such transactions. In their architectural release, they carried out much of the interesting behavior of a dozen or so transactions. The bad news was the resulting application was slower and bigger than the entire COBOL system. A tiger team investigated the problem, and discovered that the group had done exactly what every beginning object-oriented team tends to do: they overabstracted in some places (there were too many classes for the same concept) and underabstracted in others (there were too few classes for certain complex abstractions, requiring application developers to write an excessive amount of hand-crafted code). The good news was that after fixing these problems and quickly respinning the architectural release, the team validated its assumptions with an architecture that was smaller and faster.

If this team had used a more traditional non-iterative style of development and so waited until integration time to bring the application together, it simply would have been too late to recover from the systemic problems.*

Let me be very clear by what I mean regarding an executable architecture.

An executable architecture:
- Exists as a real application that runs in some limited way
- Carries out some or all of the behavior of a few interesting scenarios chosen from the analysis phase
- Is production quality code
- Either constitutes a vertical slice that cuts through the complete system from top to bottom, or goes horizontal by capturing most of the interesting elements of the domain model
- Touches upon most if not all of the key architectural interfaces
- Makes a number of explicit simplifying assumptions, yet is not so simple that it assumes away reality

Most of these properties should be fairly self-evident, but my notion of a vertical versus a horizontal slice through the system requires a bit further explanation. As I mention in the first chapter, for all but the most trivial systems, it is necessary to architect a system not in terms of individual classes, but in the form of clusters of classes. These larger units of decomposition I call a class category.

Figure 3-6 illustrates this point. Here I have a top-level class diagram illustrating the architecture of the consumer loan system. This diagram represents the major clusters of classes found in this system, arranged in a reasonably strict hierarchy. Zoom inside any one of these class categories, and you will find a set of classes that collaborate to carry out some major set of behaviors, as well as perhaps some other nested class categories that further decompose this structure. This kind of diagram serves to visualize the static structure of even the most complex systems, and it will typically appear as part of the architecture's documentation, which I discuss later in this section.

A *vertical slice* through this architecture would involve creating a small executable release that touches classes in most of these class categories from top to bottom. For example, the team might partially implement the scenarios for cre-

---

* In all fairness, I must provide a sad but true ending to this story. The team successfully finished their project ahead of schedule and on budget. They attributed much of their success to the process and the tools they were using. However, the delivered system was never fully deployed and was, in fact, ultimately canceled because of purely political reasons. The moral of this story is that even the best intentions and the most superior technology are no match for political subterfuge.

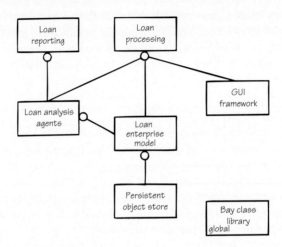

Figure 3-6   A Top-Level Class Diagram

ating a loan and for making a payment on a loan. This would require designing and building the core interfaces to loan processing, the loan domain model, and possibly the persistent data store, and then implementing them just enough to carry out some of the interesting behaviors of these two scenarios. The operative phrases here are *core interfaces* and *just enough*. The core interfaces encompass the important classes and services that live at the edge of certain class categories; just enough means that at this point in time, we implement only parts of these interfaces, in fact only those parts necessary to provide the partial behavior this initial release is targeting for, and all those parts necessary to validate the tactical policies the system's architects have established.

A *horizontal slice* cuts through this architecture broadly rather than deeply. In this example, it might mean designing the interfaces and providing partial implementations for the entire domain model. This approach touches fewer of the technology issues in the system and instead tends to focus on the logic of the system as a whole.

My experience with architecture-driven development suggests the following practice:

P 39

> During design, build an executable architectural release that forces you to consider the pragmatics of all important interfaces and all important collaborations.

What kind of slice you build in crafting this architecture depends upon the nature of the highest risks.

> If the dominant risk to the success of your system involves the technology, attack design with a vertical slice through the architecture. If the dominant risk is instead the logic of the system, take a horizontal slice.

P 40

Most often, though, the following rule of thumb applies:

> For most systems of modest or greater complexity, focus design on a broad sweep, covering some 80% of the breadth and about 20% of its depth.

R 22

In some cases, the risk in your project may be so daunting, that you have to do it both ways.

> An organization was working on a major software initiative, upon which it was essentially betting the future of the company. Moving away from mainframe technology, it was embracing client/server computing, GUI visualization, distributed data base technology, and high-bandwidth networking (not to mention making the move from COBOL to Smalltalk).* On top of all that, the organization was fundamentally reengineering the way it would use this software to run the business, employing a smaller staff backed up with much higher degrees of automation. For the first architectural release, it took a horizontal slice, because the development team wanted to validate the basic assumptions of the logic in the domain model. This was most critical to the immediate success of the project, because there was a grave concern that the team really did not understand the domain. Once it was satisfied that this risk was manageable, in just a few weeks after this first release, the team then took a vertical slice that caused it to consider their architectural decisions regarding distribution and persistence. Only once it had completed both slices, was it confident that it had made reasonable strategic decisions, and so could then commit the resources necessary to drive this architecture to production.

During design, identify the highest risks to your project's success, then deal with them by creating an executable architecture that attacks these risks head on. If correct business logic is the highest risk, implement the entire domain

---

* For those of you who have the scars to show for living inside projects such as this one, you are probably either laughing at this apparent idiocy or crying in bitter remembrance. The truth is, most projects of this complexity fail in rather spectacular ways. However, sometimes you just have no choice (as did this organization), and if you do not take the risk, you will be out of business anyway. The jury is still out on this particular project, but at least the team is deliberately trying to attack the risks it faces instead of reacting to them, as less mature organizations will tend to do.

model, and populate it with all its most interesting business rules. If the application's look and feel is more critical, then focus on the GUI part of the system. If distribution or capacity or performance are the dominant concerns, then build an executable architecture that forces you to consider all the strategic decisions that will best contribute to mitigating these risks.

The specification of all of a system's most important architectural patterns is the second most important product of design. As I describe in the previous chapter, patterns constitute a system's microarchitecture. All well-structured, object-oriented systems embody a number of patterns at various levels of abstraction, including idioms (at the level of the implementation language), mechanisms (representing important collaborations), and frameworks (which codify large functional domains).

> Why are patterns an important consideration during design? Because they:
> - Capture the architect's intent and vision, and so serve to propagate that vision in a very tangible way
> - Provide common solutions to related problems, and thus are necessary for the creation of simple systems

The successful evolution and eventual maintenance of a system can only happen if a system's microarchitecture is both explicit and understandable.

A platform vendor released an object-oriented application framework to facilitate the creation of new programs. Unfortunately, most users found it quite impossible to use. The framework had all the right abstractions, but the library was fundamentally unapproachable because the way those classes collaborated with one another was an undocumented mystery, whose secrets could only be revealed by software archaeologists who had to spend enormous amounts of time pouring over the code, trying to figure out what it did. Practically, this meant that most mortal users–who had little time for such detective work–either gave up, or used the classes in the framework in quite unnatural ways, resulting in applications that sort of worked, but were extremely fragile and impossible to understand.

Successful object-oriented projects therefore take this practice seriously:

During design, explicitly specify the system's microarchitecture, including its idioms, mechanisms, and frameworks.

P 41

As I describe in the previous chapter, an application's idioms should be stated in the project's style guide.* Similarly, the application's mechanisms should be specified in the form of an architecture document that documents these key collaborations.‡ Typically, these mechanisms are also delivered in the form of prototypes that serve to validate the design of the microarchitecture and that provide tangible examples of its form and use. Similarly, the use of certain frameworks should be described in the system's architecture document. The frameworks themselves—assuming that they are of high-quality—should already be documented in the right way, meaning that their own patterns should be both explicit, understandable, and self-evident from the implementation itself, as well as formally described in the framework's documentation.

A release plan is a later product of design, and it serves as a management planning tool that drives the next phase of development. At the very least, a release plan should prescribe explicit schedules for all incremental releases, as well as tie functionality to these releases. The best release plans additionally tie these releases to testing plans, as well as tie these releases back to the scenarios defined during analysis. In this manner, a good release plan not only serves to control the architecture's evolution, but it also provides traceability from each release back to its requirements as stated in terms of scenarios.

Test criteria encompasses a testing plan and, where possible, actual test scripts. For the most part, such scripts can often be translated directly from the system's scenarios. The risk assessment created during design is largely an evolution of the one created in the previous phase of development. A risk assessment becomes increasingly more important during this phase, simply because it is necessary for driving the rhythm of evolution. Furthermore, this assessment becomes the basis for tasking tiger teams to attack areas of high risk during the evolution of the system's architecture.

As for analysis, the activities of design may yield some executable prototypes as tangible products. This is to be expected. Design is a period of intense invention, and throwaway prototypes are one very important vehicle for exploring architectural alternatives and for trying out new ideas, such as might be found regarding to an application's look and feel.

Activities

There are three primary activities associated with design:

---

* Idioms include patterns such as naming conventions, the use of exceptions, and the style of writing and documenting class interfaces

‡ Mechanisms include patterns, such as collaborations, responsible for storage management and processing transactions.

- Architectural planning
- Tactical design
- Release planning

The purpose of these three activities is to establish a skeleton for the solution and to lay down tactical policies for implementation.

The greatest risk one project faced was balancing an ill-defined set of very slippery requirements together with an equally unchangeable schedule.* Rather than panicking and staffing the project with a horde of developers tasked with hacking away at a solution, the project instead chose to attack this risk by deliberately designing the solution's architecture and then validating that architecture in the form of an executable release. The very act of producing something real this early in the life cycle lead the team to realize that the development tools were inadequate, and that the assumptions they made about performance bottlenecks in the system were misguided. Only after correcting these oversights did the organization further grow the project with a staff sufficient to evolve this architecture through further discovery of the system's real requirements and invention of a simpler architecture. The time the team spend in architectural planning was more than made up by the elimination of an explicit and very risky traditional integration phase.

If, in the broadest sense, we say that the macro process of object-oriented development encompasses the successive refinement of an architecture, then it is fair to consider design as the production of the first iteration.

With regard to scheduling this phase, I typically apply the following rule:

R 23

For projects of modest complexity whose full life cycle is about one year, the design phase typically lasts about one month and rarely exceeds two months.‡

For massive projects, the design phase ends up looking like the whole life cycle of analysis, design, and evolution for a much more modest sized project.

---

* Sadly, this situation describes just about every project of substance that I have encountered; the demand for software indeed remains insatiable. This particular story comes from the domain of a client/server application at a telephone company, involving the analysis of customer calling patterns for toll-free numbers.

‡ For the design phase especially, the important aspect of this rule is not the calendar time itself, but rather, the actual time it takes to design a stable architecture. In large projects, I have seen the design phase take upwards of half a year or longer.

In many projects, it is common for the activities of analysis to overlap slightly with design as the team continues to explore the dark corners of the system's requirements. As I discuss in Chapter 5, it is also common to overlap the design phase with the training and indoctrination of the bulk of the development team that will join with the project during evolution.

Architectural planning is the central activity of design, and it serves to establish the basic structure of the system under development. As such, architectural planning involves inventing the layers and partitions of the overall system. Architectural planning encompasses a logical decomposition representing the clustering and collaboration of classes, as well as a physical decomposition representing a clustering of modules and the allocation of functions to different processors.

Architectural planning is fundamental to establishing a system's conceptual integrity. By creating the framework for a solution relatively early in the development life cycle, the team puts in place a tangible artifact that captures the architect's vision and provides a stable intermediate form that can be evolved as the details of the system's behavior are discovered and new solutions invented.

The activities of architectural planning can best be summarized in one practice:

> Just do it.* Resist the urge to delay building something real until you know all there is to know about your problem; by then it will be too late, and the problem will likely have changed anyway.

P 42

You would be surprised at the number of object-oriented project teams I encounter that are absolutely terrified of building anything real. These projects are so afraid of failure that they want to wait until they have the perfect abstractions in place. Applying this practice forces them to make intelligent engineering choices sooner rather than later, where there is more room to maneuver.

Critics of this practice argue that I am encouraging random acts of hacking by urging projects to rush into implementation. Not so. During architectural planning, one does not build everything. Rather, the team should focus on mitigating risk by establishing the bones of the evolving system.

> During design, focus the creation of an architecture on three things: interfaces, the intelligent distribution of responsibilities throughout the system, and the exploitation of patterns of collaboration that make the system simpler.

P 43

---

* This is known as the Nike® approach to software development.

This is not hacking: Architectural planning is the deliberate creation of a reusable artifact that serves as the center of all subsequent development.

Non-object-oriented developers may think that architectural planning is a bit like RAD (rapid application development). Sort of. Whereas RAD focuses on independently completing functionally disparate parts of an application through rapid development, architectural planning seeks to rapidly build an architecture that cuts across functional boundaries and then grows it over time to complete each function.

Architectural planning typically follows a simple chain of activities. First:

- Consider the clustering of functions from the products of analysis, and allocate these to layers and partitions of the architecture. Functions that build upon one another should fall into different layers; functions that collaborate to yield behaviors at a similar level of abstraction should fall into partitions which represent peer services.

This step is fundamentally a raw act of invention, wherein the architect decides upon the basic shape of the system and the general distribution of responsibilities throughout it. For even the largest systems, that basic shape is something that an architect should be able to express in a single diagram that illustrates the major clusters of classes in the system, such as shown in Figure 3-6.

There are three factors that influence this step: big architectural patterns, an understanding of what is likely to change, and an understanding of the pressures brought about by technological alternatives.

Big architectural patterns denote the basic framework of a system and its flow of control. For example, in a real time system, the architect might choose between a frame-based architecture (wherein time is divided into discrete frames of processing) or a message-based one (wherein external events are detected and then dispatched by a central object to subordinate objects responsible for responding to certain classes of events). Similarly, in an MIS system, the architect might choose between a centralized model (wherein the domain model lives on one large server) or a more distributed one (wherein the model is broken up among clients). The best large architectural patterns often spring from the experience of the seasoned architect, who already has an intuitive feel for what structures work and what do not. It is also the case that different domains are best served by different architectural patterns, as I discuss in detail in Chapter 7.

An understanding of what is likely to change is important in this step because things that change together should in general be grouped together in the architecture. For example, if it is expected that an application will be ported to a system with a different GUI, then it is best to separate all those elements that functionally relate to the look and feel of the system. Similarly, if there is great risk associated with the choice of a particular data base strategy, then it is best that all abstractions associated with persistence mechanisms be clustered together. In short, this aspect forces the architect to build firewalls into the architecture, so that when changes occur—and they will—they will not rip through the entire architecture, shredding any hope of conceptual integrity.

An understanding of the pressures brought about by technological alternatives means simply that the architect must take advantage of existing frameworks and standard off-the-shelf components. If a nearly perfect framework already exists for the problem's domain, or even if parts of that domain can be satisfied by the adaptation of a technology specific framework such as a for a GUI or a distributed object manager, then it's down right stupid to build something from scratch if you don't have to. In other words:

> During design, the architect should first consider how to adapt existing frameworks before setting out to build an architecture from scratch.

P 44

There is a rule that I find useful here:

> Even the most unusual application should be able to steal at least 10% of its implementation from existing simple frameworks, such as for domain-independent data structures. More mature organizations should be able to avoid writing about 30% of their whole system from scratch. The most mature organizations—those which have invested the resources necessary to develop a domain-specific framework that offers them a competitive advantage—can see in the steady state the ability to avoid writing 60% or more of their applications.

R 24

Architectural planning continues with the next step:

• Validate the architecture by creating an executable release that partially satisfies the semantics of a few interesting system scenarios as derived from analysis.

Building something executable is absolutely essential because it forces the development team to validate their design assumptions in the harsh light of reality. The danger with hanging on to a paper design for too long is that it can lull the team into a false sense of security. It is important to spend a reasonable amount of time generating models on paper, but it is seductively easy to develop models that are either too hard to build or are focused on the wrong priorities. Putting a stake in the ground in the form of an executable architectural release helps to focus the team on the right priorities, namely, the project's essential minimal characteristics.

As I describe earlier, this first architectural release can take the form of either a horizontal or a vertical slice through the system. No matter which slice is chosen, it is critical to drive this step to closure by selecting a few interesting scenarios from the analysis phase and implementing them just enough. The operative phrases here are *interesting* and *just enough*. By *interesting*, I mean selecting just a handful of primary and secondary scenarios that satisfy the following criteria:

- Collectively they demonstrate the central behavior of the system
- Their implementation touches most, if not all, of the architecture's most important interfaces

By *just enough*, I mean:

- Their implementation directly attacks the highest risk to the project, which at this stage is typically either the risk of not understanding the project's real requirements or some risk of technology, be it tools, networks, persistence, or user interfaces.
- Craft concrete interfaces for all of the abstractions necessary to implement the given scenarios, but do not try to make these interfaces complete.
- Implement the abstractions below these interfaces only to the degree necessary to achieve the goals of this first architectural release; where necessary, stub out implementations with scaffolding that can be replaced in later iterations.

This step not only serves to produce a tangible product, but as I describe further in Chapter 5, it also helps to kick-start the team's selection and use of development tools.

Architectural planning concludes with a final step:

- Instrument the architecture and assess its weaknesses and strengths. Identify the risk of each key architectural interface so that resources can be meaningfully allocated as evolution commences.

If this first release is found seriously deficient, then these newly discovered weakness should be attacked immediately and another spin of the architecture produced before moving on.

There are two subtle implications of this step. First, it means that the testing team engages in the development life cycle far earlier than tradition dictates. This is actually a good thing, because it permits early collection of quality data, as I further describe in Chapter 6. Second, it requires that the team conduct walkthroughs of the entire architecture. This step not only forces the architect to make simple and understandable strategic decisions, it also serves to communicate his or her architectural vision to the rest of the team which will be starting to ramp up for production development during the next phase.

Tactical design involves making decisions about the myriad of common policies that impact the emerging implementation. As I describe earlier, poor tactical design can ruin even the most profound architecture, and so the team must mitigate this risk by explicitly identifying the project's key policies and putting in place incentives to adhere to them. This activity thus selects the major mechanisms and idioms that shape the system and make it simple. This activity also explicitly considers how the team can avoid writing code by reusing or adapting existing frameworks.

Tactical policies are typically established by the architect and then carried out by transitory tiger teams that validate and drive those policies to closure. These policies should encompass the most important patterns in the system. Such patterns should include idioms for the implementation language (such as naming conventions and rules about documenting classes in code), as well as patterns for most if not all of the system's central mechanisms (which I describe in Chapter 2).

> During design, explicitly select, validate, and then document the common idioms and mechanisms that shape the system and bring it conceptual integrity.

P 45

This activity serves to produce three tangible artifacts: the project's style guide, an architecture document, and a set of prototypes of the system's mechanisms that serve as examples for the rest of the team from which they can learn as well as steal ideas and code.

This activity begins with the following step:

- Relative to the given application domain, enumerate the common policies that must be addressed by disparate elements of the architecture.

Some such policies are fundamental, that is, they address domain-independent issues such as memory management, error handling, and so on. Other policies are domain-specific and include idioms and mechanisms that are germane to that domain, such as control policies in real-time systems, transaction and database management in information systems, identification and migration in distributed systems, and the look and feel of user-centric systems.

There is a danger in trying to do too much at this stage, and so I offer the following rule:

> Since most object-oriented systems require less than 10 to 20 really central mechanisms, during design focus on the 5 to 7 mechanisms that have the most sweeping implications to the evolving implementation or that represent the highest risk to the success of the project.

R 25

Before rushing out to craft these patterns by hand, apply the next step in tactical design:

- Consider whether any existing frameworks can be adapted to satisfy the needs of these mechanisms.

In other words:

Aggressively seek out ways to avoid writing code. Where it makes sense, adapt existing frameworks or use application builders.

P 46

Be skeptical of any solution that seems too good to be true, however, because it probably is too good to be true. Make certain that any framework you select is mature enough that you are willing to bet your project on it. Prove to yourself that any application builder you select is comprehensive enough and scales up sufficiently to meet your production needs. Indeed, this is an essential part of tactical design: your team must develop a high level of confidence in any of the off-the-shelf components you decide to use.

In virtually all trading firms, demands by traders for applications to serve the derivatives market far outrun their development organization's ability to deliver. One company started building a solution from the ground up (at last report, they are still building it). Another company developed an architectural vision (which provided them a competitive advantage), but then it looked around for existing frameworks to carry out that vision. The development team found two candidates in the form of financial frameworks consisting of over 500 classes each that codified a major part of their domain. After assessing the technical merits of each framework (through prototyping) as well as the merits of each company (i.e. where they sufficiently stable and not likely to go out of business anytime soon), the team selected one of the frameworks and adapted it to their needs. This approach retained the firm's competitive advantage, yet allowed it to get to the market much more rapidly than starting from scratch.

This step requires some creative exploration. Typically, this means that the architect will first identify a mechanism, then a tiger team will select candidate frameworks or application builders and build prototypes against them to validate that proposal. The end of this exploration yields one of two possible outcomes:

- The selected technology is found suitable, and the team is left with a prototype that shows how it can be adapted to their use.
- The selected technology is found wanting, and the tiger team generates a custom solution that satisfies the project's needs together with a prototype that demonstrates its use.

Under either outcome, the pragmatic team will always keeps its eyes open during the rest of the development life cycle for new frameworks that might better satisfy their needs, as well as for the opportunity to turn any custom solutions into local frameworks. If any such technologies pop up later, the team's management must make an explicit business decision about whether or not to adopt them at that time.

Validating either off-the-shelf or custom approaches takes place in the next overlapping step:

- For each common policy, develop the scenarios that describe the semantics of that policy. Further capture its semantics in the form of an executable prototype that can be instrumented and refined.

Be aware of the great distance that separates the lashing together of a prototype from the building of a production system.* Remember that a prototype is not production code, but rather it is only an artifact that serves an immediate purpose (in this case, to validate an approach to the design of a mechanism) and is eventually discarded.

Once the team is satisfied with its decisions, tactical design concludes with the following step:

- Document each policy and carry out a peer walkthrough, so as to broadcast its architectural vision.

Formal walkthroughs are important in propagating the architect's vision as well as in mentoring the junior people on the team.

Collectively, the more important mechanisms should be preserved in an architecture document, which serves as a repository of all such tactical policies and provides a living artifact that the management team can use to bring simplicity to the overall system. Figure 3-7 provides an example of how one such mechanism might be documented in the form of an object message diagram.‡ In Chapter 6, I describe the structure of an architecture document in complete detail.

Release planning sets the stage for architectural evolution. This activity exposes any new areas of risk and creates the plan to evolve the system's initial architecture into a production system. Such a plan must identify a controlled series of architectural releases, each growing in its functionality and ultimately encompassing the requirements of the complete production system. A main artifact of this activity is therefore a formal development plan that specifies this stream of architectural releases together with the team tasks and risk assessments for each one. A good plan should portray the tasks, priorities, and plans for evolving the system in the face of numerous unknowns.

---

* I have encountered more than a few organizations that have adopted technologies such as Visual Basic that work well in the small, but fail to scale up as requirements grow. If the cost of ownership of software is not an issue in your domain, then such approaches are reasonable. However, do remember that small, manageable pieces of software have a tendency to grow up to be large, unmanageable ones.
‡ This figure illustrates a common mechanism used in real time systems, namely, the division of processing into frames of time. Chapter 7 talks about this mechanism in a bit more detail.

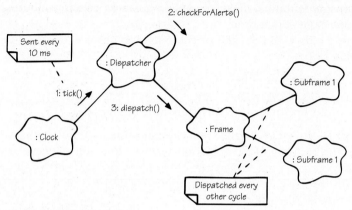

Figure 3-7 An Object Message Diagram

This activity typically begins with the following step:

- Given the scenarios identified during analysis, organize them in order of fundamental to peripheral behaviors. Prioritizing scenarios can best be accomplished with a team that includes a domain expert, analysis, architect, and quality-assurance personnel.

Prioritizing scenarios must take into account several factors, including risk, importance to the customer, and the staging of development (since certain scenarios will depend upon the services provided by other more basic scenarios). Next:

- Group these scenarios and assign them to a series of architectural releases whose final delivery represents the production system.

Grouping scenarios properly is critical. Remembering that the initial architectural release carries out the partial behavior of a small set of scenarios, think of this step as adding to that initial set in a way that grows the architecture from the inside out. In other words, each release should encompass the behavior of several new scenarios as well as more completely carry out the behavior of earlier ones. Scenarios should be grouped so that they collectively provide a meaningful chunk of the system's behavior for each release, and additionally they require the development team to attack the project's next highest risks. By attaching scenarios to releases in this manner, this provides the project a large measure of accountability (every scenario must be explicitly considered) and traceability (each scenario can be tied to an implementation).

I use the following rule when establishing the number of evolutionary releases for a project:

For most projects, plan on about five (plus or minus two) intermediate releases during evolution.

R 26

As I describe in the next section, by *intermediate* I mean major internal releases to which the team drives the selected set of behaviors to closure. Some of these releases may be exposed to customers under controlled circumstances. Additionally, as I describe in Chapter 4, these do not constitute the only releases the team will produce. Indeed, in the healthiest projects, it is not uncommon to find a new release being integrated every few days.

Continuing:

- Adjust the goals and schedules of this stream of releases so that delivery dates are sufficiently separated to allow adequate development time, and so that releases are synchronized with other development activities, such as documentation and field testing.

This step establishes the heartbeat of the project's evolution. It is critical to set the beat now, so that the entire project can begin to pace itself over its remaining life cycle.

P 47

Toward the end of the design phase, establish the rhythm of a project that drives it to the end of its scheduled life cycle by planning for a series of intermediate releases, each of which grows the architecture from the inside out.

As I discuss in the next section on evolution, keeping this rhythm requires the active involvement of management.

Release planning concludes with the following step:

- Create a task plan, wherein a work breakdown structure is identified, and development resources are identified that are necessary to achieve each architectural release.

Chapter 5 talks about the details of staffing a project.

Agents

I use the following practice when staffing a project's design activity:

P 48

Design is best conducted by a small team made up of the project's very best people, principally including an architect and one or two developers. As the complexity of the project grows, this group should be supplemented by a few other developers (who mainly concentrate upon certain technology areas), a toolsmith (responsible for the team's development environment), a member of the quality assurance/testing team (responsible for the project's quality program), and perhaps a writer (who manages the project's documentation).

As for analysis, the role of the architect on this core team is to provide a sense of conceptual integrity. Small projects can get by with a team of one, namely, the architect. Modest-sized projects need to add a developer or two to back up the architect and to focus on different areas of technology.

Responsible for processing tax returns, a European government organization decided to downsize its mainframe resources and move to a client-server architecture using a combination of Smalltalk and Visual Basic (on the client side) and C++ (on the server side). In addition to a principle architect, the core design team included a data base expert, a network developer, and a developer experienced in GUI systems.

For the largest projects, I use the following rule:

Never engage a core design team larger than about 7 to 10 people; anything bigger is almost impossible to manage. If the sheer complexity of your project demands it, however, break your project into several teams of a dozen or so people, but still coordinate their activities under the control of a single core design team.

R 27

Architecture planning is carried out by the developers on the core design team. Where the size of the project demands it, this team is backed up by the toolsmith who helps with the mechanics of the development environment and by the writer who writes the architecture document in conjunction with the principle architect. If separate people do not exist for these roles, the developers themselves must act as the toolsmiths and writers.

As part of design, the system's patterns are best planned by the architect or other senior developers and then prototyped and validated by small tiger teams who are formed as necessary and then dispersed when their work is done.

For each critical mechanism in the architecture and for every framework intended to be used in the system, create a tiger team who drives that pattern to closure within about 1 to 5 days (or 1 to 5 weeks for the more complicated frameworks).

R 28

This rule also applies to the project's style guide, which captures the system's major idioms. Be sure that you assign your best industrial-strength developers to the style guide effort. A singularly evil practice of certain loosely-managed projects is to have the style guide written by people who have never written a production line of code in their recent past. If you do not have such experienced people, then by all means try to reuse a style guide from some other successful project.

Release planning is the main responsibility of the project's development manager. Management must work in conjunction with the project's customers who advise what schedule and roll out of functionality is required as well as with the team's architect and senior developers who advise what is possible.

Milestones and Measures

There are two major milestones in this phase:

- Completion of the architectural release
- Acceptance of the release plan

Completion of the architectural release actually encompasses two intermediate milestones:

- Delivery of an executable release that satisfies the selected scenarios
- Delivery of prototypes of and documentation for the system's major patterns

As a vehicle for management control, the team can also use the review and acceptance of the system's architecture document as a major, formal milestone.

Realizing that design never finishes until the completed system is delivered, what is important here is that the development team does enough to give itself a high level of confidence in its decisions regarding the areas of highest risk to the project's success. This suggests the following recommended practice:

> The design phase should be drawn to a close only once the team has delivered an architectural release whose bones are healthy enough and whose risks are sufficiently understood such that it would be willing to bet the future of the project on it.*

P 49

Acceptance of the release plan is an equally important milestone marking the end of the design phase. It is fruitless to proceed unless management has consensus between the customer and the development team as to the schedule for refining the system's architecture.

Relative to the delivered architecture, there are three aspects to consider during design:

- Simplicity
- A balanced distribution of responsibilities throughout the system
- Stability

---

* Of course, the team will be betting its future on this architecture, whether it realizes this or not.

The tendency to over-architect is common in object-oriented systems, and thus architectural simplicity is the most important metric to look for at this stage. If your system is complex now, it is only going to get worse as you evolve the implementation. Simplicity is hard to measure, but there are a few early warning signs that point to the realization that your team is trying to build too much, namely:

- Your architectural release has a bigger-than-expected footprint (i.e., at run time it is already big and slow).[*]
- Your team gets stuck trying to prototype the system's major patterns.
- Functional decomposition sets in, with your system taking on the shape of a stovepipe architecture with a large chunk of code for every scenario and a small chunk of code for the common infrastructure.
- The team starts to panic at the perceived growing complexity and so runs to the security of coding at the expense of calm confrontation of the project's risks.

If any of these signs appear, the proper antidote is strong management intervention to drive the architecture to simplicity before proceeding.

One group was on its very first object-oriented project, and it had jumped into this technology in a big way—new language, new development environment, and new data base technology. The earliest architectural releases from this group were OK, but only just so. There were a few warning signs, such as hitting the limits on the development tools during architectural design, very sluggish performance of the first release, and longer than expected turn around times required to spin the architecture. Management did not take heed of these signals, and relentlessly pushed forward toward the scheduled delivery. Weighed down by an over-architected system, the team finally delivered a product, but only after shedding significant amounts of functionality. The original architecture was ultimately abandoned in the next major release of the system.

A balanced distribution of responsibilities is another important measure to look for in the emerging system. This simply means that no one part of the architecture is tasked with too much to do, another indication that the team has seriously over- or under-architected part of the system. Stability is also a critical measure of goodness. If you find the development team thrashing in any of

---

[*] Just knowing the executional footprint of your system this early in the life cycle is a sign of a healthy project. Too many systems suffer from software bloat simply because they ignore its footprint until it's too late to do anything about it.

its decisions about the system's idioms, mechanisms, or frameworks, this is a clear sign of architectural risk which is best attacked by assigning a tiger team to drive the decision to closure. At this stage of development, the team must realize that what remains is an engineering problem.

> When designing, always keep in mind that this is an engineering problem. Do not become obsessive about finding perfect solutions (they are an illusion) but equally, do not assume away all of the hard parts of your problem (they will come back to haunt you). Strive for adequate solutions that resolve the competing technical, social, and economic forces that shape your particular problem.

P 50

There is a corresponding rule:

> Pragmatically, strive toward an 80% solution. Achieving a 100% solution requires exponentially more effort, and the last 20% of functionality (typically representing the dark corners of a system's behavior) is often not commensurate with the required effort (often because you misunderstood the problem in the first place). Additionally, your risk of failure is much, much higher. Setting and making an 80% solution is far better than setting out for a 100% solution and achieving a 0% one.

R 29

Do not use this rule as an excuse to cut corners blindly, however. You must always be focused on achieving your project's essential minimal characteristics.

EVOLUTION

Purpose

The purpose of evolution is to grow an implementation through the successive refinement of a system's architecture.

The ultimate end of this phase is deployment of the system. Deployment involves the complete productization of the system, encompassing its (executable) software, installation mechanisms, documentation, and support facilities. For many mission-critical systems, once deployment is achieved, the released system enters into maintenance, but then main stream development returns to start another round of evolution for the next deployed release.[*]

---

[*] This leads to a "b" shaped macro process, wherein the team loops in the evolutionary phase, never to depart from it until that entire product line is abandoned.

This phase is one of continuous integration, meaning that there never exists any single big-bang integration event. Instead, this phase is populated with lots of small bangs that evolve the architecture from the inside out. Furthermore, evolution should never be viewed simply as an activity requiring only raw coding skills (although these skills do play a vital role during this phase). As evolution proceeds, discovery continues but then fades as light is shined upon the remaining dark corners of the system's desired behavior. Similarly, invention peaks but then also diminishes as strategic design issues are stabilized and the remaining tactical ones are wrestled to the ground. Finally, implementation grows to a frenzy as some developers complete the system's abstractions and policies established during design, while concurrently other developers assemble these components in ways that carry out the desired behavior of the system as established during scenario planning through analysis.

The calm and deliberate conduct of this phase is absolutely essential to the success of an object-oriented project. Indeed, it is in this stage of software development wherein pragmatics must dominate as the team focuses on satisfying the project's essential minimal characteristics. A steady hand is key because during evolution it is not rare to be blindsided by some failure of the underlying technology, a radical change in requirements, or simply a discovery that certain assumptions made earlier in the life cycle where simply wrong. During evolution, knowing what is the highest risk to the success of the project will therefore change from time to time as new data is absorbed. The task of the management team is to act both as a sorter that continually qualifies and prioritizes the project's risks and a damper that prevents the team from being wildly jerked around as each new revelation unveils some heretofore hidden risk. With the management team focused on beating a steady rhythm for the project as a whole and the development team focused on the evolving architecture as a stabilizing factor, the successful team will never panic during this phase; instead, during evolution the team will come to reach closure on all of the system's risks.

A system integrator sold the object-oriented paradigm to its big life insurance customer but quickly came to realize that it was way in over its head. Not only was the problem more complex than it had first anticipated, but the requirement for interim coexistence with legacy systems just made the problem even harder. At first, the team was on a path that yielded a fair understanding of the business's processes, but it was on the verge of panic when it realized the horrible impedance mismatch between the behavior of these processes and their existing legacy data bases. Order was restored to the project by first focusing the team on the creation of a domain model (that anchored all of their discussions about the behavior of the system), and secondly by planning and then executing upon a series of releases that built upon this model. This evolutionary plan permitted the group to move forward on an more pure object-oriented path, while at the same time preserving their legacy assets during the interim.

This story suggests the following practice:

> During evolution, beat a steady rhythm that allows the team to first approach each new risk with caution but then, once identified as real, to attack each risk with due and deliberate haste.

P 51

This phase permits management to answer the following four questions:

- What are the real requirements of this system?
- Is there certain behavior that really ought to be deferred, or perhaps new behavior that can now be provided that was once thought impossible?
- How does the implementation carry out the system's desired behavior?
- Just how good is the evolving product?

The first two questions strike at the heart of why the system is being built in the first place. Answering these questions during this phase is not meant as an excuse for doing sloppy analysis earlier, but rather it is a recognition of the fact that the existence of any new system always changes the end user's behavior and understanding of what it really wanted or believed was possible in the first place. Through the use of this iterative and incremental process, evolution aims at driving the project to a better understanding of the details of the real problem to be solved before final delivery as opposed to after production release, which is what a non-iterative process will often yield.

The third question addresses the issue of traceability: given a statement of the system's desired behavior, is every behavior carried out properly and in the simplest manner possible? The final question addresses the quality of the evolving implementation: is the chosen architecture working, and is the team building a system that is both correct and free of anomalous behavior?

Sometimes, projects ignore this stage and strike out on a program of unbridled programming. From the outside this looks good, because the team will end up spewing out reams of code that makes its programmers appear brilliantly productive. However, this is a false economy. Under such a program, the team often ends up building the wrong thing and most certainly an unnecessarily complicated thing that typically proves to be a real burden to own and maintain. Under the same conditions, a healthy project will generate less code than an unhealthy project. Evolution thus serves to mitigate the tendency toward barbarous hacking by forcing the team to keep itself focused on the right problems, as driven by the project's unique set of risks.

Products

The evolution of a system generates four distinct artifacts:

- A stream of executable releases
- Behavioral prototypes
- Quality assurance results
- System and user documentation

A release is simply a stable, self-complete, and executable version of a system, together with any other peripheral elements necessary to use that release. The primary product of evolution is thus a stream of releases representing successive refinements to the initial architectural release. Some of these releases are intermediate, that is, they are meant only for internal consumption; others of these represent deployed versions, meaning that they are meant for external consumption. Secondary products include behavioral prototypes that are used to explore alternative designs or to further analyze the dark corners of a systems' functionality.

An executable release serves to grow a system's architecture from the inside out, driven by the highest risks in the system. Unlike behavioral prototypes, each executable release incorporates production-quality code that ultimately grows into the final delivered system.

Why is it important to have a stream of executable releases?
- Each release provides a stable intermediate form upon which greater complexity may be grown
- The period between releases affords an opportunity for further discovery and invention
- Early releases offer a degree of instant gratification (essential for better engaging end users), and later releases offer points of control (essential for management to make mid-course corrections in the direction of the project).

There is an important corollary to this last point. By focusing on the development of a stream of releases, management is given the means for making trade offs between time to market and feature functionality.

This evolutionary approach to software development is based on a very simple yet profound observation: all complex systems tend to grow from simple ones.

An organization took an object-oriented approach in the development of its information management system. The customer was so pleased with the progress that it added some significant new requirements about halfway through the schedule (but offered no schedule relief or additional resources). After a quick assessment by a tiger team, project management heartily signed up to the new requirements: the architect had discovered that by adding a few new classes and reusing existing ones in creative ways, the team could easily accommodate the changes without disrupting the original schedule.

Ultimately, the products of evolution serve as a forcing function that drives the development team toward closure of a solution that satisfies the customer's real requirements. Sometimes, though, this approach can work too well:

> One organization was tasked to build a decision support system for the company's sales force. Using an incremental and iterative approach, the development team started to produce executable releases within a few weeks after the project had started. Although the project was scheduled to go on for a year, the sales force was so pleased with the early releases that it declared them sufficient. The project was disbanded, with a small cadre left behind to handle minor bug fixes and enhancements.

Of course, your mileage may vary: this example is an extreme case, but points out that evolution does drive the project toward closure.

Each executable release in this stream of successive refinement is a product marked by three properties:

- A growth in functionality, as measured by the new scenarios that each implements.
- Greater depth, as measured by a more complete implementation of the system's domain model and mechanisms.
- Greater stability, as measured by a reduction in the changes to the system's domain model and mechanisms.

These properties tend to derive from the following practice followed by successful object-oriented projects:

> During evolution, refine each new release so that it adds more flesh to the bones of the previous one. Choose where to expand each release according to the highest risk at hand.

P 52

Again, this is why a sound architecture is so important: without it, your project will collapse of its own weight into an amorphous blob that lacks any structure or substance.

Each project has its own set of risks, which is why every stream of releases tends to grow in different ways for every project. For example, if in one project messaging performance in a distributed environment is viewed as the highest risk, then its earliest releases should focus on the mechanisms associated with object distribution and migration. If in a different project the usability of the user interface has the greatest impact upon the project's success, then its earliest releases should focus on the system's look and feel.

Each release I speak of in this stream of executable releases represents a major event in the life cycle of a project. As such, in order to preserve the rhythm of the healthy project, the development team must pace itself. I tend to use the following rule to guide my planning:

For a modest-sized project, plan for a new release every 2 to 3 months.
For more complex projects, plan for a new release every 6 to 9 months.

R 30

This rule only applies to the internal releases that are exposed beyond the core programming team. As I describe in the next chapter, the needs of the micro process dictate that many more internal releases will be accomplished by the programming team, with only a few executable releases turned over to external parties.

A secondary product of evolution is a set of behavioral prototypes used by the team to further the discovery of the system's requirements or to explore technology alternatives. I make a clear distinction between executable releases and prototypes: executable releases are production quality code; prototypes are not. Indeed, prototypes are explicitly meant to be thrown away. During the evolution of a system, the ideas but not necessarily the substance of a prototype are folded into production architectural releases.

To be clear, a prototype is an experiment. As such, an effective prototype must encompass three elements, in this order:

- A problem statement   Specifies the scope of the experiment, including its functionality, the technology or tools to be explored, and the resources to be committed.

- A solution   Provides an executable model that fulfills the problem statement.

- Experimentation   Permits evaluation and further exploration of the solution.

A policy of prototyping gives the development team the opportunity to fail as it attacks the next highest risk without destroying the project's rhythm. Indeed, the purpose of a prototype is the rapid exploration of alternatives so that areas of risk can be resolved early. Prototypes by their very nature make sweeping simplifying assumptions (regarding completeness, response to corner conditions, and quality, for example), which allow them to target on a very narrow spectrum of behavior and to explore that behavior in depth. In this manner, any lessons learned from a particular prototype about some system behavior can be fed into a future architectural release, where there are no such simplifications.

Opportunities for prototyping abound: each new prototype may serve to explore some isolated element of the system, such as a new algorithm, a user interface model, or an alternative database schema. There is grave danger of rabid prototyping, however, because rapid prototyping can give the team the illusion that it is building something real and complete. If you find your team hacking rather than calmly and deliberately developing, management must invoke the following practice:

> Remember that prototypes are meant to be thrown away or cannibalized; especially in the presence of fierce schedule pressure; resist the urge to build a prototype, bless it, and then declare it as production quality. Doing so may offer the project a short term gain, but assuredly this decision will come back to haunt you.

P 53

Prototypes should be created solely for honorable reasons, of which there are only a few:

- To obtain a deeper understanding about the requirements of a system;
- To determine whether certain functionality, performance, cost, reliability, or adaptability can be achieved;
- To assess the risk associated with a certain design;
- To serve as a vehicle for communicating a design within the team to an customers;
- To serve as a learning tool for the development team.

If you find your team prototyping for any other reason, management should step in and focus its efforts to more respectable pursuits.

Another secondary product of evolution involves the artifacts of testing and quality assurance. Pragmatically, this means that the development team will generate test plans largely tied to the system's scenarios, and it will use these plans to access the system's quality and completeness. Thus, one other advantage of using an incremental and iterative development process is that the testing team can get involved relatively early in the process, and use that time to begin to collect a history of the system's quality. As I discuss in a later section, this early data is essential for the active management control of a project.

According to the particular needs of a given project, various kinds of system and user documentation make up the final artifact of this phase. Just as an implementation tracks the evolution of a system's architecture, so does the documentation of most successful systems track each successive release. As I discuss in Chapter 6, in the healthiest projects, system and user documentation is never developed in isolation, away from the stream of executable releases.

Rather, each such document is treated as a living, breathing thing that tracks with the ongoing discovery and invention that happens during evolution. Thus, rather than treating the production of documentation as *the* major milestone that marks the rhythm of a project, it is generally better to have documentation as a secondary and semiautomatically generated artifact of the evolution of the system's architecture.

Activities

There are two primary activities associated with evolution:

- Application of the micro process
- Release assessment and change management

The purpose of two three activities is to refine the system's architecture and so to raise product quality to the point where the product can be shipped.

A communications company was drowning in a sea of software, weighed down by grossly complex systems that required tremendous care and feeding, and that were flatly resistant to change. As a result, the company was losing customers at an alarming rate, because it was being beaten in the marketplace by newer companies that were far more nimble and that offered a wider range of customer services. One analysis suggested it would take a year or two to port its existing software products to a more realistic client/server topology, and at the expense of no new functionality. Such a path was immediately rejected as utterly foolish, because the company would long be out of business by then. Thus, rather than taking a sterile and monolithic approach to migrating its legacy systems, the organization attempted to regain a foothold in the market place by using a more incremental and iterative approach that allowed them to tackle their more pressing requirements first, all the while building an architecture that would serve as the foundation for all future development.

With regard to scheduling this phase, I typically apply the following rule:

For projects of modest complexity whose full life cycle is about one year, the evolution phase typically lasts about nine months.

R 31   Coupled with my earlier rule of thumb, this practically means that most modest sized projects should plan for around 3 to 5 releases during evolution.[*]

---

[*] Philippe Kruchten and Joe Marasco have observed that the duration of an iteration in weeks seems to be equal to the square root of the size of the code to be developed, as measured in thousands of lines of code.

As I discuss in the previous chapter, all successful projects tend to exhibit overlapping cycles of discovery, invention, and implementation. This is particularly evident during evolution. As I explain in more detail in the next chapter, the micro process is essentially an opportunistic process of development, during which time developers analyze a little, design a little, and implement a little, in direct correlation to the cycles of discovery, invention, and implementation. Briefly, the micro process begins with a further analysis of the requirements for the upcoming release, proceeds to the refinement of the existing architecture, and continues with the further invention and implementation of the classes and objects necessary to carry out this design. However, because the micro process is essentially one of pure creativity, its basic problem is that programmers, left to their own devices, never reach closure. What makes the micro process work is setting it in the context of the macro process which provides a disciplined and more predictable framework for management.

> Carry out the development of each new release during evolution as one or more spins of the micro process.

P 54

As I explained earlier, three things drive each such release: a clear statement of its desired behavior, a declaration of its expected completeness, and goals for its quality. In the context of the macro process, application of the micro process typically begins with the following step:

- Identify the function points to be satisfied by this executable release as well as the areas of highest risk, especially those identified through evaluation of the previous release.

Typically, this step means identifying the scenarios of interest to be completed or reworked by this next release. Focusing on scenarios gives the added advantage of traceability, since the implementation of all such behavior can in theory be traced back to scenarios established earlier during analysis.
Next,

- Assign clear tasks to the development team to carry out this release, and initiate a spin of the micro process. Supervise the micro process by establishing appropriate reviews and by managing against intermediate milestones that take on the order of a few days or a week or two to complete.

Thus, integration is the forcing function that brings the micro process to closure. As I explain in Chapter 6, the use of walkthroughs during this phase not only helps to propagate the system's architectural vision, but it also provides a means of mentoring more junior people on the team and developing their skills.

There is a subtle implication to this step that requires further explanation, and it is implied by the plural noun *tasks*. In virtually all of the successful projects I have encountered, there are usually two or more lines of development during evolution. The first line constitutes the primary activities that lead up to the next release; the other lines represent secondary activities that involve the investigation of design alternatives and the adaptation of new technologies. In larger projects, this typically means assigning a set of developers the line responsibility for generating the release and assigning another smaller set of developers these secondary tasks. In smaller projects, the same thing happens, except that the responsibilities must be shared by the same people.

An organization, focused on developing products for personal computers, was feeling double pressured because its customers were not only demanding more and more features, but its technology base was changing out from under it. In particular, the team knew that it had a hard requirement to support OLE (object linking and embedding) at some unspecified time in the future, but it couldn't risk losing momentum in the market place by trading off more product functionality for OLE support. To prevent disrupting the rhythm of the project, project management assigned one person to investigate the implication of supporting OLE. This person's first prototypes were very simple, but they helped him to learn the risks associated with the technology. His later prototypes served to bound the changes that would be required to the project's existing architecture. As the risks associated with his work became manageable, his design was eventually folded into a production release.

This story is very typical of successful projects. Establishing tiger teams to carry out secondary tasks gives the project significant degrees of freedom to actively attack its risks. Preserving a main line of development and then folding in the results of these secondary tasks as it makes sense serves to maintain the project's rhythm.

These secondary tasks may involve much more than just the exploration of new technology. In some projects, this work appeals to the social aspects of development, which may have a much larger bearing on the success of the project than any programming issues.

One organization was moving its entire staff off of mainframes with line-oriented terminals, and onto a client/server network with graphical user interfaces. Although the development team was making steady progress, there was significant unrest brewing among a vocal set of end users, who protested to any degree of change—these people were quite content to operate in a world of semi-automation, backed up by telephones and faxes.

Although the company's management recognized that it had to peruse the new technology in order to stay alive in the marketplace, there was a very real danger that the project would fail due to lack of acceptance. To mitigate this risk, the team established a secondary line of development that just focused on end-user visible prototypes, which management used to internally sell the idea of the system, as well as to make the protesters part of the solution. These prototypes were lashed together quickly using Visual Basic and GUI builders, and the results were eventually folded into the main stream development.

There is a lesson in all of this:

> During evolution, aggressively focus a main line of developers on the next release, but hedge your bets by allocating a few resources for exploring areas of risk. Preserve the project's rhythm by the planned incorporation of the results of these investigations into future releases.

P 55

The work of these secondary tasks can best be described by the following step, which takes place in parallel with the main line of development:

- As needed to understand the semantics of the system's desired behavior and to attack risks, assign developers to produce behavioral prototypes. Establish clear criteria for the goals and completion of each prototype. Upon completion, decide upon an approach to integrate the results of the prototyping effort into this or subsequent releases.

In the context of the macro process, application of the micro process finishes with the following step:

- Force closure of the micro process by integrating and releasing the executable release.

Launching intermediate releases can be quite informal, such as simply notifying the proper parties inside the organization that the release exists. Deployed releases require much more ceremony, because they must be complete enough for end users to apply.

This step is the principle forcing function that beats the rhythm of evolution. Building real things forces the team to make intelligent engineering decisions, guards against development paralysis, and permits the project to roll with the punches in its encounter with previously undiscovered areas of risk.

During evolution, the application of the micro process does not take place in isolation; rather, it requires continuous reassessment and change management, the second major activity of the macro process. After each release, it is important for the team to revisit its original release plan and to adjust the requirements and schedules for its subsequent releases as necessary. In the healthy project, this typically means shifting internal release dates by a few days or weeks, or migrating functionality from one release to another. Indeed, a sign of project decay is if the team finds that it has to radically change its plans during evolution.

Release assessment is essential to growing a mature development organization. This activity has one major step:

- Qualify each release against the project's minimal essential characteristics as well as against certain other predictors of health, such as stability, defect discovery rates, and defect density.

A later section explains these relevant measures of goodness in more detail. What is important to note here is that management cannot control what it cannot measure, and so this step puts in place a vehicle for gathering meaningful data for the team to probe what's really going on inside the project.

As I describe in more detail in Chapter 6, one implication of this activity is that in successful object-oriented projects, testing is incremental. In other words:

During evolution, carry out unit testing of all new classes and objects, but also apply regression testing to each new complete release.

P 56

This is another benefit of an incremental and iterative approach to development: a policy of continuous integration of release gives the team an ongoing log of the system's quality, which can be used to track the project's overall health.

Given a release assessment, change management concludes with the following step:

- Identify the project's next highest risks, and adjust the scope and schedule of the next series of releases as necessary.

This translates into a practice I find common among successful projects:

During evolution, maintain a regular release schedule as much as possible. All things being equal, shift functionality rather than schedules, but never ever let functionality creep out of the picture altogether.

P 57

Sometimes you have to make mid-course corrections to your projects:

Early releases of one project's personal productivity tools were well received, and there was a clear plan for growing its functionality over time. However, these early releases to a few select clients changed the ways end users thought they would interact with the system. As a result, clients began to demand immediate support for a particular feature that was planned for a much later release. Reorienting the project so abruptly would have meant not doing a number of other important things. To preserve the momentum of the project, management set up a tiger team to explore the necessary changes in parallel with development of the current release, and then the feature was added to the very next release. End users won, because their needs were met in a predictable fashion; the development team won, because the change was accommodated with minimal impact to their architecture.

There's a rule of thumb that I apply when assessing the scope of such changes:

> A change that affects just a handful of classes is minor (and typical). A change that affects the basic structure of only one or two class categories has a modest impact (and is not uncommon). A change that effects the basic structure of three or more class categories is major (and should be rare in healthy projects).

R 32

Given this rule, the following practice applies:

> During evolution, minor changes can be handled by the owner of the affected classes. Modest changes should be handled by collaboration among the abstractionists who own the corresponding class categories with a sign off by the architect. Major changes should first be validated by a tiger team lead by the system's architect and then incorporated by collaboration with all of the system's class category owners.

P 58

These team roles are explained further in the next section as well as in Chapter 5.

Change will happen: that is the nature of iterative development. Brooks observes that in the process of building a complex system, you should plan to throw one away. In the context of object-oriented development, I find that his recommendation still rings true, but with a twist:

> Throw away a little as you go along, so you do not have to throw it all away at the end.

P 59

From my experience, there are two rules that will help guide your way:

> With each iteration, if you throw away less than 10% of your work, you are not throwing away enough; if you throw away more than 20%, it probably means you are not integrating enough of your prototypes into the final product (your actual mileage may vary).

R 33

R 34

If at your first iteration you find you must trash more than 30% of your work, this is a sign that your architecture has never really achieved a stable state.

No matter how much advance planning a team does,[*] reality is that during evolution, you may sometimes discover that your architecture is broken in very fundamental ways, representing a kind of systemic decay in the system.

A project built a system centered around an object-oriented data base. There were early warning signs, but it was not until the first production release that the team realized that this technology was just fundamentally a wrong match for the problem. Reworking the system effectively required the team to abandon the original architecture and to start from scratch.

There's a lesson in this story as well:

P 60

Don't panic. No matter how broken your system is, the world will still go on.[‡] The worst thing management can do is overreact and spread hysteria throughout the team; the rational thing management can do is assess the damage, pick up the broken pieces, and develop an intelligent plan for reestablishing the project's rhythm.

Agents

Staffing reaches its peak during evolution. In the healthy project, most of the team is actively engaged in driving each new release to closure.

R 35

During evolution, a full 80% of the team should be focused on pumping out each new release. The remaining 20% or so should be assigned to secondary tasks that attack new risks and that prepare the ground work for the next series of releases.

In the healthy project, the roles and responsibilities of the development team reach a steady state during this phase. The architect continues in his or her role of maintaining the conceptual integrity of the system as it evolves. Abstractionists are typically assigned ownership of various class categories to serve as defenders of its interfaces and the architect of its structure. Collectively, the architects and the abstractionists collaborate to further shape the bones of the implementation.

---

[*] Yes, even one using object-oriented technology.
[‡] Assuming the complexity of contemporary systems, that is. Given the growing pervasiveness of software, I offer no predictions as to the scope of damage of future failed systems.

The bulk of the team acts as application engineers who carry out any one of three tasks:

- Implementation of the classes and collaborations of classes specified by the architect and abstractionists.

- Completion of system functions through the assembly of the classes and patterns invented by the abstractionists and implemented by other application engineers.

- Creation of behavioral prototypes used to explore design alternatives or new avenues of technology.

All three tasks require good, raw programming skills. The first task requires the most mature programming talent. The second task requires average programming skills, but also demands a basic knowledge of the problem domain, since the essential task here is the assembly of small programs in the context of the vocabulary of the problem space as provided by the classes and objects in the system. The third task requires developers who are good at rapid development and who have an innate ability to discover simplifying assumptions that allow them to cut corners without compromising reality too much.

For all three of these tasks, it is typical to find specialization among application engineers: some may be focused on user interface design, some may be experts in networking, and some may be experienced in data base technology. Each skill set contribute to the goals of the project as a whole in the context of the classes, objects, and collaborations that serve as the system's framework.

In addition to these three traditional roles, individuals may be assigned to various tiger teams throughout the life of a project. As I describe further in Chapter 5, a tiger team is a transitory organization, established to investigate some clearly defined issue. Such teams are transitory in two dimensions. First, they are explicitly created and then disbanded as the need arises. Second, their membership is not fixed, but instead may be drawn from the entire development organization. Indeed, it is wise to shift the assignment of developers among various tiger teams. This not only helps to propagate the system's architectural vision, but it also addresses the social aspects of development by helping to build team unity (through the creation of new lines of personal communication) and by giving individual developers a change of pace (especially in high pressure projects, the team can get very fatigued, and assignment to a tiger team can give the individual a change of venue).

> Organize tiger teams as the need arises to attack some risk in the project. Explicitly create such a team with clear goals as to its mission, scope, and schedule, then disband the team when its work is done.

P 61

There is a corresponding rule:

R 36

The typical tiger team has from one to three members, with one and one-half being a median size.[*]

A stream of executable releases is the basic product of evolution, and the disposition of these releases requires the involvement of much more than just the team's developers. Early in the development process, major executable releases are turned over by the development team to quality-assurance personnel, who begin to test the release against the scenarios established during analysis. In so doing the team gathers information on the completeness, correctness, and robustness of the release. This early data-gathering aids in identifying problems of quality, which are more easily addressed during the evolution of the subsequent release. Later in the development process, executable releases are turned over to select end users (the alpha and beta customers) in a *controlled* manner. By controlled, I mean that the development team carefully sets expectations for each release, and identifies aspects that it wishes to have evaluated.

P 62

Never throw an interim release over the wall to a customer: not only will you get large amounts of low quality feedback, but you will eventually alienate all of your customers by forcing them to do the testing your team should have done in the first place.[‡] Therefore, when exposing releases to end users during evolution, be certain to set expectations as to what each release does and does not do.

Not only is this practice technically sound, it is also the most ethical.

Milestones and Measures

During evolution, there is one series of obvious milestones:

- The release of each intermediate executable form

Managing the scope, completeness, and quality of each such a release is the primary means whereby management exerts its control over the object-oriented project. By forcing the team to pump out a steady stream of real artifacts, management avoids the illusion of progress that is typical of organizations that do not practice an incremental and iterative approach to development.

As I have explained earlier, each release is more than simply a hunk of object code. A release consists of a full package, including executable software, documentation, and test results.

---

[*] One-half, meaning the part-time assignment of an individual.
[‡] World-class chutzpah is when an organization can get away with charging a customer for the privilege of receiving an early and undertested beta release.

When does evolution end? In one sense, good software never dies, it just continues to evolve. However, every project needs a sense of closure, which is offered by the following practice:

> Evolution should be drawn to a close only when the functionality and quality of the releases are sufficient to ship the product to an average customer who requires little or nohand-holding to use the system.

P 63

Ultimately, this desired functionality and quality are defined as a part of each system's minimal essential characteristics.

Measuring the goodness of each release during evolution is absolutely fundamental to the conduct of a project. Indeed, a number of predictors of health can be used by management to diagnose the state of a project; some of these measures are universal, and some of them apply specifically to object-oriented systems:

- Completeness of each release
- Defect discovery rate and defect density
- Stability

The primary measure of the quality of each release is the degree to which it satisfies the behaviors required of it, and how well its schedules are met. Missing any of these intermediate milestones is a clear warning sign to the development team that there are gremlins in the system that must be found and eliminated.

Defect discovery rate is a measure of how rapidly new errors are being detected. By investing in quality assurance early in the development process, it is possible to establish measures for quality for each release which the management team can use to identify areas of risk and also to calibrate the development team. After each release, the defect-discovery rate generally surges. A stagnant defect-discovery rate usually indicates a cache of undiscovered errors. An off-scale defect discovery rate is typically an indication that the architecture has not yet stabilized, or that there are new elements in a given release that are incorrectly designed or implemented.

Traditionally, defect density is a measure of the number of errors per thousand lines of code. In object-oriented systems, experience suggests that it is far better to measure defect density as the ratio of errors per some unit of classes (typically, per one hundred classes). This leads to the following rule:

> 80% of the errors in an object-oriented system will be found in 20% of its classes.

R 37

Tracking errors to associated classes and collaborations of classes helps management apply its scarce development resources intelligently during evolution.

Specifically:

P 64

> During evolution, use a bug tracking system to identify the minority of classes and collaborations of classes that are the source of the majority of the system's errors. Conduct design walkthroughs against each of these key abstractions to work on improving their quality.

Stability is perhaps the best predictor of the health of an object-oriented system. In most successful projects, stability manifests itself in two forms:

- Relative to individual classes, artifacts tend to stabilize in the following order:
  - Distribution of responsibilities
  - Relationships among classes
  - Class interfaces
  - Class implementations
- Relative to clusters of classes (that is, class categories), stability works its way from the bottom up: lower-level categories tend to stabilize first, and top-level categories tend to stabilize last.

Measuring the rate of change of architectural interfaces and tactical policies is the primary measure of architectural stability, a measure I call architectural churn. Architectural churn is relatively easy to quantify: in the context of a configuration management system, simply track how often individual classes and groups of classes are checked out for modification.

Of course, in any real system, changes are to be expected. This is especially true of object-oriented systems: it is almost impossible to get a class exactly right the first time. What is important, therefore, is for the development team to recognize the kinds of changes that a successful object-oriented project will naturally undergo. Briefly, local changes to the interface or implementation of an individual class are normal, but if complete inheritance lattices or the boundaries between class categories change wildly, this is an indication of architectural decay in the system that should be recognized as an area of risk when planning the next release.

In practice, I find that the following kinds of changes are to be expected during the evolution of an object-oriented system:

- Adding a new class or a new collaboration of classes
- Changing the implementation of a class
- Changing the representation of a class
- Reorganizing the class structure
- Changing the interface of a class

Each kind of change comes about for different reasons, and each has a different cost.

A developer will add new classes as new key abstractions are discovered or new mechanisms are invented. The cost of making such changes is usually inconsequential in terms of computing resources and management overhead. When a new class is added, consideration must be given to where it fits in the existing class structure. When a new collaboration is invented, a small domain analysis should be conducted to see whether this is actually one of a pattern of collaborations. Beware of excessive invention, however: adding lots of new classes without ever touching existing ones is usually a sign that your team has actively ignored opportunities for reuse and has struck out on a path of development in spite of the existing architecture:

> In one project, the team started with an absolutely beautiful architecture. Its abstractions were intelligently grouped in class categories, and its mechanisms were clearly identified. Once this base architecture got into the hands of the main line development team, management happily found them generating new subclasses. However, later in the project, development ground to a halt; the team found the system ponderous and almost impossible to change. A project post-mortem revealed the disease: developers had subclasses off the existing class hierarchies without regard for new commonality, resulting in a structure that graphically looked like a jellyfish with long tentacles. In short, the team had invented lots of new classes that were so deeply subclassed that they had virtually no connection to the original set of base classes.

Changing the implementation of a class is also generally not costly. In object-oriented development, the team usually establishes the responsibilities of a class first, then creates its interface, and then stubs out its implementation. Once the interface stabilizes to a reasonable degree, developers can choose a representation for that class and complete the implementation of its methods. The implementation of a particular method may be changed later, usually to fix a bug or improve its performance. Developers might also change the implementation of a method to take advantage of new methods defined in an existing or newly added superclass. In any case, changing the implementation of a method is not generally costly, especially if one has previously encapsulated the class's implementation.

In a similar vein, one might alter the representation of a class. Usually, this is done to make instances of the class more space-efficient or to create more time-efficient methods. If the representation of the class is encapsulated, as is possible in most object-oriented programming languages, a change in representation will not logically disrupt how clients interact with instances of that class, unless, of course, this new representation does not provide the behavior expected of the class. On the other hand, if the representation of the class is not encapsulated, as is also possible in any language, a change in representation is much more dangerous, because clients may have been written that depend upon a particular representation. This is especially true in the case of subclasses: changing the representation of a superclass affects the representation of all of its subclasses. In any case, changing the representation of a class incurs a cost: one must recompile its interface, its implementation, all of its clients (namely, its subclasses and instances), all of its client's clients, and so on.

Reorganizing the class structure of a system is common, although less so than the other kinds of changes I have mentioned. The reorganization of a class structure usually takes the form of changing inheritance relationships, adding new abstract classes, and shifting the responsibilities and implementation of common methods to classes higher in the class structure. In practice, reorganizing the class structure of a system usually happens frequently at first, and then stabilizes over time as its developers better understand how all the key abstractions work together. Reorganizing the class structure is actually to be encouraged in early stages of design because it can result in great economy of expression, meaning that the system has smaller implementations and fewer classes to comprehend and maintain. However, reorganization of the class structure does not come without a cost. Typically, changing the location of a class high in the hierarchy makes all the classes below it obsolete and requires their recompilation (and thus the recompilation of the classes that depend on them, and so on).

An equally important kind of change that occurs during the evolution of a system is a change to the interface of a class or a class category. A developer usually changes the interface of a class either to add some new behavior, to satisfy the semantics of some new role for its objects, or to add an operation that was always part of the abstraction but was initially not exported and is now needed by some client. In practice, building quality classes as I have described in the previous chapter (and as I expand upon in the next chapter) reduces the likelihood of such changes. However, my experience is that such changes are inevitable. I have never written a nontrivial class whose interface was exactly right the first time.

It is rare but not unthinkable to remove an existing method; this is typically done only to better encapsulate an abstraction. More commonly, developers add new methods, change the signature of existing methods, or override a method defined in some superclass. In all these cases, the change is costly, because it logically affects all clients, making them obsolete and forcing their recompilation. Fortunately, these latter kinds of changes—adding and overriding methods—are upwardly compatible. In fact, in practice I find that the majority of all interface changes made to well-defined classes during the evolution of a system are upwardly compatible. This makes it possible to apply sophisticated compiler technology, such as incremental compilation, to reduce the impact of these changes. Incremental compilation allows developers to recompile single declarations and statements one at a time, instead of entire modules, meaning that the recompilation of most clients can be optimized away.

Why, you may ask, is recompilation cost even an issue? Given an evolutionary approach to development, long complication times mean long turn around times, a measure of the time it takes for developers to make a change and then execute the system again.[*] For small systems, turn around time is simply not an issue, because recompiling an entire program might take only a few seconds or minutes. However, for large systems, it is an entirely different matter. Recompiling a multiple hundred-thousand line program might take a few hours of computer time.[‡] In the extreme, recompilation costs may be so high as to inhibit developers from making changes that represent reasonable improvements. Recompilation is a particularly important issue in object-oriented systems because inheritance introduces compilation dependencies. For strongly-typed object-oriented programming languages, recompilation costs may be even higher; in such languages, one trades off compilation time for safety.

The compile-time cost of recompilation is one thing, but even that factor is increasingly less important as computers get faster and incremental compilers get smarter. The larger issue is that the semantic changes that trigger such recompilation tend to disrupt the team's work flow. Changes in one place of the code may affect the behavior of other code. Similarly, interface changes made by one development may result in other developers having to do lots of tedious and sometimes subtle changes to their code in order to accept these new changes.

There is an obvious lesson in all of this:

> During evolution, seek to stabilize key architectural decisions as early as possible. In particular, track the stability of the key classes and clusters of classes in the system that encompass its domain model and essential mechanisms.

P 65

During evolution, there is one final measure of goodness that I occasionally apply to certain hyperproductive object-oriented projects, but which I am

---

[*] In fact one of the main reasons why some developers like Smalltalk over C++ is that the Smalltalk environment encourages fast turn around times. Please do not misquote me on this issue, however, the differences are not due to language issues, but rather they are due to environmental issues.
[‡] Can you imagine making a change to the software for a shipboard computer system and then telling the captain that he or she cannot put to sea because you are still recompiling?

reluctant to explain for two reasons. First, it is a measure that I only find in the healthiest of projects (and less sophisticated projects get a complex if they don't feel they measure up). Second, it is a measure that involves lines of code, a quantity that is easy to abuse.* Given that warning, let me proceed by way of an example:

> The first release by this hyperproductive project involved some 50,000 lines of code. Over time, as early users demanded new features, subsequent releases grew to about 70,000 lines of code. This code bloat was not viewed as a good sign, because the measure of new functionality was not commensurate with the amount of new code. Analysis revealed common patterns whereby clients subclasses abstractions and used existing classes in novel collaboration with one another. The team reacted to these findings by removing the system's latent redundancy and codifying these common patterns in a set of new classes. The ultimate result was a modest increase in the number of classes in the system but a radical decrease in the lines of code. In fact, later releases involved only about 30,000 lines of code with greatly increased functionality.

This example, and many others like it, leads me to state the following practice that at first glance appears contrary:

P 66

> If you find your application getting too complex, add more classes.

As evolution nears an end, it is actually a good sign to find the raw lines of code in your project start to tail off. Although traditional management policy would decry throwing away perfectly good lines of code, this is a trend to be encouraged by all successful object-oriented projects, because it represents the fact that the development team has found opportunities for reuse that they simply could not have seen before.

---

* What exactly is a line of Smalltalk code, anyway?

MAINTENANCE

Purpose

The purpose of maintenance is to manage postdelivery evolution.

This phase is largely a continuation of the previous phase of development (evolution), except that architectural innovation is less of an issue. Instead, more localized changes are made to the system as some new requirements are added and lingering bugs stamped out.

Once a system is deployed, it enters into maintenance, although, as I have indicated, the team as a whole may return to further evolution leading up to the next deployed release. Thus, every industrial-strength system requires this phase, for two reasons:[*]

- A program that is used in a real-world environment necessarily must change or become less and less useful in that environment (the law of continuing change).
- As an evolving program changes, its structure becomes more complex unless active efforts are made to avoid this phenomenon (the law of increasing complexity).

I distinguish the preservation of a software system from its maintenance. During maintenance, the maintenance team will be asked to make continual improvements to an existing deployed system. Preservation, on the other hand, involves using excessive development resources to shore up an aging system that often has a poorly-designed architecture and is therefore difficult to understand and modify. In such cases, a business decision must be made, as I explain in the following practice:

> If the cost of ownership of a software system is greater than the cost of developing a new one, then the most merciful course of action is metaphorically to put the aging system out to pasture or, as conditions dictate, either to abandon it or to shoot it.

P 67

Maintenance permits management to answer the following two questions:

- How have requirements changed now that the system is in production?
- Is the system's architecture still resilient to change, or is it time to start over?

This first question addresses behavior that was deferred from the main line of development as well as any truly new requirements that arose because the

---

[*] Lehman and Belady, as quoted in Sommerville, I. 1989. *Software Engineering, Third Edition.* Wokingham, England: Addison-Wesley, p. 546.

current system changed the rules of how end users perceived and articulated their needs. The second question addresses the business issue: are we still in maintenance, or are we just performing unnatural acts to preserve this system for purely sentimental reasons?

Products

Since maintenance is in a sense the continued evolution of a system, its products are identical to those of the previous phase, with one addition:

- A punch list of new tasks

A punch list is a concept taken from the construction industry. Immediately upon release of the production software system, its developers and end users will probably already have a set of improvements or modifications that they would like to carry out in subsequent production releases, which for business reasons did not make it into the initial production release. Additionally, as more users exercise the system, new bugs and new patterns of use will be uncovered that quality assurance could not anticipate.[*] A punch list serves as the vehicle for collecting bugs and enhancement requirements, so that they can be prioritized for future maintenance releases.

Activities

Maintenance involves activities that are not very different from those required during the evolution of a system. Especially if the development team does a good job in refining the original architecture, adding new functionality or modifying some existing behavior comes naturally during maintenance.

In addition to the usual activities of evolution (but now in the face of new requirements), maintenance involves one other planning activity:

- Prioritization and assignment of tasks on the punch list

There is no magic to this activity; a typical order of events for this task is as follows:

- Prioritize requests for major enhancements or bug reports that denote systemic problems, and assess the cost of redevelopment.
- Establish a meaningful collection of these changes and treat them as function points for the next evolution.

---

[*] Users are amazingly creative when it comes to exercising a system in unexpected ways.

- If resources allow, add less intense, more localized enhancements (the so-called low-hanging fruit) to the next release.
- Manage the next maintenance release.

Agents

Typically, maintenance of a software system is carried out by a truncated cadre of the original development team, or by an entirely new team that had no part in the system's initial development. In either case, the makeup of the maintenance team is virtually identical to that of the development team during evolution, with two exceptions: there is no architect, and there are few if any abstractionists.

Thus it is fortunate, as I have already observed, that maintenance requires less focus on architectural innovation; instead, most changes are more local in nature. However, for any group to maintain a complex system successfully and to make changes that preserve the conceptual integrity of the original architectural vision, it must have knowledge of its patterns. This is again why I have emphasized the importance of architecture. In the absence of a clear architectural vision that carries through to maintenance, the maintenance team must take on the role of software archeologist in order to rediscover the system's patterns. Not only is this job difficult, it is also error-prone, which is why preserving tangible artifacts of the system's architecture is so important.

Milestones and Measures

The milestones and measure of maintenance are identical to those of evolution.

We know that we are still maintaining a system if the architecture remains resilient to change; we know we have entered the stage of preservation when responding to new enhancements begins to require excessive development resources.

The Micro Process

Chapter **4**

The Micro Process

Just do it.
NIKE®

In the successful object-oriented project, development is swept along through the successive refinement of the system's architecture. As the last chapter makes clear, this is by its very nature a controlled iterative and incremental process that generally works on the time scale of months (or in some cases, years). Ultimately, this macro process is risk-driven, meaning that the products and process of development are adapted as risks are identified, and then are overcome. In essence, the macro process provides the basic means for management to measure the health of a project and to control its rhythm.

However, the individual developer follows a very different rhythm. In this micro process, the traditional phases of analysis, design, and implementation are blurred, and daily activities are under opportunistic control. At any given moment, a myriad of tactical decisions must be made as part of the ongoing fabrication and adaptation of the system's software.

Successful projects recognize that these two competing processes exist. I speak of them as *competing*, because they have very different agendas and activities. Whereas the macro process is concerned with strategic issues of schedule and function, the micro process focuses on the more tactical issues of building quality software that works. Organizations that overemphasize the macro process work in an atmosphere of high ceremony, where it sometimes seems that developing software is only a minor activity. Organizations that overemphasize the micro process work in an atmosphere of institutionalized chaos, which some people thrive on, but which is not sustainable, and which often leads to the team building the wrong thing. Successful organizations find the right balance between these two processes, according to their particular problem domain, the organization's culture, and the essential minimal characteristics of the current project.[*]

Many books on management ignore the individual developer, assuming that each is a replaceable part that can be directed at will. As I explain in the next chapter, however, this is simply not reality: software development is ultimately a human activity, and as such, it is more affected by the nature of the development team than by anything technical. Furthermore, what the individual developer does in an object-oriented project is quite different than in a non-object-oriented project. For these reasons, this chapter focuses on the conduct of the micro process, detailing the goals, products, activities, agents, milestones, and measures that are relevant to the individual team member.[‡]

The time scale of the micro process can be measured in hours, days, or weeks. The rhythm of the micro process can be summarized in the following practice:

---

[*] As I explain in the first chapter, this balance is what Parnas means by faking a rational design process.

[‡] Since this is a book on management, this chapter does not discuss the technical details of how to build good object-oriented models and how to turn them into code. Rather, these topics are studied at length in *Object-Oriented Analysis and Design with Applications*.

> The micro process of the object-oriented project should comprise the overlapping waves of discovery, invention, and implementation.

P 68

In the remainder of this chapter, I will concentrate on the rhythm of the micro process.

I'M OK, MY PROGRAM'S OK

The individual developer is rarely interested in non-technical things such as return on investment or risk management. Rather, most programmers have their professional worth wrapped up in the software artifacts they so lovingly create. The best developers I know all exhibit a fair pride of ownership in their work, and they are genuinely pained when that work is found wanting, such as when bugs are uncovered or, even worse, when they realize that they had built the wrong thing.

> I was working closely with a colleague on the development of a modestly complex framework. We had subjected the code to some vigorous testing, and we were confident of its quality. However, shortly after it was deployed, we received a handful of bug reports from a customer who had used the framework in some totally unexpected ways. My colleague was in a blue funk all the rest of the day (we had tracked the problem to code she had written). The next morning, it came to light that she had stayed up until the wee hours of the morning chasing down a solution that not only eradicated the bug, but ultimately made the framework even simpler and therefore better.

In the most successful organizations, individual developers thrive on challenge and seek recognition of their work as an individual contribution to some shared goal. In the end, most developers simply want to write hard-core code for some cool projects. Anything that gets in the way of that goal is viewed as a distraction.

This is why I said earlier that the macro process and the micro process involve different agendas and activities. This is not to say that either one is more important than the other. Rather, in successful projects, both views and both processes are respected.

What are the agendas of the micro process?
- To select the right abstractions that model the problem at hand
- To determine the proper distribution of responsibilities among these abstractions
- To devise a simple set of mechanisms that regulate these abstractions
- To concretely represent these abstractions and mechanisms in the most efficient and elegant way

In that light, it is fair to say that the macro process is a management process, whereas the micro process is a technical one, focused on building real things. The macro process provides the context for the micro process, by establishing the intermediate products and milestones that the team works toward. Thus, the macro process serves as a forcing function for the team, and it is the responsibility of the project manager to select the right milestones that keep the team properly focused. Similarly, under the micro process, it is the responsibility of the development team to contribute to establishing this set of milestones according to the project's current risks, and then, once there is a shared vision, to deliver against these milestones. Realize that these two processes are never disjointed, but indeed they continuously interweave with one another. The products and milestones of the macro process are created and achieved through the efforts of the micro process.

In addition, in every one of the successful projects I have encountered, there exists a spirit of open communication that encourages all members of the development team to question aggressively any assumptions made in the context of the macro or the micro process. This healthy attitude makes the overall development process self-regulating because it prevents the team from telling lies to itself which, over time, may actually begin to believe.[*]

Use the macro process to control the activities of the project as a whole; use the micro process to iteratively carry out these activities and to regulate the future conduct of the macro process.

P 69

The micro process represents a reasonable characterization of what goes on with the individual developer throughout the life of a successful project. Thus, the micro process carries on throughout the macro process, but each spin of the

---

[*] Innocent lies, such as "this feature is really not that critical" or "my guess is that it will only take a day or two to implement these classes" have a way of escalating and then suddenly turning on your project when you least expect it. In the passion of development, human error is quickly amplified by technology, so no one wins if the project is not honest with itself—particularly with regard to risk assessment, realistic schedules, and levels of effort.

micro process has a subtly different emphasis, depending upon where the project is relative to its macro process. For example, during analysis, the developer will begin to discover, invent, and then implement—albeit with a far greater emphasis upon discovery than implementation. During design, the developer's focus will turn to invention, although discovery and implementation will continue. During evolution, implementation dominates, yet there is still an ongoing role for discovery and invention.

> The major phases of the object-oriented micro process include:
> * Identifying classes and objects
> * Identifying the semantics of classes and objects
> * Identifying relationships among classes and objects
> * Implementing these classes and objects

In non-object-oriented projects, the conduct of the micro process primarily involves the successive refinement of big functions into smaller ones. As Figure 4-1 illustrates, however, the object-oriented micro process is fundamentally different. Indeed, this process is distinguished by four important attributes:

* It is cyclic, with each path through the process focusing on different partitions of the system or bringing light to a different level of abstraction.
* It is opportunistic, meaning that each cycle begins with only that which is best known, with the opportunity to refine that work on every subsequent pass.
* It is focused on roles and responsibilities rather than on functions and control.
* It is pragmatic, meaning that it achieves closure by regularly building real, executable things.

In the remainder of this chapter, I explain each phase of the micro process in detail.

IDENTIFYING CLASSES AND OBJECTS

Purpose

The purpose of this phase is to select the right abstractions that model the problem at hand.

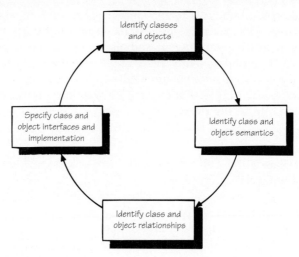

Figure 4-1   The Micro Process

This phase is largely one of discovery. During analysis, this step represents the first stage in establishing the boundaries of the problem. Specifically, the development team focuses on discovering the abstractions that form the vocabulary of the problem domain. In so doing, it starts to constrain the problem by deciding what is and what is not of interest. During design, this step serves to begin the object-oriented decomposition of the system's architecture, during which time the team begins to uncover abstractions that are elements of the solution domain. During evolution, this phase is the first step in adding meat to the system's architectural bones, by identifying the lower-level abstractions that make up the higher-level ones, and by leveraging commonality among existing abstractions in order to simplify the system's architecture.

It is a hard lesson to grasp, but identifying classes and objects is an open-ended activity, because, as I have discussed earlier, there is no such thing as a perfect abstraction. Fail to recognize this lesson, and development will come to a grinding halt.

 A development team embarked on its first full-scale object-oriented project. It entered the new undertaking with a bit of wild-eyed innocence, having just successfully completed a small pilot project. However, within just a few weeks, it was clear that the project was one the verge of meltdown. There were a number of obvious warning signs. For example, it seems that during a particular CRC card exercise, one developer swept the cards off the table and stormed off, angry about the naming of certain classes. A handful of other developers were just plain stuck, so overwhelmed with the complexity that seemed to grow every time they uncovered a new class that they were afraid to start writing any code, for fear of doing something wrong. The project finally got back on track when the architect declared that the analysis was good enough and when management temporarily banned all further scenario planning, directing instead that the team build an executable, throw-away prototype that required it to validate the model it had built thus far.

Intelligent classification is a problem common to all good science. As such, I can offer some practices and rules that can guide the identification of classes and objects. Ultimately, however, it is an activity that must be subject to practical realities.

> Remember that identifying classes and objects is fundamentally an engineering problem, not a theoretical one. Seek to find a set of abstractions that are good enough, and let the iterative nature of the object-oriented development process provide a mechanism of natural selection that forces these abstractions to become better as the project unfolds.

P 70

Products

During this stage of the micro process, there is one primary artifact that is produced:

- A dictionary of abstractions

Although the intent is the same, I hesitate calling this a data dictionary, because here its scope is much larger. In the object-oriented project, this dictionary encompasses classes and objects, as well as the mechanisms that denote collaborations of these classes and objects.

In most cases, a project's dictionary of abstractions is either an intellectual product that lives in the minds of its developers, on a collection of CRC cards, or in the form of any related notation, or it is a byproduct of other artifacts, such as a view upon the system's domain model or its executable architecture. As development proceeds, this dictionary will grow and change, reflecting the team's deeper understanding of the problem and its solution. Initially, it may be sufficient to enumerate a "list of things" consisting of all significant classes, objects, and mechanisms, using meaningful names that imply their semantics. As development continues, and especially as the dictionary grows, it may become necessary to formalize a representation of this dictionary, perhaps by using a simple *ad hoc* database to manage the list, or a more focused tool that supports the object-oriented development method directly. In these more formal variations, the dictionary can serve as an index into all the other products of the development process, including the various diagrams and specifications associated with any particular abstraction.

This dictionary of abstractions thus serves as a central repository for the vocabulary of the problem domain and it solution. Initially, it is common to keep this dictionary open-ended: some things in this repository might turn out to be classes, some objects, and others simply attributes of or synonyms for other abstractions. Some abstractions in this dictionary might not ever manifest themselves as software, and serve only to designate things in the domain's context. As development continues, then, this dictionary will be refined by adding new abstractions, eliminating irrelevant ones, and consolidating similar ones.

There are number of benefits to creating an implicit or explicit dictionary during this phase of each pass through the micro process. First, maintaining such a dictionary helps the development team to establish a common and consistent vocabulary that can be used throughout the project. Second, a dictionary can serve as an efficient vehicle for browsing through all the elements of a project in arbitrary ways. This feature is particularly useful as new members are added to the development team, who must quickly orient themselves to the solution already under development. Third, a dictionary of abstractions permits architects and abstractionists to take a global view of the project, which may lead to the discovery of commonalties that otherwise might be missed.

Activities

There is one primary activity associated with this step: the discovery and invention of abstractions.

This activity is essentially a problem of classification for which there are no right answers, just some good answers, and occasionally a few profound ones, according to the engineering tradeoffs of the context.

In teaching the techniques that help developers gain classification skills, I often use the following example: Consider the following four things, and select the one that is most different: horse, painting, sky, and car. Now, this is a trick question, because there is not enough context to state an intelligent classification. Indeed, that is the very point of the exercise. People will struggle with this problem for a while, with some brave souls offering an answer based on obvious properties, such as the horse (the only one that is alive) or the sky (has no crisp boundaries) or the painting (the only one that can represent itself and the other three). Midway through this exercise, I will change the requirements[*] and state

---

[*] Just like a real software project.

that this is actually a problem of modeling insurance policies. Immediately, most people shout out that the sky is the most different thing, because it's the only one that cannot be insured. Perhaps the most profound answer I received to this problem came from a programmer who calmly stated that it was obviously the horse, because it was the only one that was never the color blue.

As I explain in Chapter 2, there is really no magic to discovering the classes, objects, and mechanisms germane to a problem. Most classes are easy to find, although getting their boundaries right is much more difficult.

> How are most classes, objects, and mechanisms found?[*]
> - By examining the vocabulary of anyone familiar with the domain
> - By pooling the wisdom and experience of interested parties

This is indeed the experience of most successful projects, which can be summarized in the following practice:

> Use scenarios to drive the process of identifying classes and objects; CRC card techniques are particularly effective at getting interested parties together to work through scenarios.

P 71

At any point in the macro process, your first pass through the micro process will reveal many of the relevant abstractions. The remaining ones are often overlooked, and furthermore, applying any additional effort at this point to find them will yield diminishing returns. Indeed, these leftover abstractions typically can be found only by living and working with an executable artifact, and even then, only by those development teams willing to drag their architecture along as they improve their understanding of the problem. In the later stages of development, the successful teams will sometimes have the delightful experience of seeing accumulated complexity melt away when a just-right abstraction is introduced.

A typical order of events for this activity is as follows:

- Generate a set of candidate abstractions by applying classical approaches to object-oriented analysis, namely, by looking for things with common properties.

Early in the life cycle, tangible things are good starting points. Later in the life cycle, tracing external events will yield other first- and second-order

---

[*] Ward Cunningham, *private communication.*

abstractions: for each event, there must be some object that is ultimately responsible for detecting and/or reacting to that event.

Continuing:

- Starting with the system's outwardly observable behaviors (that is, its function points), find the roles and responsibilities of the things in the domain that carry out these behaviors. As with events, for each outward behavior, there must be abstractions that initiate and participate in each behavior.

- Walk through the relevant scenarios generated in the macro process. Early in the life cycle, follow initial scenarios that describe broad behaviors of the system. Later in the life cycle, consider more detailed scenarios as well as secondary scenarios that cover the "dark corners" of the system's desired behavior.

Again, expect that some of the abstractions you identify during early phases of the macro process to be wrong, but that is not necessarily a bad thing. Many of the tangible things, roles, and responsibilities that are encountered early in the life cycle will carry through all the way to implementation because they are so fundamental to any conceptual model of the problem. As the development team learns more about the problem, it will end up changing the boundaries of certain abstractions by reallocating responsibilities, combining similar abstractions, and—quite often—dividing larger abstractions into groups of collaborating ones, thus forming the new mechanisms for the solution.

Agents

Not every developer has the skills to perform this step, but then, not every developer needs to perform this step. Rather, this activity is primarily the work of a project's architect and abstractionists, who are responsible for a system's architecture. Analysts, usually working in conjunction with other domain experts, must also be good at discovering abstractions, and they must be capable of looking at the problem domain in order to find meaningful classes, objects, and mechanisms. Application engineers, mainly responsible for implementing and assembling classes, will do some identification, although most of their abstractions will be more tactical in nature.

Milestones and Measures

This phase is finished for the current iteration of the micro process when the team has reached reasonable consensus on a dictionary of abstractions. Because of the iterative and incremental nature of the micro process, do not expect to complete or freeze this dictionary entirely until very late in the development process. Rather, it is sufficient to have a living dictionary throughout the macro process, containing an ample set of abstractions, consistently named and with a sensible separation of responsibilities.

A measure of goodness, therefore, is that this consensus of abstractions does not changing wildly each time the team iterates through the micro process. Indeed, a rapidly changing set of abstractions is a sign either that the development team has not yet achieved focus, or that the architecture is in some way flawed. As development proceeds, management can track stability in lower levels of the architecture by following the local changes in this dictionary.

IDENTIFYING THE SEMANTICS OF CLASSES AND OBJECTS

Purpose

The purpose of this phase is to determine the proper distribution of responsibilities among the classes and objects identified up to this point in the development process.

This phase involves a modest amount of discovery (to understand the deeper meaning of each abstraction), an equal measure of invention (to determine the right set of roles and responsibilities in the domain and then to attach them to the right abstraction), and a sprinkling of implementation (to drive these decisions to a concrete form). During analysis, this means that the team identifies the roles and responsibilities of each abstraction and allocates these roles and responsibilities to different parts of a domain model, or to different layers in the system. During design, this step serves to establish a clear separation of concerns in the architecture by ensuring that abstractions that are semantically close are grouped together, and that abstractions with semantics that are likely to change independently are kept apart. During evolution, this phase seeks gradually and consciously to refine these semantics, transforming them first from free-form descriptions to concrete protocols for each abstraction, to, in the end, a precise signature for each operation and a clear specification of the collaborations that define each mechanism.

This phase focuses on behavior and considers issues of representation as secondary. This is in fact a general principle:

> Do not let the internals of an abstraction leak out to its externals. When considering the semantics of classes and objects, there will be a tendency to explain how things work; the proper response is "I don't care."[*]

P 72

---

[*] Kent Beck, *private communication.*

Products

There are generally three artifacts produced in this phase of the micro process:

- A specification of the roles and responsibilities of key abstractions
- Software that codifies these specifications (that is, their interfaces)
- Diagrams or similar artifacts that establish the meaning of each abstraction

By implication, each of these products may suggest a refinement of the project's dictionary of abstractions.

The specification of each abstraction's roles and responsibilities is the most important product at this stage, especially early in the development life cycle as the team struggles with finding an intelligent distribution of responsibilities. This product may take any number of forms, ranging from sketches on a white board, to text on a CRC card, to elements of a more rigorous notation. As design and evolution proceed, these roles and responsibilities are transformed into specific protocols and operations that carry out these contracts.

As soon as possible, it is wise to generate the second product of this phase, namely, software that concretely captures each specification. Practically, this means writing the interface of each interesting class in the chosen implementation language. In C++, for example, this means delivering *.h* files containing class declarations. With Ada, this means delivering package specifications. For Smalltalk, this means declaring, although not implementing, the methods and method categories for each class. For persistent, data-centric abstractions, this product may manifest itself as rudiments of the domain model's schema. Later on, these specifications will be refined and their implementations completed.

As useful as it may be, it is not possible to capture all of the interesting semantics of an abstraction directly in code or in CRC cards. Furthermore, it is particularly difficult to illustrate the semantics of mechanisms directly in software simply because, by their very nature, mechanisms represent collaborations that may span many individual classes and objects. For this reason, in many projects, the development team finds producing diagrams that capture these broader semantics useful. During analysis, scenario diagrams, such as illustrated in Chapter 3, are quite useful products at this stage to formally capture the team's storyboarding of key scenarios. During design and evolution, it is common to introduce class diagrams, scenario diagrams, state machine diagrams, and other kinds of diagrams as well.

P 73

Start with the essential elements of any notation and apply only those advanced concepts necessary to express details that are essential to visualizing or understanding the system that cannot otherwise be expressed easily in code.

The primary benefit of these more rigorous products at this stage is that they force each developer to consider the pragmatics of each abstraction's deeper meaning. Indeed, the inability to specify clear semantics at this stage is a sign that the abstractions themselves are flawed.

Activities

There are three major activities associated with this step:

- Scenario planning
- Isolated class design
- Pattern scavenging

As I explain in the previous chapter, scenario planning is an essential part of the macro process. In that context, the focus is upon selecting the right set of scenarios and using them to drive architectural design and evolution. In the context of the micro process however, scenario planning refers to the tactical issues of how one uses scenarios to identify the semantics of key abstractions. Thus, the primary and secondary scenarios generated at various levels of abstraction and at various times during the macro process are the main drivers of scenario planning in the micro process.

Under this activity, most object-oriented developers track the following series of events:

- Select one scenario or a set of scenarios related to a single function point; from the previous step in the micro process, identify those abstractions relevant to the given scenario.
- Walk though the activity of this scenario, assigning responsibilities to each abstraction sufficient to accomplish the desired behavior. As needed, assign attributes that represent structural elements required to carry out certain responsibilities. CRC cards are a particularly effective technique to use here.
- As storyboarding proceeds, reallocate responsibilities so that there is a reasonably balanced distribution of behavior. Where possible, reuse or adapt existing responsibilities. Splitting large responsibilities into smaller ones is a very common action; less often, but still not rarely, trivial responsibilities are assembled into larger behaviors.

Early in the life cycle, it is common to specify the semantics of classes and objects by writing their responsibilities in free-form text. Usually a phrase or a single sentence is sufficient; anything more suggests that a given responsibility is overly complex and ought to be divided into smaller ones.

R 38

> Most good responsibilities can be written with approximately a dozen words; any more, and you probably should divide the responsibility; far fewer, and you probably need to combine responsibilities.

As developers begin to specify the protocol of individual abstractions, they start by turning these responsibilities into a set of named operations, but without their full signatures, which should be added as soon as practical. In this manner, the development team achieves traceability: a specific responsibility is satisfied by a set of cooperative operations, and each operation contributes in some way to an abstraction's responsibilities.

As this activity unfolds and developers begin to wade deeper and deeper into the complexities of their system, there is a curious practice that I find common among most successful projects:

P 74

> Sometimes, the best way to solve a problem is to expand it. If you find yourself getting stuck in the complexity of a scenario, add more classes.

> A particular developer was getting bogged down in the algorithmic details of a ray tracing problem. Although a reasonable object-oriented domain model existed, incorporating the algorithm for tracing from light sources to reflecting and refracting objects was proving to be a bottleneck, manifested by the fact of a lot of ugly code repeating itself through the system. After walking through a scenario on paper, the developer's colleague pointed out that by objectifying elements of the algorithm (namely, items such as points and lines) and delegating some of the responsibilities to them, the implementation of the algorithm would collapse into something much simpler. These new classes were added, and the problem indeed got simpler.

Why does this seemingly contradictory practice work? The simple answer is that introducing a few well-placed classes can shift the placement of responsibilities in a system so that there is greater sharing and a better balance of power. This is again why an architectural foundation is so critical: a system's architecture provides the arena for developers to carry out this intelligent distribution.

As I have already explained, at this stage of the micro process it is critical to focus upon behavior, not structure or representation. Attributes represent structural elements, and so there is a danger, especially early in analysis, of binding implementation decisions too early by requiring the presence of certain attributes. Attributes of classes and objects should be identified at this point only insofar as they are essential to building a conceptual model of the scenario.

Whereas scenario planning looks at the semantics of an abstraction from the top down in its context, isolated class design is an activity that focuses on the bottom-up identification of semantics. Both activities are important because together they cover the two most important views of an abstraction: its outside view (achieved through scenario planning which concentrates upon the uses of an abstraction) and its inside view (achieved through isolated class design which concentrates upon the subclasses and delegations of a single abstraction). This activity is much more tactical in nature, because here developers are concerned with good class design, not architectural design. For this activity, developers typically follow this order of events:

- Select one abstraction and enumerate its roles and responsibilities.

- Devise a minimal and sufficient set of operations that satisfy these responsibilities. (Where possible, try to reuse operations for conceptually similar roles and responsibilities.)

- Consider each operation in turn, and ensure that it is primitive, meaning that it requires no further decomposition or delegation to other abstractions. If it is not primitive, isolate and expose its more primitive operations. Composite operations may be retained in the class itself (if it is sufficiently common, or for reasons of efficiency) or be migrated to a class utility (especially if it is likely to change often). Where possible, consider a minimal set of primitive operations.

- Particularly later in the development cycle, consider the life cycle of the abstraction, particularly as it relates to creation, copying, and destruction. Unless there is compelling reason to do so, it is better to have a common strategic policy for these behaviors, rather than allowing individual abstractions to follow their own idiom.

- Consider the need for completeness: add other primitive operations that are not necessarily required for the immediate clients, but whose presence rounds out the abstraction, and therefore would probably be used by future clients. Realizing that it is impossible to have perfect completeness, lean more toward simplicity than complexity.

In the early stages of development, isolated class design is exactly what it says it is: isolated. However, once the development team begins to populate the system's architecture with inheritance lattices and other kinds of hierarchies, this step must also address the proper placement of operations in these hierarchy. Specifically, as a developer considers the operations associated with a given abstraction, he or she must then decide at what level of abstraction it is best placed. The following common practice applies in this matter:

Good class design requires an intelligent distribution of responsibilities. Specifically, operations that may be used by a set of peer classes should be migrated to a common superclass, possibly by introducing a new intermediate abstract class. Operations that may be used by a disjoint

P 75

set of classes should be encapsulated in a mixin class. Operations that are unique to specific classes or that represent specializations of other operations should be pushed lower in a class hierarchy.

The third activity of this step, pattern scavenging, is also an activity of the macro process, but in the context of the micro process, represents the tactics of how to exploit any commonality that may found throughout a system. As the development team continues to elaborate upon the semantics of its abstractions, it is important to be sensitive to patterns of behavior, which represent opportunities for reuse. Making this activity a part of the micro process institutionalizes the search for patterns so that it happens continuously throughout the development life cycle.

Developers will typically follow this order of events to carry out pattern scavenging:

- Given a reasonably complete set of scenarios at the current level of abstraction, look for patterns of interaction among abstractions. Such collaborations may represent implicit idioms or mechanisms, which should be examined to ensure that there are no gratuitous differences among each invocation. Patterns of collaboration that are nontrivial should be explicitly documented as a strategic decision so that they can be reused rather than reinvented. This activity preserves the integrity of the architectural vision.

- Given the set of responsibilities generated at this level of abstraction, look for patterns of behavior. Common roles and responsibilities should be unified in the form of common base, abstract, or mixin classes.

- Particularly later in the life cycle, as concrete operations are being specified, look for patterns within operation signatures. Remove any gratuitous differences, and introduce mixin classes or utility classes when such signatures are found to be repetitious.

As I explain in Chapter 2, all good object-oriented architectures are full of patterns. This is indeed why pattern scavenging in the micro process is so absolutely critical.

P 76

Employ pattern scavenging as an opportunistic activity to seek out and exploit global as well as local commonality. Ignore this practice and you run the high risk of architectural bloat which, if left untreated, will cause your architecture to collapse of its own sheer weight.

Realize that the activities of identifying and specifying the semantics of classes and objects apply to individual classes as well as to larger architectural components, such as class categories and mechanisms. Just like an individual class, the semantics of a class category encompasses its roles and responsibilities as well as its operations. In the case of an individual class, these operations may eventually be expressed as concrete member functions; in the case of a class category, these operations represent the services exported from the category, which are ultimately provided not by just a single class, but by a collaborative set of classes exported from the category itself.

Agents

This step spans the work of a project's abstractionists and application engineers. As in the macro process, scenario planning is typically conduced by domain experts in conjunction with developers. As development proceeds and there is less risk in understanding the problem and more risk in crafting a solution, scenario planning turns more internal and tactical and can be carried out by individual developers or small teams of developers.

This is especially true of isolated class design, which is really a manifestation of the individual blocking and tackling that each developer must accomplish daily. As such, this is indeed a relatively isolated activity, best accomplished by one developing working apart or two developers in a mentoring relationship. Either way, this work must not be hidden; it should always be subject to peer reviews.

Pattern scavenging is also an activity for the individual developer, but as condition warrant, may call for the creation of tiger teams who are tasked with searching out opportunities for simplification. This strategy not only yields a better architecture, it also helps to propagate the architectural vision and a sense of ownership, by allowing specific developers to get a more global view of the problem.

Milestones and Measures

Developers successfully complete this phase when they have devised a reasonably sufficient, primitive, and complete set of responsibilities and/or operations for each abstraction or partition at this level. Early in the development process, it is satisfactory to have an informal statement of responsibilities. As development proceeds, there must be more precisely stated semantics, eventually manifesting themselves in code.

> Responsibilities and operations that are neither simple nor clear suggest that the given abstraction is not yet well-defined. An inability to express a concrete header file or other kinds of formal class interfaces also suggests that the abstraction is ill-formed, or that the wrong person is doing the abstracting.

P 77

A number of tactical measures of goodness apply to this step, with the metrics of sufficiency, primitiveness, and completeness as I describe earlier being perhaps the most important in the context of designing individual abstractions.* One rule that applies in this regard helps scope the size of these abstractions:

R 39

> Most interesting classes will, on the average, have about a dozen operations. It is not unusual to find classes with only one or two operations, particularly if they are subclasses. Finding classes with statistically far more operations is not in itself a bad thing, but it is a warning sign that perhaps you have underabstracted.

This number may be slightly larger for languages such as C++ (due to its rules about construction and destruction, overloading and type conformance) and slightly smaller for languages such as Smalltalk (because it is typeless, and so is semantically simpler).

IDENTIFYING RELATIONSHIPS AMONG CLASSES AND OBJECTS

Purpose

The purpose of this phase is to devise a simple set of mechanisms that regulate the classes and objects identified up to this point in the development process.

This phase is largely one of invention, involving decisions about the semantic dependencies among each class and object, and among groups of classes and objects. Some amount of discovery must go on at this stage as the boundaries of abstractions are adjusted to make classes and objects fit together. There is also some amount of implementation that must be carried out in this stage, because paper designs have their limits, and the practical implications of certain decisions cannot be known until they are tried in the context of something executable.

During analysis, this step primarily helps to stabilize a system's domain model, by forcing a consideration of the associations among its classes and objects. Among other things, these associations specify how clients navigate among objects in the model, how certain classes and objects are structurally related to other abstractions, and how behavior is delegated among objects during the conduct of various scenarios. During design, this phase serves to

---

* For a much more detailed treatment of these kinds of tactical metrics, see *Object-Oriented Software Metrics* by Lorenz and Kidd.

specify the collaborations that are important in the system's architecture, by establishing the connections among groups of classes and objects that work together to carry out some higher level behavior. During design, this phase also serves to specify the grouping of classes into class categories, and the relative layering of one category upon another. During evolution, this phase continues to add details to the system's architecture, as certain associations are expanded into instances of underlying collaborations, or are transformed into specific programming idioms.

No object is an island, and so this phase forces the development team to consider the implications of each decision as it relates to every other abstraction. Please understand that identifying the relationships among classes and objects involves much more than just refining the artifacts identified in earlier stages of the micro process. Rather, identifying the relationships among classes and objects involves taking a gestalt view that seeks to identify patterns of relationships, whose exploitation can yield simpler architectures.

> I had taken over the development of a class category consisting of a couple of dozen classes responsible for providing a common error handling mechanism for a larger system. The mechanism was well-designed, but it was also fragile. As more and more clients started using this mechanism, some of them in novel ways, it became clear that the existing design was problematic, manifested by the fact that it was difficult to introduce new kinds of errors and new kinds of behaviors in responses to those errors. A study of a few key scenarios revealed that two of the base classes were deeply entangled. Without changing the semantics relied upon by any existing client (only the code had to be recompiled), I discovered that I could vastly simplify the mechanism by introducing a new class that took responsibility for this shared behavior. This meant delegating certain responsibilities of the two base classes to this new class and then establishing the right relationships among the three. The resulting implementation was not only simpler, it was easier to use and easier to adapt.

I have see this same kind of situation again and again in successful projects, and therein is a practice worth following:

> While identifying the relationships among classes and objects, seek to discover common patterns of relationship, and invent ways to exploit these patterns. Specifically, maximize the connections among things that are semantically related, and minimize the connections among things that are semantically distant and that are subject to change.

P 78

Products

Much like the previous phase, there are generally three artifacts produced in this phase of the micro process:

- A specification of the relationships among key abstractions
- Software that codifies these specifications
- Diagrams or similar artifacts that establish the meaning of each relationship as well as larger collaborations

Once a set of classes and objects have been identified and their semantics specified, the development team can turn its attention to identifying the relationships among them. To a large degree, therefore, these three products serve to capture the patterns of collaboration among a system's classes and objects, forming the mechanisms that, as I describe in Chapter 2, represent an important dimension of any system's architecture. As before, these products contribute to a refinement of the project's dictionary of abstractions.

The specification of the relationships among key abstractions is the most important product at this stage. During analysis, this generally means the identification of any associations among these abstractions. During design and evolution, this means the identification of more specific kinds of relationships, such as inheritance, aggregation, and so on. This first product may take any number of forms, ranging from transitory ones such as CRC cards, to more rigorous notations.

As before, successful projects try to capture these relationships concretely in the form or code or similar executable artifacts. Typically this means refining the interfaces of classes specified in the previous phases, by introducing semantic connections from one class to another.

Because these relationships by their very nature span many individual abstractions, various kinds of diagrams become an even more important product at this phase. One well-placed diagram can speak volumes about some aspect of an architecture. The best use of such diagrams is to illustrate relationship semantics that are important to the problem, yet cannot be easily enforced by the linguistics of any programming language.[*]

During analysis, this step often involves producing class diagrams that state the associations among abstractions, and that add details from the previous step (in particular, the operations and attributes of certain abstractions). During design, the team may also generate class diagrams at the level of class categories to illustrate the system's logical architecture, showing the allocation of

---

[*] For example, the event-ordered behavior of an object, the flow of control in a mechanism such as MVC (Model-View-Controller), and timing assumptions in the synchronization of two concurrent threads are all things that can be expressed in code, but that are better visualized in some diagram that can spatially represent semantics distributed over several classes.

abstractions into layers and partitions. During design and evolution, other diagrams, particularly scenario diagrams and state machine diagrams, may be employed to visualize and reason about the groups of abstractions that work together. As evolution proceeds, the development must make other kinds of relationship decisions, such as the mapping of classes and objects to files, or the allocation of distributed objects and processes to certain processors. Both of these kinds of relationship decisions are often best expressed in module and process diagrams.

At this or any stage of the micro process, it is not desirable, nor is it possible, to produce a comprehensive set of diagrams that express every conceivable view of the relationships among the abstractions in a system. Rather, the development team must focus on the "interesting" ones, where the definition of *interesting* encompasses any set of related abstractions whose relationships are an expression of some fundamental architectural decision, or that express a detail necessary to complete a blueprint for implementation.

Activities

There are three major activities associated with this step:

- Association specification
- Collaboration identification
- Association refinement

Together, these three activities represent an increasing refinement in the semantics of how classes and objects relate to one another. An association is simply a statement of semantic dependency between two or more things.[*] Therefore, because they are so fundamental, this step begins with simple associations, adorns them with their detailed semantics, and then eventually culminates in producing a concrete representation for each association.

> Start identifying the relationships among abstractions by considering their associations first. Once these are reasonably stable, begin to refine them in more concrete ways.

P 79

The identification and specification of associations is primarily an activity of analysis and early design. However, at these stages in the life cycle, it is often sufficient to be imprecise, and so simple association can be used to capture

---

[*] Associations generally represent peer dependencies, the role and cardinality of each participant in the relationship, and possibly a statement of navigability. For example, consider the association between an employee and an employer. Both play distinct roles in the relationship, and, given an instance of one, you can navigate to the other.

enough interesting details about the relationship between two abstractions, yet developers are not required to make premature statements of detailed design.

Developers in a project found themselves getting stuck, because their analysts and their developers were speaking two different languages. In this particular problem (dealing with the flow of customer orders through the business), the analysts were talking in terms of business processes, whereas the developers were getting wrapped up in the details of how they were going to represent these processes. The project finally got unstuck when an outside mentor stepped in and coerced the group into building a domain model that spoke only of responsibilities and associations. At the end of the day, dozens of mangled CRC cards lay scattered on the floor, yet the team left with a common understanding such that the analysts could go back and talk to some end users, and the developers could proceed with augmenting their architecture.

Developers typically follow this order of activities when specifying associations:

- Collect a set of classes that are at the same level of abstraction or that are germane to a particular family of scenarios; populate this set (via CRC cards, in scenario diagrams, or in class diagrams) with each abstraction's important operations and attributes as needed to illustrate the significant properties of the problem being modeled.

- In a pair-wise fashion, consider the presence of a semantic dependency between any two classes, and establish an association if such a dependency exists. The need for navigation from one object to another and the need to elicit some behavior from an object are both cause for introducing associations. Indirect dependencies are cause for introducing new abstractions that serve as agents or intermediaries. Some associations (but probably not many) may immediately be identified as specialization/ generalization or aggregation relationships.

- For each association, specify the role of each participant, as well as any relevant cardinality or other kind of constraint.

- Validate these decisions by walking through scenarios and ensuring the associations that are in place and are necessary and sufficient to provide the navigation and behavior among abstractions required by each scenario.

The identification of collaborations at this step in the micro process is related to the activities of pattern scavenging from the previous step, although here the focus is upon patterns that span peer abstractions. Thus, collaboration identification shares the same activities as pattern scavenging, with the addition that developers also seek out patterns of communication and message passing among classes and objects.

Collaboration identification is primarily an activity of design and evolution. Because it is also largely a problem of classification, this step requires significant creativity and insight. Building executable artifacts is especially important at this stage to validate the assumptions one has made about these collaborations. Depending upon where the development is in the macro process, developers must consider a number of different kinds of collaborations:

- Mechanisms (which represent patterns of collaboration that yield behavior that is greater than the sum of the individual participants in the collaboration)
- Generalization/specialization hierarchies
- The clustering of classes into categories
- The clustering of abstractions in modules
- The grouping of abstractions into processes
- The grouping of abstractions into units that may be distributed independently

The first three kinds of collaboration above derive from views of a system's logical architecture; the last three kinds of collaboration derive from the mapping of this logical model into the physical system.

Association refinement, the third activity of this phase of the micro process, is an activity found throughout analysis, design, and evolution. During analysis, developers evolve certain associations into other more semantically precise relationships to reflect their increasing understanding of the problem domain. During design and evolution, they will similarly transform associations as well as add new concrete relationships in order to provide a blueprint for implementation.

As associations are refined, inheritance, aggregation, instantiation, and use are the main kinds of relationships to consider. A typical order of events for this activity is as follows:

- Given a collection of classes already related by some set of associations, look for patterns of behavior that represent opportunities for specialization and generalization. Place the classes in the context of an existing inheritance lattice, or fabricate a lattice if an appropriate one does not already exist.

- If there are patterns of structure, consider creating new classes that capture this common structure, and introduce them either through inheritance as mixin classes or through aggregation.

- Look for behaviorally similar classes that are either disjointed peers in an inheritance lattice or not yet part of an inheritance lattice, and consider the possibility of introducing common parameterized classes.

- Consider the navigability of existing associations, and constrain them as possible. Replace with simple using relationships, if bi-directional navigation is not a desired property. Expand these associations if navigation requires significant underlying behavior to carry out.

- As development proceeds, introduce tactical details such as statements of role, keys, cardinality, friendship, constraints, and so on. It is not desirable to state every detail: just include information that represents an important analysis or design position, or that is necessary for implementation.

Agents

The identification of relationships among classes and objects follows directly from the previous step. As such, the activities of this stage are carried out by the same kinds of agents as for the identification of the semantics of classes and objects.

Milestones and Measures

Developers successfully complete this phase when they have specified the semantics and relationships among certain interesting abstractions sufficiently to serve as a blueprint for their implementation.

Measures of goodness at this stage include tactical metrics of cohesion, coupling, and completeness, dictated by the following practice and rule:

P 80

Seek to build logically cohesive and loosely coupled abstractions. Abstractions that are clumsy to use or to implement represent a failure to properly identify the right semantics or the right relationships for a given abstraction.

R 40

Be sensitive to balance. As a rule, good architectures are composed of forests of classes, rather than trees of classes, wherein each hierarchy is generally no deeper than 5±2, and no wider than 7±2 at each intermediate node.

IMPLEMENTING CLASSES AND OBJECTS

Purpose

The purpose of this phase is to represent each abstraction and mechanism concretely in the most efficient and elegant way.

Not surprisingly, this phase is largely one of implementation, yet be assured that it is not void of creativity. Choosing the right representation for a class or a mechanism requires stamping out any lingering ambiguities and thus may require further discovery regarding the dark corners of each abstraction's semantics. Similarly, selecting an efficient and elegant representation is an act of invention that cannot be automated easily.

During analysis, the successful project will proceed with a modest amount of implementation, primarily as a means of scoping risk and as a vehicle for unveiling new classes and objects to be refined in the next iterations. During design, this phase serves to create tangible and executable artifacts, by which the system's architecture takes form.* During evolution, activity in this phase of the micro process accelerates, as more substance is added to each successive refinement of the architecture.

The ordering of this step is intentional: the micro process focuses first upon behavior, and defers decisions about representation until as late as possible. This strategy avoids premature implementation decisions that can ruin opportunities for smaller, simpler architectures and also allows for the freedom to change representations as needed for reasons of efficiency, while limiting any disruption to the existing architecture.

> Encourage pragmatic engineering decisions: implementing classes and objects means moving to practical abstractions.

P 81

Products

During this stage of the micro process, one primary artifact is produced:

- Software that codifies decisions about the representation of classes and mechanisms

Simply put, this means cutting some executable code. Secondary artifacts (namely, more detailed diagrams) may exist, but ultimately this is the phase at which abstractions meet reality, and so they should driven to a physical manifestation in code.

---

* Philippe Kruchten stated this eloquently: "I code to better understand what I design."

There is little doubt of the importance of this product during evolution, or even during design, but it may seem curious to include such a concrete artifact as early as analysis. However, as I have mentioned before, being forced to cast one's abstractions in a concrete, unambiguous form is perhaps the best way to ensure that it is useful.

Activities

There is one primary activity associated with this step: the selection of the structures and algorithms that complete the roles and responsibilities of all the various abstractions identified earlier in the micro process. Whereas the first three phases of the micro process focus upon the outside view of an abstractions, this step focuses upon its inside view.

A company had been using object-oriented technology for some time, although these practices had not yet spread to every part of the organization. As a result, it was common for new projects to be staffed with a mixed set of skills: some developers were quite experienced in objects, and others would not have recognized a class even if it had stood up and talked to them. However, the development manager used this fact to her advantage. By pairing up every junior developer with a senior one, a mentoring relationship was established that allowed the junior developer to learn about all things object-oriented. Similarly, each senior developer ended up with a helper who could focus on the details of coding an implementation with the right time and space complexity. This arrangement leveraged the skills of the senior developers (who were all good abstractionists) as well as the skills of the junior developers (many of whom were fresh out of college and still remembered most of the things they had learned in their classes on data structures and algorithms).

During analysis, the results of this activity are relatively abstract: individual developers are not so concerned at that point about making representation decisions; rather, they are more interested in discovering new abstractions to which they can delegate responsibility. During design, and especially during evolution, this activity accelerates as more concrete decisions are made.

Under this activity, most object-oriented developers track the following series of events:

- For each class or each collaboration of classes, consider again its protocol. Identify the patterns of use among its clients in order to determine which operations are central, and hence should be optimized.

Next:

- Before choosing a representation from scratch, consider adapting existing classes, typically by subclassing or by instantiation. Select the appropriate abstract, mixin, or template classes or create new ones if the problem is sufficiently general.

I cannot emphasize the importance of this step strongly enough: before implementing any class and mechanism from scratch, hunt around for components to reuse. If you can reuse parts without modification, then you have just vastly simplified your work. If you find a reusable part that is close to your needs, consider spending a little additional effort to make it closer, because small adjustments like that spread over the entire development life cycle will lead to an architecture that is highly adaptable, at low cost and little additional risk.

> Remember that successful developers seek to write small amounts of quality code, rather than massive amounts of mediocre code. Thus, during implementation, aggressively search for parts to reuse; if you find some that are close to your needs, spend the effort to make them just right.

P 82

What constitutes "close enough"? I use the following rule to guide my actions:

> Adapting a class or mechanism that is just 5 - 10% off from your needs is a no-brainer: do it without question unless there are extenuating circumstances. Adapting an abstraction that is 20 - 30% off from your needs requires a bit more consideration: do it if you expect you will be able to reuse it in one or two more additional ways. Abstractions that are 50% or more off from your needs are not likely candidates for reuse: but if you find a number of such near-misses, then you have the wrong set of components, and so you ought to reconsider their microarchitecture before you move on.

R 41

Continuing:

- Next, consider the objects to which you might delegate responsibility. For an optimal fit, this may require a minor readjustment of their responsibilities or protocol.
- If your abstraction's semantics cannot be provided through inheritance, instantiation, or delegation, consider a suitable representation from primitives in the language. Keep in mind the importance of operations from the perspective of the abstraction's clients, and select a representation that optimizes for the expected patterns of use, remembering that it is not possible to optimize for every use. As you gain empirical information from

successive releases, identify which abstractions are not time- and/or space-efficient, and alter their implementation locally, with little concern that you will violate the assumptions clients make of your abstraction.

- Select a suitable algorithm for each operation. Introduce helper operations to divide complex algorithms into less complicated, reusable parts. Consider the trade-offs of storing versus calculating certain states of an abstraction.

If you have done everything right up to this point—most importantly, meaning you have got a balanced distribution of responsibilities in your system—then you should find that the implementation of most classes and mechanisms is relatively simple.

R 42

Most individual operations associated with a class can be implemented in a dozen or so lines of code. It is not unusual to find some implementations that require only one or two lines of code. If you find implementations that require a hundred or more lines of code, then you have done something very wrong.

Agents

This phase requires substantially different skills than the other three of the micro process. For the most part, these activities can be carried out by application engineers who do not have to know how to create new classes, but at least must know how to reuse them properly and how to adapt them to some degree.

Milestones and Measures

During analysis, developers successfully complete this phase once they have identified all the interesting abstractions necessary to satisfy the responsibilities of higher-level abstractions identified during this pass through the micro process. During design, this phase is completed successfully when there exists executable or near-executable models of these abstractions.

The primary measure of quality for this phase is simplicity. Implementations that are complex, awkward, or inefficient are an indication that the abstraction itself is lacking, or that it has a poor representation.

Chapter 5

The Development Team

The Development Team

Two are better than one, because they have a good return for their work.
ECCLESIASTES 4:9

It is time that I come clean and unveil one of the dirty little secrets of software engineering:

People are more important than any process.

This is especially true of very small teams, wherein the ability of individual team members contributes to the success of the project far more than any other factor. However:

- On larger teams, the law of large numbers forces management to deal with fewer exceptional people and far more average people.
- A good process will leverage the talents of average people.
- Good people with a good process will outperform good people with no process every time.

This is why, in the last two chapters, I describe the macro process and micro process of object-oriented software development in excruciating detail. Of course, successful processes are never carried out by mindless groups of drones. Rather, the successful project requires both a good process and a cohesive team. This, then, is the focus of this chapter:

How should management organize its development team so that it becomes a cohesive unit and becomes larger than the talents of its individual contributors?

Simply hiring some smart men and women is not enough to ensure the success of a project. I know; I have seen projects try it time and time again.

An organization embarked on a project to build a next generation payroll system. They brought in a team of approximately 30 of the best and most experienced people in the company. They trained them in object-oriented stuff. They loaded them up with the latest tools. And they utterly failed. After about a year into the project, it was painfully evident that the team was absolutely stuck in implementation. They had devised a reasonable architecture, but each individual contributor kept hacking away at it, adding more and more cool features that he or she individually thought were interesting. Ultimately, they over-engineered the thing, until it was so bloated with complex features such that no mortal user could ever effectively use it. The company finally threw the project manager out the door, abandoned the system under development, and started all over again, this time a lot wiser but several million dollars poorer.

This example illustrates the culture of the cowboy programmer that prides itself on individual contribution and views every problem as a simple matter of programming.* Don't get me wrong, however: I would much rather have a team of all A+ players rather than a multitude of B players. Furthermore, reality is that many real software innovations seem to come from a mixture of A++, A, and B players‡ organized in small teams that provide a fertile ground for their unrestrained creativity to take root.

However, this simplified model often breaks down, because is it neither repeatable, nor does it scale up, nor does it represent a sustainable business practice. To be precise, there are three problems with merely organizing a development team around a bunch of smart men and women thrown together in the same room. First,

- There are not enough smart men and women to go around.

I do not mean to imply that most of us in the software industry are mentally underpowered. In my experience, I have encountered perhaps only a couple of dozen or so truly world-class developers who not only were experts in their domain, but who could also program circles around their peers.

> In one particular organization, I had the honor to briefly work with a hyperproductive developer who, for the purposes of this example, I will call Howard.** Howard was an off-scale developer, who could write more lines of production quality code in a weekend than most of his peers could write in a month. We measured his work in "Howard days", wherein one Howard day was equivalent to a week or two of a mere mortal developer's time.

This suggests a rule:

> Hyperproductive developers are, on the average, 4 to 10 times more productive than the average developer.

R 43

---

* Found written on the whiteboard of one such programmer's cubicle: *Methods are for wimps.*

‡ And often with some C players mixed in, who handle a variety of the tedious and thankless jobs of production software development that the A and B players either will not do or are not highly leveraged at doing.

** I won't tell you Howard's last name, because you would try to hire him.

Developers like Howard are rare; if you have the good fortune to have people such as he in your organization, treat them well, because their impact upon the success of your project is beyond measure.

However, there's another rule of thumb that applies here:

> Hyperproductive developers constitute less than about 1 or 2% of the entire developer population.

R 44

In other words, there are not many of these kind of people to go around. You may debate whether or not such people are born or made, but either way it is clear that they are a very limited resource. Therefore, practically, most projects simply cannot afford to staff itself with all hyperproductive developers.

Continuing,

- There is a big difference between creating a simple, brilliant program that demonstrates one cool concept very well, and productizing that program so that it meets the needs of industrial strength users.

Building simple, flashy things is easy. Indeed, teams of smart men and women often excel at rapidly crafting such software innovations. However, for most complex domains, this is simply not enough. As the last two chapters should have made clear, building production quality software is an engineering process that requires far more than just raw programming talent, rather, it demands a lot of tedious blocking and tackling to drag an inspired architecture out of the lab and into the real world. Furthermore, dealing with the multitude of details that go into productization is something that some hyperproductive developers find odious, largely because it's A) not as fun and B) requires engineering compromises.

Finally,

- Some problems are so complex that they simply require a lot of hard, sustained labor, more than can be carried out by a small team of smart men and women.

I am a great fan of small teams: they are easier to work with, they are more nimble, and they generally are more successful than larger teams. However, imagine trying to develop an entire national air traffic control system with just 10 people; imagine reengineering a multinational organization's entire billing system with only a two or three really good programmers. You simply cannot do it. Well, actually, you can, but it would take these small teams most of their lifetimes, and by the time they delivered, the world would have changed so much that their work would be irrelevant. Object-oriented technology is great, but no technology is so great that it provides that much leverage to any single small team.

This suggests another rule:

A small object-oriented project can be carried out with a team of only 1 or 2 people. A slightly larger project requires around five people. A modestly-sized project requires a development team of dozen or two. A team developing a moderately complex project will typically reach a peak staff of around 50. Projects of geopolitical scope may require the efforts of a few hundred developers.

R 45

Realize that this is just a general rule: most projects tend to have rather inflexible deadlines and inflexible budgets, and most start with varying amounts of infrastructure. Thus, the size of the team is often as much a function of these three factors as it is the nature and size of the problem to be solved.

The bad news is that the larger the staff, the more likely it is the project will fail. The good news, as I discuss later in this chapter, is that on the average, object-oriented projects tend to require smaller staffs and a less aggressive staffing profiles as compared to non-object-oriented ones. Still, it is the case that as complexity grows, so must the size of your development team. Understaffing a complex project will mean you will never have enough raw horsepower to complete the task in a timely fashion.

For all these reasons, the dirty little secret I revealed earlier is itself not so pure. You cannot simply expect a project to succeed by staffing it with a bunch of smart men and women, arming them with powerful tools, showing them where to stand, and then expect them to move the world. There is not enough leverage. Individuals are important, but in the world of industrial strength software development, teams are even more important. In turn, process is important in building teams, because it is repeatable, it helps to address issues of scale, and it leads to a sustainable business practice.

MANAGERS WHO HATE PROGRAMMERS, AND THE PROGRAMMERS WHO WORK FOR THEM

My experience with successful object-oriented projects suggests the following practice:

> Remember that software development is ultimately a human endeavor.

P 83

Successful object-oriented projects require a skill set, an allocation of resources, and a staffing profile subtly different than for non-object-oriented projects. These topics represent the tactical issues of organizing a cohesive development team, which I discuss in the following sections. However, before I do that, it is important to establish the mindset of the cohesive team. Even if you organize a team with the right roles and responsibilities, your project will flounder if you fail to recognize that development is indeed a human activity.

The mindset of the successful development team has three elements which I can best illustrate through some war stories:

> One organization staffed its projects according to the Mongolian horde principle: sheer numbers would allow management to overwhelm any technical problem by throwing sufficient bodies at it. Furthermore, the more developers you had, the more important the project would seem to be. In one particular object-oriented project for a major new product line, management allocated 300 programmers.* My first recommendation to the project was to get rid of at least 250 developers. Management politely declined my advice, in retrospect because it was more interested in building empires than in building software. I walked away from this project, because with this attitude, it was beyond help.

Thus:

- A project must recognize that its developers are not interchangeable parts, and that the successful deployment of any complex system requires the unique and varied skills of a focused team of people.

Ignoring this principle was a large measure of the reason that the project in this example failed. In this case, management imposed some degree of structure by blindly assigning certain senior programmers as managers. Most absolutely fell flat at their task, simply because they were not skilled in leading other programmers.

Managers are not the only ones who sometimes forget that their developers are human; in a number of failed projects, I have seen senior developers share this distressing attitude:

> I was called in to a project in crisis, and I began my investigation by spending some time with the architect in order to diagnose the problem. We spent a few hours talking about certain key abstractions in the domain, and then I asked him if he would take one of these abstractions that he had outlined, and capture it in a C++ header file. He refused, with words to the effect "No! Damn it, I'm an architect, not a coder!" It took me about three picoseconds to realize why this project was in crisis. When developers say such things, it is usually a sign of arrogance or ineptness. Unfortunately, this "architect" was both.

---

* Honest. I'm not making this up.

I never engaged with this project again. One of my spies on the project reported back to me later that this project eventually died a very slow and painful death.

- A project must honor the role of every one of its developers.

A coder is not a lesser person than an architect; a programmer is not a lower life form than a project manager (or, from the programmer's perspective, a manager is not a lower life form than a programmer). Indeed, the success of every project depends upon the efforts of every team member, no matter how humble their contribution.

This mindset extends to individual contributors:

> At the onset of a large object-oriented project, the architect set out to jell the development team. One interview uncovered a brilliant young programmer who came highly recommended, having saved a number of projects. The interview revealed that she was smart and energetic, but she did not know one thing about the object-oriented programming language, the domain, or any project larger than 50,000 SLOC. The architect advised her to spend at least one or two iterations in the trenches in order to learn about pragmatic object-oriented stuff. She was furious. She came back the following week, saying that she had read the Booch book over the weekend and did not see why she should waste a year in the trenches, because "this object-oriented stuff was not all that different." She very reluctantly took on the job anyway. Six months later, she joined the architecture team. At the next performance review, she admitted that this six months in the trenches had been a most formative one, allowing her to really understand what object-oriented stuff was all about. She added that, despite the fact that she hated the architect's guts for a while, she thought now that this was in fact the right path to grow as a productive member of the team.

The happy ending to this story is that the programmer in question ended up being one of the best team players on the architecture team. This story suggests a third element of a project's mindset:

- Individuals on a development team must be honest about their strengths and weaknesses, and not let their ego take them to places beyond their ability.

As a developer, admitting that you have certain strengths and weakness is the first step in growing as a professional. Every new project that a developer encounters changes that person. Successful developers recognize that fact, and in truth they welcome the challenge each new project brings because it represents an opportunity for professional growth.

ROLES AND RESPONSIBILITIES

Although there may be a limited pool of hyperproductive developers in the world, it is possible—and indeed desirable—to build a hyperproductive team using developers of average talents. The key to this approach is recognizing that different people have different skills and every complex software project requires a balanced mixture of these skills. Furthermore, my experience suggests that the object-oriented development process requires a subtly different partitioning of skills as compared to traditional methods. In small projects, the same people may play several different roles; in larger projects, each role may be carried out by a different person or persons.

The development team includes any person who has an impact upon the success or failure of a project. Every successful team encompasses three general sets of roles:
- Core   Responsible for actual software production
- Supplemental   Supports the activities of the core developers
- Peripheral   At the boundary of the project and its context

---

In traditional approaches to software development, the work of the core team would typically be divided among a group of people who gather and interpret requirements from the real world, some who translate those requirements into a blueprint of software artifacts, and coders who write code against these blueprints. There are lots of problems with this monolithic model, not the least of which that it almost forces a very strict waterfall process, wherein perfectly formed requirements are transformed into complete and unchangeable designs that are then mechanically implemented by largely unskilled coders. As I explain in Chapter 1, this utopian model of development is pure folly.

Furthermore, this traditional model is absolutely the antithesis of the incremental and iterative development process found in all successful object-oriented projects, wherein the conventional activities of analysis, design, and programming are blurred. In successful object-oriented projects, a very different partitioning of skills is found.

A conservative COBOL organization found itself being dragged into the object-oriented world because of an external dictate. Management took a calm and deliberate approach to transitioning the team through a combination of mentoring, formal training, and pilot projects. Much to the surprise of the team itself, the group quickly became a cohesive unit, manifest by the fact that the project soon found its own rhythm. Ultimately, the core development team organized itself around three different groups: an architect who established the system's structure, class and class category designers who managed the system's microarchitecture, and general engineers, who both implemented these classes as well as assembled them into larger parts. The health of this team was made clear when they were thrown a whole new set of requirements without schedule relief, yet did not panic.

In the successful object-oriented project, the core team is typically made up of individuals with three different roles:[*]

- Architect
- Abstractionist
- Application engineer

This suggests a common practice:

Organize your core development team among three groups: an architect who is responsible for the system's overall structure, abstractionists who manage the system's microarchitecture, and application engineers who implement and assemble the classes and mechanisms found in the system.

P 84

I also have a general rule about the mixture of these roles in successful projects:

Approximately 10% of the development team should be a full or part time member of the architecture team. About 30% of the team are abstractionists. Application engineers constitute about 50% of the whole team. The remaining 10% serve in supporting roles.

R 46

An architect is the person or persons responsible for evolving and maintaining the system's architecture. The main activities of the architect include:[‡]

---

[*] I do not include the project manager in this group because, by my earlier classification, the core team is made up of people who cut code. However, as I discuss later, the role of the project manager is just as important as any of these core roles.
[‡] Kruchten, P. April 1994. *Software Architecture and Iterative Development*, Santa Clara, California: Rational Software Corporation, p. 53.

- Define the architecture of the software.
- Maintain the architectural integrity of the software.
- Assess technical risks relative to software design.
- Propose the order and content of the successive iterations and assist in their planning.
- Consult to various design, implementation, integration, and quality assurance teams.
- Assist marketing regarding future product definition.

The architect typically is responsible for producing a number of deliverables, including the architecture document, parts of lower-level design documents, design and programming guidelines, elements of release plans, meeting and review minutes, and design audits of the released system.

The architect is the project's visionary. Ultimately, every project should have exactly one identifiable architect, although for larger projects, the principle architect should be backed up by an architecture team of modest size. The architect is not necessarily the most senior developer but rather is the one best qualified to make strategic decisions, usually as a result of his or her extensive experience in building similar kinds of systems. Because of this experience, such developers intuitively know the common architectural patterns that are relevant to a given domain and what performance issues and other forces apply to certain architectural variants. Architects are not necessarily the best programmers either, although they should have adequate programming skills. Just as a building architect should be skilled in aspects of construction, it is generally unwise to employ a software architect who is not also a reasonably decent programmer.[*] Project architects should also be well-versed in the notation and process of object-oriented development because they must ultimately express their architectural vision in terms of clusters of classes and collaborations of objects.

The architect must possess four skills:[‡]

• Experience	Expertise both in the domain and in software design are essential.
• Leadership	The architect must have the focus, confidence, charisma, and authority to drive the technical effort.
• Communication	Architects must do a lot of preaching, convincing, mentoring, and teaching in order to carry the architectural vision to

---

[*] Borrowing a story from civil engineering, it is said that an architect must be a person willing to be the first to walk across every bridge he or she designs. An architect who suffers no consequences from his or her architectural decisions has no skin in the game; indeed, the best architects have a lot of skin in the game.

[‡] Kruchten, pp. 52–53.

the rest of the development team as well as to customers.

- **Proactive and goal-oriented** The architect is neither a staff researcher nor a technologist; he or she must possess the drive to build something tangible and complete and the guts to make the engineering compromiss nessary to cope with building systems for the real world.

An architect should also be a person who sometimes likes to "color outside of the lines." As I have mentioned, every good architecture requires some element of risk, and therefore, architects should not be afraid to take bold or novel actions that might lead to a breakthrough that generalizes or simplifies the architecture.

This suggests the following practice:

> Choose an architect who possess a vision large enough to inspire the project to great things, the wisdom born from experience that knows what to worry about and what to ignore, the pragmatism necessary to make hard engineering decisions, and the tenacity to see this vision through to closure.

P 85

An abstractionist is a person responsible for class and class category design. In other words, an abstractionist is charged with evolving and maintaining the system's microarchitecture. The main activities of the abstractionist include:

- Identify classes, clusters of classes, and mechanisms relevant to the domain and to the implementation.
- Devise, defend, and negotiate the interface and services of individual class categories and direct their implementation.
- Carry out class category level testing.
- Advise the architect with regard to the order and content of the successive iterations and carry out his or her planning.
- Direct tiger teams to investigate design alternatives and to stamp out technical risks.
- Mentor and lead application engineers working on the artifacts under the abstractionist's control.
- Back up the architect in his or her absence.[*]

---

[*] Jim Coplien has suggested "truck number" as a measure of catastrophic risk to the architect. This is a little morbid, but truck number measures the number of negative events that it would take to wipe out the architecture team (*c.f.*, a truck flattening an architect as he or she crosses the road). Projects with a truck number of one are at high risk for losing their vision. Using abstractionists as lieutenants that back up the architect increases a project's truck number and therefore decreases its risk. Every successful project should be able to survive the loss of key individuals, although it will certainly take the project time to regain its rhythm.

An abstractionist typically is responsible for producing a number of deliverables, including elements of the architecture document, design documents, class and class category interfaces, some class and class category implementations, and walkthroughs of certain important classes and mechanisms.

An abstractionist is ultimately an engineer who turns the architect's vision into reality. An abstractionist can look at the world and say, "yea, verily, here is a class," and turn that class into a piece of code. Whereas an architect has dominion over the entire software system, an abstractionist reigns over individual class categories. Every class category should be controlled by exactly one abstractionist, although one abstractionist may control many class categories. An abstractionist is therefore the ultimate owner of a cluster of classes and its associated mechanisms and is also responsible for its implementation, testing, and release during the evolution of the system.

An abstractionist must possess skills quite similar to that of an architect. Abstractionists are usually faster and better programmers than the project architect, but lack the architect's broad experience. The role of abstractionist also requires some skills at analysis, for he or she must be able to look at the real world while walking through scenarios in order to extract the abstractions that live there and to specify their boundaries.

With regard to this role, I find many successful object-oriented projects that follow this practice:

P 86

Select abstractionists who are skilled at identifying, specifying, and implementing classes and mechanisms that are germane to the domain and to the implementation.

An application engineer is a person responsible for implementing the classes and mechanisms invented by the architect and abstractionists and who assembles these artifacts in small program fragments to fulfill the requirements of the system. The main activities of the application engineer include:

- Implement the design of the classes and mechanisms in the context of a class category under the leadership of an abstractionist.
- Write small programs that work in the language of these classes to fulfill scenarios defined for the system as well as for the class category itself.
- Carry out tactical class design.
- Carry out class-level testing.
- Advise the abstractionist with regard to tactical risk.
- Participate in tiger teams to prototype design alternatives.
- Participate in walkthroughs.
- Back up the abstractionist in his or her absence.

An application engineer is largely responsible for producing code. Application engineers will often also contribute to design documents and user documentation.

An application engineer is ultimately a programmer who turns an abstractionist's microarchitecture into reality. An application engineer can look at the design of a class or a mechanism and say "yea, verily, here is some code."[*] In smaller projects, application engineers are also abstractionists. In larger projects, the roles of the abstractionist and application engineer are explicitly separate. Furthermore, as the complexity of the project grows, it is common to find different kinds of application engineers. For example, in the information systems domain, one might find specialists such as:

- GUI designer
- Database programmer
- Network programmer
- Transaction programmer
- Security and administration programmer

In the engineering domain, one might find other specialists such as:

- Device driver programmer
- Process programmer
- Mathematician and/or algorithm developer

With regard to skills, application engineers should be familiar with but not necessarily experts in the notation and process of object-oriented development. However, application engineers are ultimately very good programmers who understand the idioms and idiosyncrasies of the given programming languages. The best application engineers are also articulate, able to network with their peers and communicate their positions through mediums other than just naked code.

This suggests another practice:

> Assemble the implementation team from application engineers who love to code and who are able to turn abstractions into reality.

P 87

The core team of architects, abstractionists, and application engineers is responsible for actual software production. The supplemental team supports the activities of these core developers and typically includes people in a number of different roles:

- Project manager
- Analyst

---

[*] Bumper sticker found on the motorcycle of an application engineer: *Live to code, code to live.*

- Integration
- Quality assurance
- Documentation
- Toolsmith
- System administrator
- Librarian

Not every project requires all of these roles, and in smaller projects, many of these roles are assigned to the same individuals.

This suggests another practice common among successful projects:

P 88

> Surround your core development team with people responsible for the daily care and feeding of the project's artifacts.

This practice lets the core team focus on its primary mission, namely, producing quality software that serves some meaningful purpose. As an analogy, consider the structure of a professional soccer team: the players on the field are on the line for winning the game, but their task would be impossible without all the coaches, trainers, medical personnel, and equipment handlers on the sidelines.

Perhaps the most important of these supplementary roles is the project manager who is ultimately responsible for the project's success and so carries out the active management of the project's deliverables, tasks, resources, and schedules. I have called this role supplemental only because it does not directly contribute to the activity of cutting code. However, the following practice must be kept in mind:

P 89

> Treat the architect and the project manager as peers; they should effectively be joined at the hip.

Do not confuse their roles, however: the architect is in charge of the architecture, whereas the project manager is in charge of the team, the schedule, and the process. Consequently, the project manager drives the rhythm of the project, not the architect. Indeed, just because a project applies the most sophisticated development method or the latest fancy tool does not mean a manager has the right to abdicate responsibility for hiring developers who can think or to let a project run on autopilot.

This can be summed up in the following practice:

P 90

> Do not confuse the roles of project management and development; they encompass very different activities. Remember that a team's architects, abstractionists, and application engineers are responsible for designing software and that the project manager is responsible for designing the team of software developers.

The main activities of the project manager include:

- Negotiate, establish, coordinate, and oversee the project's deliverables.
- Establish and drive the project's schedules.
- Staff the project.
- Assign the team's work break down.
- Manage the project's budget.
- Coordinate with the project's patrons and user community.

The project manager is typically responsible for producing a number of deliverables, including schedules, staffing plans, budgets, and meeting minutes, and project reports.

The project manager is the project's director. Every project should have exactly one identifiable project manager, separate from the architect. The project manager should be technically astute, but more importantly, he or she must have the necessary people skills to direct a group of high-energy and highly creative technophiles.

The project manager must first possess the same four skills as the architect. The best managers I have worked with were also:

• Risk-aversive	Managers must always challenge assumptions. They must also be on the lookout for anything that adds risk to the project, yet they must not be so scared of change as to reject any thing new.
• Politically sensitive	Managers must understand that the project's patrons, user community, and developers may have different and sometimes hidden agendas, and so they must be able to set expectations and manage conflict.
• An enlightened dictator	As a manager, sometimes you have to shoot the developer: real systems require engineering compromises. Furthermore, *sometimes* you have to give users what they really need, not just what they tell you they think they need.

When the pragmatism of a bold project manager finds balance with the intense vision of a hyperproductive architect, the results are magical.

I was invited to spend some time with a team building a successful and very large Smalltalk application involving semiconductor wafer fabrication. From the moment I came on to the site, I could almost feel the electricity in the air. Although this was the first real Smalltalk project for most of this team, the programmers I spoke with consistently exhibited pride and enthusiasm for their work. They were clearly under the strong leadership of a forceful and dynamic project manager, yet his presence was not so overpowering that the rest of his team cowered in his sight, nor were they afraid to tell him when he was full of hot air.

The other supplemental roles are not quite as important to the success of a project as that of the project manager, yet each is still important in its own way.

The analyst is responsible for evolving and interpreting end users requirements. True, to some degree, each member of the core development team must be an analyst. However, for larger projects, it is often useful to identify the analyst as a distinct role; for the largest projects, the team may require a handful of such analysts. An analyst must be an expert in the problem domain, yet he or she must not be isolated from the rest of the development team. Analysts typically are responsible for conducting user interviews, identifying functional and performance requirements, resolving conflicts and ambiguities in the project's requirements, and building analysis models. In the context of object-oriented development, the analyst must also be adept at building and refining scenarios, since these are the primary artifacts of object-oriented analysis.

The role of integration sounds traditional, but it has a role peculiar to object-oriented development, wherein integration is a continuous activity rather than a monolithic one. In hyperproductive projects, integration might take place as often as a few times a week. Rather then underusing the programming skills of a core developer, it is often best to assign the role of integration manager to a separate individual responsible for assembling compatible versions of released artifacts in order to form a deliverable and executable release. This role requires clerical skills as well as proficiency with the project's development tools because its work largely involves maintaining configurations of released code. This role also requires people skills because the integrator sometimes has to cajole, plead with, and otherwise coerce some members of the development team to reach closure in their work, so that integration can proceed.* For projects of moderate complexity and in the presence of good tools, integration typically requires the labor of one person who works in spurts: between releases, there is only a little clean up to do, but when a release is being built, it is all-consuming.‡

The role of quality assurance is often a thankless one. Core developers sometimes feel they get in the way, and managers outside the project often view

---

* For this reason, my organization sometimes calls the person in the role of integrator the project's *ramrod*.

‡ Software (and a software integrator) never sleeps. In fact, I swear that releases seem to come together faster in the wee hours of the night.

them as overhead.* As the last two chapters should have made clear, however, it is impossible for a development organization to mature unless it measures what it is doing. For smaller projects, quality assurance, including testing, should be the shared responsibly of the development team. For larger projects, it is useful to have people in this distinct role, responsible for measuring all the products of the development process and for directing system-level testing of all prototypes and production. The next chapter has more to say about testing.

As I described in Chapter 2, a successful software project is more than the sum of all its code. The world has seen more than a few brilliant projects utterly fall flat in the market place because they were incomprehensible to its users. Thus, the role of documentor involves the responsibility for producing end-user documentation of the project and its architecture. In small projects, the trend is often for core developers to write this documentation. This practice is OK to a point, but if you find your programmers writing more text then they are writing code, you have your priorities all wrong. In most successful projects, the documentor is a professional technical writer. He or she should be able to work with the core development team to devise a comprehensible model of the solution and then explain it in prose in ways that make that model accessible. Modest-size projects may require only one or two part time writers; larger projects may require a small staff of writers for a limited duration.

A project's toolsmith is responsible for creating and adapting software tools that facilitate the production of the project's deliverables, especially with regard to generated code. For example, a project might need common test scaffolding to test certain aspects of a user interface, or it might need to integrate the project's selected commercial development tools with the organizations standard yet proprietary configuration management tool.

Especially in the presence of an incremental and iterative development process, having an independent toolsmith allows for a resource that can provide creature comforts to the core development team, which, in the heat of battle, simply do not have the time to write even the simplest tools that might in the long run give them a lot of leverage. The role of toolsmith requires intimate knowledge of the organization's tools, and the programming and systems skills sufficient to bend and shape them to the needs of the project. For smaller projects, the toolsmith is typically the part-time job of one of the application engineers. In larger organizations, one dedicated toolsmith can be shared among modest sized projects. Only the larger projects require a full-time toolsmith.

A project's system administrator is responsible for managing the physical computing resources used by the project. Just as the toolsmith is responsible for the care and feeding of the project's tools, the system administrator is responsible for the care and feeding of the project's hardware. This role may sound rather mundane, but reality is that programmers cannot program if their com-

---

* A common complaint from such people: "If my developers were hired to write good code in the first place, why do I need a separate staff to measure quality?"

puter is down or generally sick. For most organizations, this role is provided by some centralized organization, although larger projects may have their own dedicated system's administrator.

Lastly, the librarian is a supplementary role that I sometimes find in larger organizations that are serious about large-scale reuse. A librarian is responsible for managing the organization's repository of reusable artifacts, including code, architectures, and even documentation. At the very least, the duties of the librarian include maintaining the contents of and access to this repository. Without active effort, such a library can become a vast wasteland of junk that no developer would ever want to paw through. In more mature organizations, the librarian's duties encompass participation in reviews and walkthroughs, actively seeking opportunities for commonality, and then acting as an advocate for exploiting this commonality. As such, a librarian may acquire, produce, and adapt frameworks for general use within the organization. In smaller projects, this role is shared with the toolsmith. In the largest projects, the librarian may include a small staff or two or three.

Beyond the core and the supplemental roles, peripheral roles exist that are far removed from software development, yet still have a distinct impact upon the success or failure of a project. These peripheral roles include:

- Patron
- Product manager
- End user
- Tech support

These four roles represent people who are ultimately consumers of the system being built by the core development team. Thus, the following practice applies:

P 91

> Executing a project in a technically flawless manner is a laudable goal, but never forget for whom you are building the system.

A patron is someone who champions a particular project and who, in many cases, controls its main source of funding. The role of the patron was common during the Middle Ages and the Renaissance, wherein a wealthy benefactor would commission an artist to execute certain works, sometimes culminating in a relationship that spanned the artist's lifetime. This analogy holds true in larger software development organizations as well. Here, a patron is typically someone in the higher echelons of the company who promotes the project's concept, identifies its funding, and in general blesses the effort. Patrons are important to the success of a project for two reasons. First, a good patron will go to bat for you when your project is faltering and the future looks gloomy. Second, because the patron typically lives at stratospheric levels in the organization, he or she likely has a vision that goes beyond the dominion of your particular project and so may provide useful insight into the project's real context. Without a doubt, it is very important for a project to keep its patrons happy, for without them, the project would likely not exist.

A product manager is one who, in a larger organization, typically manages an entire product line for a vertical line of business. A product manager's activities not only include supervising individual projects, but also coordinating marketing, training, and support activities. In smaller organizations, the product manager and the project manager may be one and the same person.

To no great surprise, end users are the ultimate client of every project, and their acceptance or rejection of a project's artifacts provide an unequivocal measure of success or failure. Unhealthy projects typically take one or more of the following attitudes towards end users:

- Distant

  End users get in the way; they slow down the "real" work that has to get done.

- Condescending

  Users are essentially clueless; it is our job to tell the customer what they need.

- Adversarial

  End users create conflict; it is our job to neutralize their complaints.

- Codependent

  The customer just told us to jump; although it screwed up all our plans we asked "how high?"

None of these attitudes are very productive. The healthiest projects I have encountered aggressively seek a professional liaison with its end users. This means seeking insight, actively soliciting feedback from them regarding early prototypes, and involving them in strategic project decisions, especially those involving tradeoffs between what is desirable and what is possible. In the most successful projects, end users are exposed to early prototypes and incremental architectural releases in a controlled fashion. By *controlled*, as I have said before, I mean that the project never throws the product over the wall to the end user, but rather sets expectations about what the release does and what it does not do. Additionally, the project will hold the hand of the end users when necessary to guide them through the early learning curve. When a project has the resources, the following practice applies:

> Assign someone to act as a liaison between the core development team and its clients, especially its patrons and end users.

P 92

For many commercial projects, even internal ones, the end user community may be big enough to warrant the existence of a technical support group independent of the core development team, whose role is to manage post-delivery activities. Thus, from the perspective of the core development team, technical support is one of its clients. An analogy drawn from car manufacturing applies here: car companies design cars not just for the driving public, but also with the needs of manufacturing and car maintenance in mind. So it is with software. Technical support is on the front line once a product is released, and must cover for any gaps weaknesses, and outright flaws in the product. Technical support is always the first to suffer the consequences of a project's short comings, for support is the first to register end user complaints.[*] Involving technical support during development helps the core team design for support. Practically, this means exposing technical support to early architectural releases, letting them sit in on design reviews, and generally exposing them to the product before its end users do. This early involvement has the social benefit of forging personal relationships between the core development team and the technical support team, which really helps when times are rough, and difficult end user complaints come streaming in. Of course, in the successful object-oriented project, there should never be any such large stream of complaints. This suggest the following rule:

R 47

> Although your project may be an economic success, you have failed your end users if you require a technical support team an order of magnitude larger than your core development team.

By implication, the cost of ongoing technical support must be a development consideration.

RESOURCE ALLOCATION

My discussion thus far should have helped you understand the subtly different roles that make up the object-oriented development team. Three questions remain, however:

> As I organize my development team:
> - How do I structure these roles?
> - How do I deal with larger projects?
> - What staffing profile makes sense?

My experience suggests that all healthy teams encompass, to varying degrees, all of the roles that I describe earlier, and with these roles form webs of relationships that spontaneously yield smaller identifiable subgroups. In fact,

---

[*] For most commercial products, end users rarely call up technical support, telling them just how utterly delighted they are to be using their products.

in his study of organizations, Coplien has found that many hyperproductive teams seem to exhibit a common pattern of communication, as illustrated in Figure 5-1.[*]

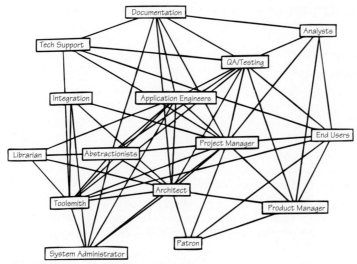

Figure 5-1   Patterns in the Hyperproductive Team

In this figure, the boxes represent different team roles, and the lines represent informal and formal paths of interaction. Notice the tight interconnection among the project manager, architect, abstractionists, and application engineers (forming the core development team), and the non-hierarchical relationship of this core team to the supplemental and peripheral roles. This is the sign of a very focused project.

> Organize your development team so that its center of gravity lies within a tight grouping of the project manager, architect, abstractionists, and application engineers.

P 93

As I have already mentioned, you will find a number of identifiable subgroups formed from collections of people in different roles. In the most healthy projects, these groups are quite fluid, springing up when necessary to actively attack some newly identified risk, and then being dismantled when their purpose is served. Because they thrive on bureaucracy, high ceremony projects tend to unnecessarily extend the life of such groups. Zero-ceremony projects, on the other hand, often go to the other end of the spectrum and aggressively

---

[*] This figure is adapted from some of Jim Coplien's studies, with the names of a few of the roles changed to match my terminology.

avoid any hint of subteam structure, since every developer is treated as an independent, heroic figure, capable of epic feats of programming. Neither such extreme is a good thing. Rather, inside most healthy projects, you will find the following subteams:

- Architecture team
- Analysis team
- Design team
- Implementation team
- Deployment team
- Tiger team

There is a very important practice that underlies the concept of the architecture team:

P 94

Control the conceptual integrity of your system by assigning responsibility of each class category to exactly one abstractionist and assigning responsibility of the overall structure to exactly one architect.

Under this practice, the overall architecture is controlled by the architect, and the microarchitecture of each class category is controlled by an abstractionist (although each abstractionist may have responsibility for more than one class category). Collectively, the architect and these class category owners form the architecture team, which is supplemented with other roles as their services are required. For example, in larger projects, it is useful to include someone from quality assurance (responsible for driving the system testing), someone from integration (responsible for driving each release to closure) and an analyst (responsible for reminding the team of its real world focus).

To clarify an earlier rule:

R 48

In a well-balanced project, 1 out of 7 developers is a full time or part time member of the architecture team. In smaller projects, 1 in 12 is satisfactory, since communication within the team is easier.

The architecture team should be created at project inception and continued through maintenance (although on a smaller scale, and perhaps with different people than the original developers), only to be dismantled when the software system is put out to pasture.

An analysis team forms early in the life cycle as requirements are being gathered and sifted through. This team is generally populated by the analysts, and supplemented by quality assurance (who must test against these requirements) and a subset of the architecture team (who must become intimately familiar with all the dark corners of these requirements). The analysis team scales back or potentially dismantles as design proceeds, only to be resurrected as necessary in the early stages of each iteration during evolution.

Design teams spring up in the macro process late during analysis, as the team begins to play with its tools and starts to explore design alternatives. Design teams are mainly populated by abstractionists and some application engineers, with mentoring supplied by the architect. To no great surprise, such teams peak during the design phase as the system's mechanisms are solidified. These teams also form during evolution, only to diminish in number over time, as lower-level design issues are solved.

Implementation teams start up slowly during analysis (as the team starts to flex its muscles against the emerging problem), begin to gain steam during design (as selected mechanisms are fleshed out), and thrive during evolution (when the project achieves its rhythm, and begins to pump out code). In an object-oriented architecture, you will typically see lots of small implementation groups, focused either on completing the behavior of selected scenarios (which involve application engineers assembling classes into small programs), or on completing the implementation of various class categories (which involve abstractionists working alone or with other application engineers to refine their microarchitecture). As I describe in the previous chapter, the life cycle of the implementation teams tends to follow a micro process.

Deployment teams are responsible for wrestling releases out the door and putting them in the hands of users. Deployment teams are lead by an integrator and may occasionally be supplemented by abstractionists or application engineers who help file off the rough edges, especially during early releases, as well as documentors, who help make the release accessible. Deployment teams begin to form during early design, so that the deployment process can be ironed out far before the first release has to be moved out the door. These teams hit their stride during evolution as the project catches it rhythm.

Tiger teams are the free agents of a project. They are formed as necessary to investigate some dark corner of the system, to validate some design alternative, or to track down and kill some bug. In other words, tiger teams provide the resources for project managers to attack any unforeseen risks that may arise.

> If your project is of modest risk, set aside about 10% to 15% of your
> development resources for tiger teams.

R 49

Tiger teams, like their name, are powerful, nimble, and often solitary groups. Populate such teams with the person or persons in your project who has the best skills for the problem at hand. Depending upon the issue, you may need a tireless detective able to search out and destroy bugs, a software archeologist patient enough to decipher the remains of some ancient piece of legacy code, or a hyperactive coder capable of lashing together prototypes in just a few hours or a few days.

R 50

For most projects, the median size of a tiger team is one or two people. The median lifetime of a tiger team is one or two weeks.

This concept of fluid teams scales down as well as scales up. For small projects with a team size of one, that one person must take on every development role, although usually not at the same time. For slightly larger projects,—around two to three people—the roles are still usually shared, although one typically does begin to see some specialization. In particular, one of the group will likely be identified—by capability and not by title—as the system's architect. In groups numbering around 5 to 7 people, the roles begin to become much more crisply defined. In particular, the division of architect, abstractionist, and application engineer is usually evident in systems of this size.

Modest-size projects, with a dozen or two developers, start to see more distinct individuals in the secondary roles, whereas in smaller teams, these secondary roles would typically be shared by the core development team. It is also at this team size that the direct mapping of architecture to team structure becomes obvious: the hierarchy of class categories tends to be mirrored by the hierarchy of architect to abstractionists to application engineers.

The really wonderful thing is that this model even scales up to much larger projects. The key here is that each abstractionist, as the owner of some set of class categories, becomes the architect for a piece of the larger system. Thus, in a project requiring 50 to 75 developers, there is still one architect, but perhaps 10 abstractionists each of whom control a system microarchitecture, and as such has control over a subteam. This approach thus addresses the problem of span of control. Of course, there is a practical limit to the number of people (or class categories) that one manager (or architect) can manage (or develop). By applying the architect/abstractionist/application engineer model to all levels of the system, the object-oriented project ends up with a manageable and repeatable team structure.

One of the larger (although not the largest) object-oriented project I encountered had well over 100 developers assigned to it. Early on, I hated to use this project as an example, because people believed that object-oriented meant never having to write much code. However, this was a system that spanned several countries, and thus the complexity of this project was such that it demanded a lot of raw code to be written. At first, management staffed the project along traditional lines: analysts, designers, coders. This quickly proved to be inadequate, represented by the fact that the project could not find its rhythm. Once management started to form teams that cut across these more rigid roles, under the direction of an architecture team, they found that the project was much more responsive to change, and was able to produce releases on a more regular basis.

This example suggests the following practice:

> As the complexity of your problem rises, grow a layer of middle level development management by letting abstractionists act as the architects of their piece of the system. Retain the role of the system architect to preserve a simplicity and a harmony that cuts across all of these microarchitectures.

P 95

No matter what the complexity of your project, however, one of the more delightful aspects of managing an object-oriented project is that, in the steady state, there is usually a reduction in the total amount of resources needed and a shift in the timing of their deployment relative to more traditional methods. The operative phrase here is steady state. Generally speaking, the first object-oriented project undertaken by an organization will require slightly more resources than for non-object-oriented methods, primarily because of the learning curve inherent in adopting any new technology.

> All other things being equal (and they never are), your first object-oriented project will likely cost you 10%–20% more resources (people and/or schedule) than your usual non-object-oriented projects. By the time you hit your second or third project, if you have done things right, you should see a need for 20%–30% fewer resources than traditional staffing would suggest.

R 51

A return on investment begins to manifest itself during the second or third project, because at that time the development team is more adept at class design and harvesting common abstractions and mechanisms, and the management team is more comfortable with driving the iterative and incremental development process.

> A large European telephone company traditionally staffed its projects on the order of hundreds of developers. As an experiment to validate its move into the object-oriented worlds, the company funded an almost parallel development effort, in which a team of a couple of hundred developers using traditional techniques worked beside a smaller group of just 30 developers solving the same problem, but using object-oriented technology. The smaller team consistently delivered its products on schedule and on budget while the larger, traditional model was slipping.

Part of the dramatic difference shown in this example can be attributed to the Hawthorn effect, but that is only a minor factor.[*] Indeed, most of this

---

[*] The Hawthorn effect in effect state that groups under study will show some imporvement, simply because they are being studied.

change can be attributed to the use of an architecture-driven, iterative and incremental object-oriented life cycle.

Above, I refer to a shift in the timing of the deployment of resources in object-oriented projects, relative to more traditional methods. Whereas role allocation and scale are issues of space, staffing profile is an issue of time.

Figure 5-2 maps staffing against the phases of the object-oriented macro process. Here we can see that, in the successful project, the team gets deployed in three major waves, reflecting the structure of the core development team. First we engage the architect, who plays a role throughout development. This is quickly followed by the engagement of the abstractionists, who begin the process of discovery during analysis and back up the architect during design. The third wave is made up of the application engineers, who are fully engaged by evolution. Individuals with supplementary roles are deployed as their skills are needed, as I describe earlier.

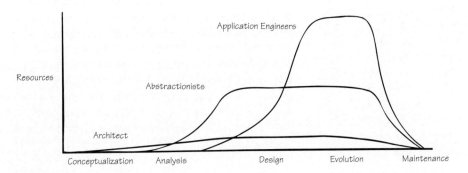

Figure 5-2 Staffing Profile

Stated as a practice followed by most successful object-oriented projects:

Staff your project in three overlapping waves. The architect leads the charge, the team's abstractionists follow, and the mass of application engineers provide the main body of resources.

P 96

TECHNOLOGY TRANSFER

The practices and rules that I describe thus far regarding the development team assume that you have got a level playing field, as far as the maturity and skills of your team members are concerned. However, because of the controlled panic under which most software development organizations operate, one rarely has it so easy. Often, as new projects are staffed, managers are faced with a heterogeneous skill set: some members may be quite adept at object-oriented technology, some may be just beginners, and some may be painfully wrenching themselves away from relatively ancient technologies.* For the team to jell, it is important that the team quickly achieve some minimal common abilities. Simply immersing a developer in a one-week course on object-oriented stuff is not enough to teach the necessary skills, nor will just handing out a book do the job.‡ If you try to move your project into the brave new object-oriented world either of these ways, you are destined to fail.

> An organization wanted to show off its cool new tool that reversed engineered C++ into Booch diagrams. We approached one company that allegedly had been developing in C++ for a couple of years and in fact had written several hundred thousands of lines of code. We asked this company for a chunk of code, so that we could reverse engineer it. "Does it matter what kind is it?" they asked. "No, it, doesn't," we said. "OK, here's some media with a few tens of thousand of lines of C++," they said. "Great!" we said. "Oh, by the way, does it have to have any classes in it? We don't have a lot of those," they said.

> I was brought in to yet another project in crisis by a team that had migrated from C to C++. I began my investigation by studying their architecture. The good news was that they had classes. The bad news was that most of these classes smelled funny. I ran a quick metric over most of their classes, and to my dismay found that the average number of member functions per class was one. Visual inspection revealed that most of these member functions were named as a form of the verb "to be" with "doit" being the most common name. Clearly, the team had missed the point, by doing a functional decomposition and only wrapping classes around their functions to make them look object-oriented.

Both of these projects tried to do the right thing, yet both failed because they simply missed the point of object-oriented stuff.

Trying to purify your organization by purging it of all those who simply do not grasp the concept of objects is not a particularly good idea either, as the following example shows:

---

* A year ago, Bjarne Stroustrup reported that the number of C++ developers worldwide was doubling every 12–18 months. Simple math will show that the means about 50% of the world's C++ developers at any one time had only 6–9 months of experience.

‡ No, not even my book on object-oriented analysis and design is so good that one can make the paradigm shift to object-oriented technology by stuffing the book under your pillow at night and hoping to learn by osmosis. Becoming an excellent software devloper is something that evolves through lots of real development experience, not simply by reading.

A large, high-ceremony MIS organization decided to embrace objects from top to bottom. Triggered by an edict on high that object-oriented stuff was their future, the organization trained every one of their COBOL developers by running them through a multi-week course. At the end of the training period, everyone took a test, which allegedly tested their ability to grok objects. About 10-15% "failed" the test, by whatever perverse measure they had devised. These 10-15% were then laid off under the cover of a rightsizing move. Needless to say, morale plummeted: learning objects with a gun to your head does not make for great technology transfer.

I am violently opposed to such Machiavellian software practices. So, the issue at hand is this:

> How does one transition one's organization to the object-oriented paradigm?

To answer that question, let me first present some general rules that collectively set the context for further discussion:

R 52

It takes about one month for a professional programmer to learn the syntax and semantics of an object-oriented programming language such as C++ or Smalltalk. It takes about 6-9 months for that same developer to really embrace the object paradigm.

R 53

It takes about one month for a professional programmer to become adept with a simple class library. It takes about 6-9 months for that same developer to become really proficient with a much larger framework (for example, the Smalltalk environment). This rate is not linear; rather it is exponential, relative to the complexity of the framework.

There is a maximum rate at which any person or organization can absorb new technology. Try to exceed that rate, and you will confuse your people; try to slow that rate down, and you your competition will run over you. Thus:

P 97

Recognize that applying the object-oriented paradigm requires a change in attitude. Allow sufficient time for your team members to mature in their roles. Every developer must have the time to reach some "aha!" experience.

However, as my last example above illustrates, not every one will get it. In fact, my rule of thumb is this:

> Given a random selection of professional developers, about 10-15% will just never get it. In other words, they will never be able to make the transition to object-oriented stuff.

R 54

This does not mean that 10-15% of the world-wide developer community is pond scum. In fact, using the language of software marketing, this is not a problem, it is actually a feature, because it means that not everyone inside your development organization has to be a total expert in everything object-oriented. At the very least, each team member must be able to recognize a class if it hits them in the face, and each should be able to use existing classes to build new things. Most developers need to be able to build new classes from existing ones. A smaller number of developers should be skilled in crafting new classes. A smaller number still should be adept at discovering patterns of classes, and able to carry out their realization. Only very small number of developers need to be the authors of new, strikingly creative patterns.

Not surprisingly, this division of knowledge exactly matches the division of labor found in the roles of application engineer, abstractionist, and architect. This division of roles facilitates organizational learning. Furthermore, the fact that in successful projects these roles overlap in time permits a team that's under intense schedule pressure to overlap the learning process. Architects can kick start the project while the abstractionists are being trained. Even before the abstractionists come online, the application engineers can go through their training, so that they will mature soon after the abstractionists come online.

To follow this line of thought a bit deeper, consider some common organizational scenarios:

- Moving an organization from traditional techniques to object-oriented technology
- Honing the skills of an organization already somewhat experienced with objects
- Institutionalizing object-oriented technology so that career development is possible (this applies to the most mature organizations).

In each of these cases, the key to success is that the organization must have the ability to learn. If that will to change is not present in the organization as a whole and in each individual developer, all is lost.

If you are starting from scratch, then the first specific key to success is to bring in outsiders, unless of course you have the luxury of totally unconstrained schedules.[*]

---

[*] Any organization that has no schedule contraints probably has too much time and money on its hands for its own good.

R 55

When staffing a new object-oriented project, 2/3 of the team can come from traditional projects, and 1/3 should be "outsiders" already exposed to objects. Increase the number of traditional developers, and you slow down the technology transfer process; increase the number of outsiders, and you run the risk of leaving the traditional developers behind.

By outsider, I do not mean to suggest that your organization should rush out and simply hire a bunch of consultants. In fact, doing only this is probably the worst thing you can do, because it sends the message that your own people are not good enough. Furthermore, hiring out your key developers from a consulting organization is like renting versus buying a house: when renting, you never accumulate any equity, and when using only consultants, the experience gained is totally lost to the corporate consciousness once that consultant rides away on his or her white horse, bags of your money in hand.

Where does a project find these people then? There are three sources, in order of my preference:

- From developers drawn from earlier object-oriented projects
- From developers who have carried out some pilot project
- From outside consultants who serve as surrogate members of your development staff, mainly responsible for mentoring and gently guiding, not doing all the work

This idea of a pilot project is not earth shattering, but it represents a second key to success:

P 98

Before you bet your company on object-oriented technology, completely carry out a pilot project that lets you validate your expectations and tune the technology and your organizational culture to one another.

The greatest advantage of a pilot project is that it lets your team fail without losing the company in the bet. In my experience, the best pilot project has these four characteristics:

- It is related to some real problem to be solved
- It is not on the critical path of any other project, and so it permits some degree of freedom for experimentation
- It is bounded in time
- It is sufficiently bounded in functionality, so that the team is not set up to fail, and so can complete their task

A third key to success in moving organizations into object-oriented technology is some degree of formal training. In my experience, this means two things. First, conduct short courses in object-oriented technology, taught by trainers who are experienced with building real things. Practically, this means that if you are having your people take a language course, do not just cover its syntax and semantics, rather have that language taught in the context of analysis and design. Second, conduct boot camps that immerse developers into the object-oriented paradigm, in the context of the problem they are working on. A boot camp, just like its military connotation suggests, is a 2 to 5 day concentrated experience whose purpose is to quickly bring developers to an aha! experience by forcing them to think, eat, and sleep objects.

> This organization was staffing up to carry out a large, mission-critical software project in Smalltalk and C++. For a number of reasons, a swell of developers came on to the project at one time, and their inexperience and numbers threatened to swamp the fragile infrastructure that had been so carefully nurtured. To mitigate this risk, the team instituted a week-long boot camp, conducted by outside consultants acting as mentors, to rapidly level set the team.

The best boot camps I have encountered included some combination of lectures, paper exercises, programming, and team-building sessions. Ideally, topics should include an introduction to abstracting, patterns, CRC card techniques, coding standards, an introduction to architecture, testing, integration, performance tuning, documentation, packaging, and delivery. In this way, a week-long boot camp becomes a microcosm of the larger project for which the team will be sent out into the world to solve.[*]

> To rapidly jell your team and level set its members' skills, conduct an intense boot camp that immerses everyone into the technology. This practice can have an impact along many dimensions, not the least of which is helping grow the team by providing a shared experience.

P 99

The fourth key to success emphasizes the importance of mentoring as a path to technology transfer. Implicit in the division of responsibilities among the core development team is the existence of a built-in infrastructure for mentoring: the architect mentors the abstractionists who in turn mentor the application engineers. The use of walkthroughs, as I describe in the next chapter, is an important mentoring tool, as are regularly scheduled architecture reviews. Finally, the very existence of a project's architecture document and style guide provide a vehicle for propagating common project policies, which is in itself is a kind of mentoring.

---

[*] Furthermore, a boot camp helps to identify those who get it from those who do not. In particular, watch the conduct of CRC card exercises. Your good abstractionists will tend to really engage with these kinds of exercises, but the poor ones will tend to sit back and show distinct apathy as the process of discovery unfolds.

The fifth and final key to success is growing the management team as well as the core development team. As the last four chapters should have made painfully clear, managing an object-oriented project means applying a number of practices and general rules that may be very foreign to a manager steeped in traditional techniques. Therefore,

P 100

> Do not forget to transition your management. Bring them to an understanding of the different products and process inherent in object-oriented technology by exposing them to other projects, letting them run a pilot project, giving them formal training, and mentoring them.

In other words, the techniques that work for transitioning the development team work for the management team as well.

As you hone the skills of an organization already reasonably adept in objects, there are a few more subtle things you can do to mature them further. These ideas apply equally to new projects, except that in these new projects, there may already be so much change that these more subtle things go unnoticed. Two specific practices come to mind:

P 101

> Rotate tiger team assignments to give developers a break from the grind of main-line development and so that developers have a chance to stretch their skills.

P 102

> Do not neglect the physical setting. Put related projects down the hall from one another. Arrange cubicles so that they all open to a common work area. Install a vending machine or a library or even a pinball game or video game so that developers have a chance to separate themselves from their computers and talk with one another.

As an organization continues to mature, it is important to develop a culture that rewards the growing skills of its developers and creates a sense of technical community. If you fail to do so, you will see all of your best talent, now wonderfully experienced in object-oriented technology at your expense, start their own companies or, perhaps worse, run off to your competition.

P 103

> Invest some time and resources into developing an infrastructure that rewards and cultivates your developer's talents.

It sounds like a terribly harsh stereotype, but I have encountered more than a few companies that make their initial mark in the industry, fueled by a pool of hard core coders comprised of young men and woman, many fresh out of college who therefore are largely unconstrained by families, possessions, or any really long-term career vision other than trying to achieve total world domination in their field. Stepping into an insulated culture where 100 hour work weeks are the norm, they do not realize that there are alternative ways of working smarter.* An organization like this, without an infrastructure and without a commitment to grow its people, will never achieve success, for chaos is never a sustainable lifestyle.

The good news is that the breakdown of roles I explain earlier helps this problem head on. Recognizing a division of labor among architects, abstractionists, and application engineers offers a career path to the more junior people on the team, and so gives them a place to grow inside the organization. Specifically, junior developers work under the guidance of more senior developers in a mentor/apprentice relationship, and as they gain experience in using well-designed classes, over time they learn to design their own quality classes. The corollary to this arrangement is that not every developer needs to be an expert abstractionist, but can grow in those skills over time.

TOOLS FOR THE WORKER

Another terribly harsh but true stereotype is that most organizations woefully undersupply their developers with good tools. Indeed, most software development organizations have tools that, figuratively speaking, are at the level of banging rocks together.

> Figures vary, but the tool cost (hardware and software) for the typical developer in the United States, neutral to object-orientation, averages somewhere around 25% of labor costs plus burden. For example, a development shop paying an average of $60,000 per year burdened costs should spend about $15,000 per developer per year.‡

R 56

Capital resources should never be squandered, and thus the issue at hand is:

> What development tools does an object-oriented project really need? Specifically, which tools are essential, and which are luxuries?

With early generation languages, it was enough for a development team to have a minimal tool set: an editor, a compiler, a linker, and a loader were often

---

* Although driving a wicked problem to closure sometimes demands an occasional 100-hour work week.
‡ Tool costs seem to be declining. In the era when mainframes walked the earth, tool costs around $50,000 were often cited as the norm. Today, tool costs are typically in the $5,000 to $40,000 range. The higher end of this range seems to apply mostly to organizations with a high degree of software development ceremony, and to organizations that are pushing the technological envelope.

all that were needed (and often all that existed). If the team was particularly lucky, they might even get a source-level debugger. Complex systems change the picture entirely: trying to build a large software system with a minimalist tool set is equivalent to building a multistory building with hand tools.

Object-oriented technology changes the picture as well. Traditional software development tools embody knowledge only about source code, but since object-oriented architectures highlight a sea of abstractions and corresponding mechanisms, it is desirable to use tools that can exploit these richer semantics. In addition, the macro process, with its emphasis upon the rapid development of releases, demands tools that offer rapid turnaround, especially for the edit/compile/execute/debug cycle.

Before I recommend a set of essential tools, let me first consider one tool-related decision that every project has to make early in its life, namely, which programming language to use. Language wars are a funny thing; they are often emotional, akin to a religious debate, and commonly devoid of much scientific content. Remember that languages are not an end in and of themselves, but they are a means to the creation of computational artifacts that serve some human purpose. Therefore, seek to use languages that let you create such artifacts in the most timely and economical fashion suitable to your organization's culture, and that help you produce architectures that can endure, even in the face of uncertainty and change (in the problem being solved).

If the truth be known, you will not really go wrong in choosing any of a number of industrial strength object-oriented programming languages, be it Smalltalk, C++, or even Ada. Other languages may not be as visible, but may also be worth considering, including CLOS, object-oriented COBOL, Eiffel, or Objective-C, to name a few. In fact, in most of the larger projects I have encountered, it is rarely a homogeneous language setting. Thus, it is not unusual to see a large project with Smalltalk on the client side, C++ on the back end, and even sprinklings of Visual Basic and proprietary application builder languages here and there.

My personal experience is that I find Smalltalk wonderful for prototyping and for building quality user-centric applications quickly. I find C++ best across most domains for every kinds of systems programming, such as for codifying business rules, handling distribution and persistence, for implementing complex mechanisms such as transactions, device drivers, or for operating systems. I am quite satisfied with Ada for large scale or demanding, human-critical applications.

Transitioning from COBOL, one organization began with the assumption that Smalltalk would meet all of its needs. Performance issues caused the developers to migrate all of their transaction processing to C++; this move was also motivated by the larger availability of frameworks in C++. As they began to consider the needs of their mobile users, they then introduced some applications in Visual Basic running on laptops, which tied into their Smalltalk/C++ system.

I cannot recommend any one language, but I can offer this advice:

> Avoid writing code in the first place, but if you have to choose a language, do so based upon its expressiveness, approachability, acceptance, and staying power in the market place, and the existence of a third-party industry that feeds that market. Most importantly, consider the cost of ownership of software written in that language versus another one.

P 104

Cost of ownership is a critical factor. Languages such as Visual Basic, and various proprietary application builders offer a very high degree of productivity for certain domains, and so for a large class of applications, may be sufficient. However, once your problem steps outside of the domains codified by these languages, then cost rises exponentially. Also, you must consider how difficult it is to make changes. Under many of these kinds of languages, development artifacts are adaptable to a point beyond which it is easier to trash the application and start all over again.[*] Having to throw systems away as complexity rises dramatically increases the cost of ownership of software.

Continuing, it is also important to choose languages and tools that scale well. A tool that works for a solitary developer writing a small stand-alone application will not necessarily scale to production releases of more complex applications. Indeed, for every tool, there will be a threshold beyond which the tool's capacity is exceeded, causing its benefits to be greatly outweighed by its liabilities and clumsiness.

In my experience, I have identified eight different kinds of tools that are applicable to object-oriented projects. Not in any particular order, the first is a graphics-based system supporting some object-oriented notation. Such a tool can be used during analysis to capture the semantics of scenarios, as well as during design to capture strategic and tactical design decisions, to maintain control over the project's architecture, and to coordinate the activities of a team of developers. Furthermore, such a tool can be used through the next phase of the life cycle, as the design evolves into a production implementation. Such tools are also useful during systems maintenance. Specifically, it is possible (and desirable) to reverse-engineer many of the interesting aspects of an object-oriented system, producing at least the class structure and module architecture of the system as built. This feature is quite important: under traditional analy-

---

[*] Why is this so? It all goes back to the importance of architecture: Most of this genre of languages have zero support for the kinds of architectural structures I have found essential for successfully building complex systems.

sis and design tools, developers may generate marvelous pictures, only to find that these pictures are out of date once the implementation proceeds, because programmers fiddle with the implementation without updating the design. Reverse engineering makes it less likely that the design will ever get out of step with the actual implementation. Reverse engineering plus forward code generation permits a round-trip engineering pattern of development, which is essential to an iterative and incremental process.

The next tool I have found important for object-oriented projects is a browser that knows about the architecture of a system. Class hierarchies can become so complex that it is difficult even to find all of the abstractions that are part of the design or are candidates for reuse. While examining a program fragment, a developer may want to see the definition of the class of some object. Upon finding this class, he or she might wish to visit some of its superclasses. While viewing a particular superclass, the developer might want to browse through all uses of that class before installing a change to its interface. This kind of browsing is extremely clumsy if one has to worry about files, which are an artifact of the physical, not the logical, design decisions. For this reason, browsers are an important tool for object-oriented analysis and design. For example, the standard Smalltalk environment allows one to browse all the classes of a system in the ways I have described. Similar facilities exist in environments for other object-oriented programming languages, although to different degrees of sophistication.

Another tool I have found to be important, if not absolutely essential, is an intelligent compiler. The kind of evolutionary development that goes on in object-oriented development cries out for an incremental compiler that can compile single declarations and statements. This kind of intelligent compilation is important because it addresses the issues of scale, and furthermore is in harmony with the kinds of changes one typically finds in successful object-oriented systems, as I describe in Chapter 3. As a project gets deeper into evolution, the last thing you want to have happen is for a developer to make a relatively innocent change, and then have to wait for an hour or more to rebuild the system. Rather than calculating compilation scripts based upon obsolesced files, incremental compilers can calculate a minimal recompilation based upon changes to individual declarations or statements.

The use of an incremental development environment can reduce turn around times by a factor of 10 to 100.

R 57　Next, I have found that nontrivial projects need debuggers that know about class and object semantics. When debugging a program, one often needs to examine the instance variables and class variables associated with an object. Traditional debuggers for non-object-oriented programming languages do not embody knowledge about classes and objects. Thus, trying to use a standard C debugger for C++ programs, while possible, does not permit the developer to find the really important information needed to debug an object-oriented program. The situation is especially critical for object-oriented programming languages that support multiple threads of control. At any given moment during the execution of such a program, there may be several active processes. These circumstances require a debugger that permits the developer to exert control over all the individual threads of control, usually on an object-by-object basis.

Also in the category of debugging tools, I include tools such as stress testers, which stress the capacity of the software, usually in terms of resource utilization, and memory-analysis tools, which identify violations of memory access, such as writing to deallocated memory, reading from uninitialized memory, or reading and writing beyond the boundaries of an array.

Next, especially for larger projects, one must have configuration management and version control (CMVC) tools. As I explain in Chapter 2, in larger object-oriented systems, the class category—and not the class—is the best unit of configuration management. Furthermore, iterative development is all about managing change. Thus, from the perspective of the project manager and the core team, CMVC tools are essential elements in supporting the rhythm of a project.

The presence of an iterative and incremental process also demands the use of automatic regression testing tools. As I explain in Chapter 3, it is useful to run regression tests that verify that the functionality and quality of the system continue to grow with each new release. Some off-the-shelf tools may be found here, especially for regression testing the GUI elements of the system. Most often, however, automatic regression testing is custom software that must be developed by the project's toolsmith.

Another tool I have found important in object-oriented development is a class librarian, which helps with the approachability of frameworks. For all of the languages I have mentioned, there exist a variety of commercial, off the shelf frameworks which codify various domains. As a project evolves, this library of frameworks will grow with domain-specific reusable software components being added over time. It does not take long for such a library to grow to enormous proportions, which makes it difficult for a developer to find a class or module that meets his or her needs, or for that matter, for a novice developer even to understand where to start. If the perceived cost (usually inflated) of finding a certain component is higher then the perceived cost (usually underestimated) of creating that component from scratch, then all hope of reuse is lost. For this reason, it is important to have at least some minimal tool that allows developers to locate abstractions to different criteria and add useful classes and modules to the library as they are developed.

Yet another category of tool I have found useful for certain object-oriented systems are application builders, specifically, GUI builders and database builders. This genre of tools represent a degree of programming without programming: both the domains of user interfaces and databases are sufficiently bounded that it is possible (and desirable) to use application builders rather than write mass quantities of raw code. For example, for systems that involve a large amount of user interaction, it is far better to use such a tool to interactively create dialogs and other windows than to create these artifacts from the bottom up in code. Code generated by such tools can then be connected to the rest of the object-oriented system and, where necessary, fine-tuned by hand. The same practice applies to database access.

Finally, do not forget simple tools that provide developer creature comforts. Groupware tools which facilitate creative collaboration, especially in geographically distributed development projects can often be valuable. Scripting tools can automate tedious operations, thereby leveraging scarce developer resources. Do not be lured away by the siren song of flashy tools, however, for my experience is that:

Simple tools often yield an 80% solution; solving the last 20% generally makes the tool much more clumsy and costly.

R 58   Do not underestimate the creativity of your developers to exploit even simple tools.

No matter what tools you choose, be certain that your developers have confidence in them and understand their limits before it is too late to make any changes, as the following example illustrates:

One project selected a fancy C++ software development environment without ever really throwing any code against it. After the second iteration, at which time the team had a couple of hundred thousand lines of code, the team simply had to abandon it, because the tool was flatly unable to process an application that big.

To mitigate this risk, my advice is:

Validate your tool set early (the software equivalent of kicking the tires before you buy). Try out the complete tool set that you intend to use for production development as early in the life cycle as possible.

P 105

In fact, this is one of the reasons for early prototyping: building executable artifacts early in the life cycle gives the team an opportunity to break in its new tools.

Chapter 6

Management and Planning

Chapter **6**

Management and Planning

Don't worry, I'll think of something.
INDIANA JONES

227

Every project has selfish interests. This may sound like a terrible quality to have, but it is indeed the pragmatic viewpoint that most real software projects posses. In the worst case, these selfish interests will cause a project to avoid investing in any technology, practice, or service that does not have some direct and immediate impact upon cost, schedule, or quality. I speak of this as the worst case because, as in human relationships, blind selfishness is a terrible policy for any project to pursue. Unsuccessful projects sometimes end up isolating themselves from their users and often from their peer projects in the organization. That is a bad thing because such blind selfishness neither encourages ongoing communication (which is essential to any real project since most requirements are rarely if ever complete, correct, unambiguous, and never changing), nor does it allow room for any kind of sharing (specifically, for the sharing of experiences, ideas, technology, patterns, and even code).

Do not confuse blind selfishness (a bad thing) with a ruthless focus (a good thing), one of the properties of successful projects that I described in Chapter 1. Whereas the former takes the attitude that anything outside of the scope of the project is irrelevant, the latter takes the view that the project itself impacts and is impacted by the outside world. Furthermore, this synergy is to be encouraged because it helps the team build the right thing at the right time for the right purpose. That is the nature of focus, and one of the responsibilities of project management is to ensure that the healthy focus of a project does not degenerate into blind selfishness.

Even in the face of dangerously high risk, the next greatest enemy of success is often the team's own ability to execute. The three primary reasons for project failure—the failure to properly manage risks, building the wrong thing, and being blindsided by technology—all represent a failure to execute. Furthermore, for all projects of reasonable complexity, such failure can often be traced to ineffective management and planning.

Chapters 3 and 4 explain the basic macro and micro process of software development, but simply having a defined process is not enough. Just as successful developers engage in iterative software development, so too must their managers engage in incremental planning, an activity that is characterized by continuous risk management and continuous adaptation.

Thus, it is a sign of project immaturity for management to blindly follow any process without adaptation. It is equally a sign of project immaturity to aggressively reject any hint of process, instead relying upon heroic feats of programming willingly provided by over-achieving developers. In the successful project, management is neither overcontrolling (a practice that tends to stifle all creativity and that tends to panic in the face of unexpected risk) nor is it distant (a practice that often causes the development team to become distracted and so lose their way.

Ultimately, the fundamental quest of every project manager is predictability: predictability of schedule, predictability of resources, and predictability of quality. To that end:

What is the role of software project management?
- To keep the development team focused on the project's essential minimal characteristics
- To shield the team from anything that might distract them and otherwise waste their unique skills
- To make the necessary business and engineering decisions needed to resolve conflicts

These three roles are accompanied by several different responsibilities:

- Risk management
- Planning and scheduling
- Costing and staffing
- Monitoring, measuring, and testing
- Documenting

These responsibilities are the topic of this chapter.

EVERYTHING I NEED TO KNOW I'LL LEARN IN MY NEXT PROJECT

I have seen my share of lousy managers, and I have worked with many good managers, too. I have even been graced with the opportunity to work under two or three really great managers over my career. In retrospect, what I find fascinating is that the lousy ones and the great ones can easily be distinguished by their perspective on the selfishness factor. Specifically, the bad managers were all extremely defensive and tended to focus on their personal self-interests, whereas the good managers were all forward-looking leaders who actively shaped their project's focus, continuously measured their project's health, and periodically instituted mid-course corrections to keep their project on focus.

Good software management is not rocket science, but too many projects seem to forget its common sense practices. A manager with an in-your-face style are like the bully who terrorizes a schoolyard to get his or her own way and generally makes life unpleasant for all who come near. Managers who try to direct their projects unarmed with any knowledge are like Little League baseball players who compete in the big leagues: they are competing far beyond their abilities, and they wind up getting many people hurt along the way. Managers who prefer playing political games to building quality software

are like the bad kids in school who cheat on their exams, and if left undetected, get better at cheating every year.

In short, good project management is simply a call for adult supervision in a project, which is best described by the following practice:

P 106

> Make it the development team's responsibility to aggressively seek out risk and to question all assumptions. Similarly, make it management's responsibility to judge these issues without passion and prejudice, weighed against the project's essential minimal characteristics.

Now, if you are reading this book and are lucky enough to be a part of an organization that is already successful and simply trying to get even better, then congratulations, for injecting other good object-oriented practices into your organization will be relatively painless. On the other hand, if you are not so lucky, you can still be of good cheer, for it is never too late to turn your organization around.*

Because its practices are sometimes subtle and sometimes radically different, introducing object-oriented technology into an organization is as much a management issue as it is a technical one. Throwing this technology at an ongoing project in crisis is a sure path to failure simply because it adds risk to an already risk-filled situation. It is an equally bad idea to introduce this technology in a frictionless environment, such as in the context of a toy project that poses no real challenges that are germane to the company's business.

> A modestly sophisticated company found itself behind the software power curve, never having really invested back into its software development organization. As a result, its developers were growing stale, with many of the good ones having already left. Management decided that object-oriented technology was exactly the right way to jump start the organization. Management dictated the use of an object-oriented language for an upcoming mission-critical project that had to be delivered in a couple of months. Not surprisingly, the team did not even come close to meeting the schedule.

There is a simple lesson in this that successful projects tend to follow:

P 107

> Introduce object-oriented practices to your organization in the form of a pilot project that affords the team the opportunity to fail.

---

* Unless, of course, your company is already in bankruptcy proceedings. If your organization is in dire straits yet not quite over this line, then the last section of this chapter (dealing with projects in crisis) should be of particular interest.

The ideal pilot project is one that has some importance to the business, yet is not mission-critical; has some modest degree of complexity, yet not so much as to exceed the team's ability, and is in a domain that the organization already understands.* Starting in this manner gives the team the degrees of freedom necessary to explore the limits of the technology and to learn how to adapt it to the organization' particular culture. This approach also gives management a forum which to calibrate itself and its team and to learn its lessons in a controlled environment.

MANAGING RISK

Every real project takes on its own unique collection of risks; that is one reason that managing an object-oriented project is never a dull activity. However, unsuccessful projects are typically outright scared of facing up to these risks. That is a bad thing because pretending that there are no risks does not make it so. Furthermore, risks have a way of multiplying when left alone, which is why I note in Chapter 1 that successful projects tend to actively acknowledge and attack its risks.

> What are the most serious risks factors that face any real project?‡
> - Inaccurate metrics
> - Inadequate measurement
> - Excessive schedule pressure
> - Management malpractice
> - Inaccurate cost estimating
> - Silver bullet syndrome
> - Creeping user requirements
> - Low quality
> - Low productivity
> - Canceled projects

The intensity of each of these risk factors increases as the complexity of a project grows. This creates a bit of a dilemma because every new hardware or software advancement pushes a team to build systems of greater complexity, and every new complex system demonstrates to users the possibilities of automation that cause them to pull for yet more complex systems. This creates an

---

* Barbara Moo, *private communication*.
‡ Jones, pp. 46–61.

insatiable demand for complex software which by its very nature means that these risk factors will continue to grow.

Thus, as far as industrial-strength software development is concerned, one can never fully eliminate risks; at best, one can manage them. This is why in earlier chapters I make the case for an architecture-driven approach; it forces risk factors to the surface early in the development process where, once identified, management can take steps to mitigate them. This is best summarized in a practice I find among virtually all the successful object-oriented projects I encounter:

Maintain a running list of your project's top ten risks, and use this list to drive each release.

P 108

Another aspect of risk management is acknowledging the natural rate at which elements in the context of your project change. This too is an element of risk because things that change rapidly represent sources of risk. From the perspective of information management systems, for example, the world is very stratified:

How fast do things change?
- User applications and interfaces   very rapidly
- Business rules   rapidly
- Technical world   rapidly
- General industry   slowly
- General business   very slowly

There are two lessons to be drawn from these observations. First every organization has a natural inertia that governs its ability to absorb these changes. Second, this stratification makes it desirable to organize systems with firewalls between each layer, in order to isolate areas the change at different rates.

This again points to the importance of conducting software development as the successive refinement of an architecture. Well-structured object-oriented architectures provide a stable artifact with which an organization can respond to changes without fear of rending the entire fabric of the system.

In an object-oriented project, early releases were met with an unexpected level of acceptance that led to a flood of requests for enhancements most of which the team had already thought about, but had deferred (time to market was a more important factor in this business case). The volume of these requests threatened to overwhelm and distract the team. Two practices were instituted to mitigate this risk. First, these requests were classified according to their importance and difficulty and then were attached to future releases in an ordering that minimized rework and emphasized a natural growth of the underlying architecture. Second, the underlying architecture was split in a way that exposed interfaces that were necessary to accommodate a certain very large class of requests (namely, dealing with queries to the domain model). This split permitted a tiger team to accommodate many of these "one-off" requests without requiring the involvement of the whole team.

There is an important phrase buried in this example that is worth repeating as a practice:

> Remember that the response to every risk is ultimately a business decision, not necessarily a technical one. Figuratively speaking, this means that sometimes you must shoot the engineer.

P 109

Relax any given constraint (such as cost, schedule, quality, or functionality) and other alternatives open up; tighten any given constraint, and certain alternatives become intractable.

PLANNING AND SCHEDULING

Planning and scheduling address two key questions: how do I best deploy my development team, and how do I organize its work and the artifacts it creates across the life cycle? In the successful object-oriented project, planning and scheduling are the active responsibilities of the management team:

> In the successful project, remember that planning is a continuous activity that is driven by risk factors and that focuses on the control of key artifacts.

P 110

By "continuous," I mean that planning is never a static activity. Rather, in the successful object-oriented project, management establishes concrete deliverables and milestones, measures them, and then adjusts future activities and schedules accordingly. These deliverables and milestones are in fact the key artifacts that management uses to exert its control. As I describe in Chapter 2, in the object-oriented project there are a small number of such artifacts, the most important of which is the system's evolving architecture. The creation, review, and completion of these artifacts all represent important milestones that management uses as measures of the project's health, as gates to regulate future work, and as forcing functions to drive the project in the right direction. Ultimately, all of this planning is affected by risk, meaning that the management team continuously directs the work of rest of the development team so as to directly attack the project's highest risks.

Management must be very careful not to catch the process disease, the symptoms of which are a blind and dogmatic acceptance of any development process. In fact, this is even true relative to the macro and micro processes I describe in Chapters 3 and 4. It is a sign of organizational immaturity to not tailor its development process to the organization's culture and the needs of the specific project.

No matter what tailoring, however, the essential feature of successful object-oriented projects is the successive refinement of a system's architecture. As Figure 6-1 illustrates, this feature tends to shape all of a project's planning and scheduling.

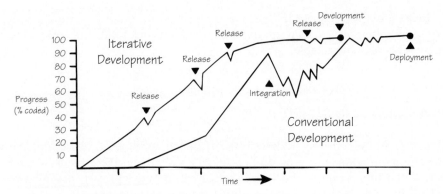

Figure 6-1   Progress Across the Life Cycle[*]

Note the contrast. In conventional development, measurable progress tends to be delayed, and then later there is one major big bang integration event, immediately after which there is a long period of instability as the development team drags the project to completion. In the iterative style practiced by object-oriented projects, progress is more steady, with tangible progress starting sooner and only minor instabilities occurring across the life cycle, each representing small mid-course corrections to the project. The main implication of

---

[*] Walker Royce, *private communication*.

this iterative style is that risk is spread more evenly across the development life cycle, with the highest risk factors addressed earlier when there is actually time to do something about them.

Another important implication of this style of planning is that the development team is incentivized to throw away bad designs and poor code a little bit at a time, rather than all at once late in the life cycle, as one typically finds in conventional development planning. In the early releases of object-oriented projects, more design is cast away than code, simply because the object-oriented development process tends to concentrate upon architectural design. This is a good thing, because unwinding code that is already written is not only expensive, one must also overcome individual inertia, arising from the fact that developers have a strong attachment to their code creations, and they really hate to throw away software they have put so much of their hearts into.

Speaking of the individual developer, perhaps the most important thing the management team can do is summarized in the following practice:

> Shield your developers from any and all distractions that keep them from their primary mission, namely, writing quality software.

P 111

This practice has absolutely nothing to do with object-oriented systems in particular, but it has everything to do with keeping your development team focused. In reality, this translates into common-sense planning:

How do you keep your development team focused?
- Actively keep them out of useless meetings
- Minimize or eliminate any activity that does not contribute to meeting the project's goals or to professional development
- Encourage each team member to lead a balanced life.

This latter point opens a whole set of issues that go far beyond the scope of this book, but it reflects my observations of successful projects: the most creative teams are those that know how to work hard, but who also know when to play hard.

This suggests a general rule:

> A strong warning sign that you have misplanned or misscheduled your project is the observation that most of your team is working a steady 60 to 80 hour work week. For most projects, an occasional hard week is to be expected. For some critical projects, several such weeks can be tolerated. For all projects, overtime as a common practice is not only unsustainable, it is an indication of severe management malpractice.

R 59

Even in the presence of object-oriented technology, there is a natural limit to productivity, and no amount of heroic programming will be sufficient to meet unrealistic schedules.

COSTING AND STAFFING

In this section, I would like to give you a rule of thumb that says that if your requirements contain a certain number of function points, a project employing object-oriented technology will require x number of developers y weeks to write the z number of classes that make up this system.

However, I cannot.

The truth is that even in non-object-oriented systems, such accurate economic models are found only among a few very sophisticated organizations that have collected lots of development data over many years in certain narrow problem domains. Unfortunately, there simply is not yet that large a body of experience in object-oriented technology to generalize a similar model. Furthermore, even if there were such a body of data, your mileage will vary widely, depending upon the maturity of your development team.

That fact is actually the key to costing and staffing an object-oriented project:

Calibrate the productivity of your team in a pilot project. Continuously recalibrate it at every release during evolution.

P 112

By "calibrate," I mean to gain a model of performance for every team member and for the team as a whole. Programmers are notoriously optimistic and most will tend to underestimate the amount of work needed to implement some feature. Calibrating gives the management team a multiplier factor so that if a certain developer (or the team as a whole) says it will take n weeks to do something, you can translate that to m (the multiplier factor) times n. If m is greater than one, then you have a typical optimistic developer. If m is less than one, then you have either got a hyperproductive developer or one who consistently pads his or her schedules. If m is always exactly one, you should stand in awe.

From my experience (not from any empirical data), I can offer these general rules:

For your team's first object-oriented project, take the schedule you would have planned with traditional development, and inflate it by 10-30%.

R 60

In the steady state, plan for your object-oriented project to require 10-50% fewer resources than traditional practices. Expect your development schedules to stay the same (but with increased functionality and quality) or be slightly compressed (but at the same level of functionality as tradition would provide).

R 61

Both of these rules assume that your object-oriented project is in a domain your team already understands.

MONITORING, MEASURING, AND TESTING

Having a policy of continuous planning is meaningful if the management team keeps its eyes on certain measures. These measures are the instrument panel of the project, and planning and scheduling are the knobs that management turns to direct the project.

In Chapters 3 and 4 I describe a number of measures of goodness associated with each phase of the life cycle. Individually, these represent the parts of a project's instrument panel. Collectively, they can be collapsed into four different kinds of measures:

- Complexity   Typically measured in terms of function points
- Size   Generally measured in terms of numbers of classes and/or lines of code as well as the run time footprint and performance
- Stability   Measured in terms of the rate of change in the project's complexity or size
- Quality   Best measured in terms of absolute numbers of errors, defect discovery rate, and defect density

The complexity of a project will tend to remain stable in most projects unless substantial new requirements are added late in the life cycle. The size of a project will tend to grow gradually in an object-oriented project, as Figure 6-1 illustrates, with some noise introduced at each release. As I mention in Chapter 3, in the healthiest projects, the numbers of classes in a project will tend to continue to grow through the life cycle, even through the number of lines of code may actually drop toward the end. Also as I describe in Chapter 3, stability is perhaps management's most important measure as to the health of a project, since rapidly changing parts of the architecture suggest systemic or more local problems, depending upon the extent of the changes.

Many of these measures are amenable to automation. Size is easily calculated by simple tools, stability can be measured by tying in to your project's configuration management tools, and quality metrics can be collected through regression tests. Indeed, the most successful projects I have encountered run automatic regression tests with every release, meaning that this data gathering happens at least every week and in some cases every night.

Institute a policy of automated regression testing, tied to each release.

P 113

I say more about testing later in this section.

A few formal reviews and many more informal ones are also an essential tool of the successful project. Such reviews are a common in non-object-oriented systems, but here, reviews tend to focus upon architectural artifacts. In practice, this means conducting formal architectural reviews on a regular basis, and reviews of the microarchitecture much more often.

In a project of modest size, a typical architecture review will take one or two days scheduled every quarter. Other reviews will take an hour or so, and these are scheduled as needed.

R 62

Peer reviews should never be treated as opportunities for seeking out and punishing developers who are not producing good code. Rather, the best reviews in object-oriented systems tend to focus on interfaces and mechanisms and serve as a vehicle for mentoring. The conduct of a typical review will be to first walk through scenarios germane to the area under review, followed by a study of the key classes, their protocols, and their patterns of collaboration, and ending with going deep in the implementation of some of these scenarios. This style is common of both architecture reviews as well as other reviews.

Keep in mind that for most projects, it is simply impossible to review every line of code. The nature of object-oriented systems helps, however, according to this practice:

Focus formal reviews upon the most complex classes as well as these mechanisms (involving collaborations of classes) that are of greatest strategic importance to the architecture.

P 114

Reviews are good, but do keep in mind this general rule as well:

The usefulness of a formal review is inversely proportional to the number of people attending beyond five.*

R 63

Testing is in a way a very formal kind of review that measures the quality of a project's artifacts and the degree of compliance with the projects' require-

---

* Airlie Software Council, *private communication*.

ments. One of the key benefits of an iterative development life cycle is the fact that testing can be a continuous activity, and testing can start very early in the process—in fact as soon as the system's architecture begins to stabilize.

Otherwise, there is no real magic associated with the testing of object-oriented systems; much of this is just good development practice, with some small twists to accommodate object-oriented architecture. Specifically, testing is conducted at three levels. At the lowest level is unit testing, which means testing individual classes and mechanisms. This is typically the responsibility of the individual developer. Next up is subsystem testing, which means testing large clusters of classes that work together. This is typically the responsibility of the abstractionist who owns that cluster. System testing is the highest level, and this involves testing the entire system against scenarios that specify the system's desired behavior. This is typically the responsibility of a semi-independent testing team. Ultimately, however, these different levels of testing mean that quality is every developer's job.

Informal bug hunts are a useful practice, during which time anyone in the organization can exercise a release in random, unplanned ways, incentivized by awarding small prizes to individuals who find the most new bugs or the most obscure bugs. Naturally, for most systems, it is wise to plan a more formal alpha and beta testing period.

DOCUMENTING

In the healthy project, documentation serves two purposes. First, certain kinds of documentation provide a reasonably permanent statement of a system's structure and behavior. From the perspective of end users, this includes reference manuals and user guides that explain how to use the software; from the perspective of maintainers and future developers who reuse this software, this includes documentation of the system's architecture. Second, other kinds of documentation are transitory, living things that are simply part of the infrastructure involved in running a real project. From the perspective of end users, this includes scenarios and other documentation that are used to evolve an understanding of the system's requirements; from the perspective of the project's developers, this includes internal design documentation, meeting reports, bug reports, and so on, all used to communicate the myriad of strategic and tactical decisions that must be made.

In a very real sense, the first kind of documentation serves as the project's memory which transcends the team that developed the original system, whereas the second kind of documentation is part of the temporary scaffolding erected by the team as it creates the system, some of which gets transformed into the former, more permanent legacy. In either case, the trend among successful projects is to minimize the need for hard copy artifacts and instead develop systems that are both intuitive and self-documenting.

In terms of end user documentation, this means that the needs of many kinds of systems can be satisfied solely by a reference manual and user guide, perhaps supplemented by online help. Writing this genre of documentation is an art unto itself and is fertile ground for all sorts of creative options, such as guided tours and anthrophromorphized on line help agents. However, this kind of documentation has little to do with the art of software development, and so I ignore this topic, except to offer the following practice that I find common among many successful object-oriented projects:

P 115

Especially for user-centric systems, write your system's reference manual and user guide early in the development process. This not only forces end users to become involved in the development process, it also forces developers to build friendly systems, since user-visible behavior that is difficult to explain is probably the wrong behavior to provide.

I am also going to ignore a considerable amount of the documentation associated with the infrastructure of a project for three reasons: most of this kind of documentation has little to do with anything object-oriented, most of it is a factor of a project's culture, and most of it probably should not be written in the first place. This is indeed the practice I find in most successful projects, but since it may sound inflammatory, let me explain my position in reverse order.

Software is a domain whose products are essentially all intellectual, and therefore any ancillary documentation is generally obsolete the moment it is committed to paper. Furthermore, most such documentation is indeed ancillary and has nothing to do with creating the primary product of a software project, namely, the software itself. Hence, there are really only three noble and honorable reasons for writing any kind of documentation:

Useful documentation is one that:
- Furthers an understanding of the system's desired and actual behavior and structure
- Serves to communicate the system's architectural vision
- Provides an description of details that cannot be directly inferred from the software itself or from executable artifacts

Ask yourself if your organization's documentation meets this criteria. If it does not, then there is a good chance that it has more to do with the politics of your business than the business of writing good software.

Now, as I have already explained, it is true that there are different organizational cultures, and each has its own comfort level of documentation. High-ceremony projects have very formal rituals for documentation, requiring programmer's folders, minutes of every meeting or trip, detailed design documentation that must be written and reviewed before a single line of code can be cut, and even written engineering change orders that must be reviewed before any code can be changed. In my experience, I can justify this culture only for systems upon which human lives depend. At the other end of the spectrum are low-ceremony projects, characterized by an utter disdain for any documentation beyond the delivered executable system. In my experience, I can justify this culture only in systems for which the cost of ownership is negligible or zero.*

When it comes to documentation, most of the successful projects I have worked with are medium- to low-ceremony, meaning that the following rule applies:

> Most successful projects spend about 5-10% of their development resources on both internal and external documentation.

R 64

In practice, this means that most good projects generate and manage only a few documents. Of these, there are three that, for object-oriented systems, have a particular role and structure:

- Requirements document
- Architecture document
- Design documents

What are my thoughts about requirements documentation in general? It is a good thing. Without some statement of requirements, it is utterly impossible to schedule a project or to properly allocate development resources because you never know if you are building the right thing. Indeed, the only case for which a project can justify not having any kind of requirements document is when the very purpose of the project is exploratory; it involves writing innovative software for the sole purpose of experimenting with what requirements are desirable and what are possible. That in fact is the purpose of conceptualization as I explain it in Chapter 3.

In all other cases (namely, in most cases), a requirements document is an essential artifact. However, it need not be a ponderous, formal tome. In fact, in successful projects, is it quite the opposite:

> Treat a requirements document not as a statement of objective, unchangeable fact, but rather as a living contract between the users and

P 116

---

* Systems with a near-zero cost of ownership are ones that have a very short life (*i.e.,* days or weeks) and so are in effect largely disposable. With such systems, the cost of writing any documentation would be greater than the cost of writing the software itself.

> the developers of a system. As a contract, a requirements document infers obligations of both parties and are open for negotiation.

A requirements document infers obligations. Specifically, end users (or the analysts who represent them) are responsible for providing both the vocabulary of the problem space and statements of the system's desired behavior. In most cases, this means describing scenarios that illustrate or bound the system's externally visible behavior. Similarly, developers are responsible for asking hard questions about the dark corners of these scenarios, so that both parties come to a common agreement of this vocabulary and behavior. Furthermore, developers are responsible for pointing out requirements that are particularly expensive to carry out, or those that, if changed slightly, would vastly reduce the cost or the risk of developing the system.

A requirements document is open for negotiation. That is what I mean by it being a living artifact. In successful projects, a requirements document is established and baselined during analysis through a dialog between end users and developers. During design and evolution, it is then used to drive the successive refinement of the system's architecture. This document is also used as the basis of system testing, which is quite reasonable since it is indeed a testable contract.

A good requirements document is inherently object-oriented. Put another way, the language of object-orientation, in which the world is seen through the eyes of classes, objects, and scenarios, is particularly well-suited to writing a good requirements document. In many successful projects, I have seen requirements documents follow this basic structure:

- Introduction   Sets the context for the system
- System functions   Describes the essential large-scaled behaviors required of the system
- Scenarios   Details the meaning of each system function in the form of primary and secondary scenarios
- Non-functional requirements Provides statements of time and space, performance, and interoperability

Where possible, it is best to supplement a written requirements document with executable artifacts that serve as models of the system's desired behavior.

An architecture document is also a living artifact that, as I describe in Chapter 2, serves to document the key class structures and mechanisms important to a project. An architecture document is established and baselined during design, at which time it is used to codify and propagate the vision of the system's architecture. During evolution, it is used to control and track the successive refinement of the system's architecture. After deployment, it serves as a statement of the system's as-built architecture.

Provide a simple architecture document that describes the essential structural patterns that permeate the system. Evolve this document so that it tracks the evolving architecture, and use this document as a means of architectural control.

P 117

In many successful object-oriented projects, I have seen architecture documents follow this basic structure:

- Introduction   Explains the basic architectural style
- Key classes   Describes the main groups of classes that form the domain model and the layers of underlying technology
- Mechanisms   Describes the main collaborations that pervade the system's architecture
- Scenarios   Provides scenarios that serve to explain the architecture as a whole

This document should always track the system's executable architecture, and vice versa.

Whereas an architecture document records a system's essential and evolving structure over the entire development life cycle, many successful projects use smaller design documents to record a system's microarchitecture and to serve as the contract that launches each iteration of a system's evolution. As such, the best design documents are simply smaller versions of an architecture document. In fact, when an iteration is finished, the essence of the more important design documents will get folded into the larger architecture document. In general, a design document is established and baselined during evolution, at which time it is used to codify the requirements for each feature to be delivered in the next release and to document the microarchitecture that satisfies these requirements. The creation, review, and implementation of each such document is thus an important point of control in the evolving system.

A large object-oriented project was struggling because it had failed to find its rhythm. Part of its problem was that the team was so overwhelmed with requests for new features, it was difficult to decide what to do next. Randomly responding to requests from the most vocal end users would have been the easy thing to do, but it would have also undermined the integrity of the system's architecture (which was just beginning to stabilize) and which, in the long run this would have made it difficult to react to future requirements. To bring some control to the project, the project manager instituted a policy that required developers to prepare short (less than 10 pages) design documents that explained how each new set of features was to be designed and implemented. There were a handful of each such document per release, and their formal review helped the team to understand the impact of each feature upon the evolving architecture. This policy also helped management to better schedule new features.

Realize that because of a variety of schedule pressures, a lot of important details never get written down in real projects. Therefore, when planning the documentation for its projects, management must chose its battles carefully.

P 118

> Make documentation an essential, albeit a secondary, artifact. Concentrate upon those documents whose creation and evolution helps drive the project to closure and serves either as a means of project control or as a measure of the project's health.

PROJECTS IN CRISIS

I was tempted to name this book *Projects in Crisis*, because it seems that every interesting project of reasonable complexity is a project in crisis, no matter what its technology base. What seems to distinguish the successful project, however, is the fact that no real or imagined crisis ever disrupts its rhythm. Indeed, one of management's tasks must be to shield its developers from the din of daily minor crises, each of which may be quashed easily yet collectively might overwhelm and frighten the team.

Of course, the basic lesson is never to reach the point of a major project crisis. In fact, there are three simple predictors of an impending crisis that serve as an early warning to management:

- Complete radio silence from the development team, which often indicates that it is either stuck, or it is frantically throwing bodies at a situation that is unraveling.
- Instability in the architecture, denoted by parts of the system that are changing wildly.
- The presence of a day-to-day slip in the schedule

If you see any of these signs, or if you are in the midst of an outright total project meltdown, it is time to invoke the following practice:

P 119

> If you find your project in crisis, above all, do not panic. Immediately conduct a software triage that identifies the project's showstoppers and the top two or three risks to the life of the project. Appoint small tiger teams to drive these risks to the ground, and in parallel, get the rest of the team focused on recovering its rhythm.

Although it is really painful to get to this point, it does happen, and so when a project is in crisis for whatever reason, management must take bold steps to recover. In most cases, that means regaining control of the system's architecture. In that context, there is a related practice that must not be forgotten:

> If your development schedule is slipping yet your deployment schedule is inflexible, do not try to make up time by forcing your developers to work even harder; it will exacerbate the problem. Rather, acknowledge reality, regain control of the architecture, and either relax the schedule constraint or relax the system's required functionality. To do neither is pure folly.

P 120

Thus, for the project in crisis, there are two inevitable paths: the project really ends up failing, or the project regains its rhythm. In either case, it is advisable to conduct a project postmortem to determine what went wrong and what to do to prevent that species of crisis from ever rising again.

> Here is a classic case of a project in crisis: schedules were already off by several months, project quality was terrible, programmers were working long hours, and managers were wringing their hands in long meetings. Eventually, management broke up the development team, because it was clear that an unhealthy environment had been allowed to develop. Before starting a new project, the management team conducted a one day, off-site postmortem, which allowed the remaining programmers to vent their wrath (which was psychologically beneficial) and allowed the management team to figure out what went wrong. In this case, they determined that they were blindsided by marginal technology from a third-party vendor, and management never acknowledged the problem until it was too late. In the end, core members of this team went on to staff their company's next object-oriented project, using explicit practices gathered from this postmortem.

Chapter 7

Special Topics

Chapter 7

Special Topics

We don't like what we don't understand; in fact it scares us.
GASTON

The mark of a good project is that its development team follows a number of well-defined practices, collected over years of experience and tuned to the culture of the particular organization. That is what the last six chapters have been all about. The mark of a wildly successful project is that its development team knows when to bend or break these rules. That is what this chapter is all about.

P 121

Remember that sometimes you have to break the rules; some risks to the success of your project may be so daunting, you may have to make up new rules along the way. Realize, of course, that in so doing, you will always be trading off one set of risks for another.

This last point is key: changing the rules in order to mitigate one risk will introduce other challenges.

The information systems development organization of a bank was installing a global system for funds management. Theirs was a classical global architecture, for which issues of object distribution and migration dominated. They wanted to build upon emerging standards for distributed object-oriented systems but found that none of the commercial products were quite ready to be used. Thus, the team made the hard decision to roll its own middleware. On the one hand, this meant that it would have to do more development from scratch than it really wanted to; on the other hand, the team could make enough simplifying assumptions that its work was reasonably bounded. In the end, the team ended up with a simpler solution than it would have, had it relied upon more general frameworks.

As I explain in the Preface, I can point to a myriad of successful and some admittedly unsuccessful projects that have used object-oriented technology, and it is from these projects that the recommended practices and rules in this book have been drawn. Another useful observation that can be made from these projects is that most of these practices and rules are fairly universal, but that there are also certain identifiable genres of projects that lend themselves to their own variations of these practices and rules. In particular, if one considers the center of gravity of an application—that is, the focus of the application as observed from the outside—it appears that most applications can be placed in one of three categories:

- User-centric   The focus of the system is upon direct visualization and manipulation of the objects that define a certain domain.

- Data-centric   The focus of the system is upon preserving the integrity of the persistent objects in the system.

- Computation-centric   The focus of the system is upon the transformation of objects that are interesting to the system.

Of course, no one system is ever wholly user-, data-, or computation-centric. Rather, every interesting application tends to have some elements of all three. What is at issue here is which of these three elements is dominant. Thus, a personal productivity tool running standalone on a personal computer is largely user-centric, although there will certainly be elements of persistent data and manipulation of that data. A system that manages customer records for an insurance company is certainly most focused upon its data; a graphical user interface (GUI) is an important, although clearly a secondary, issue. Finally, an engineering application that analyzes the acoustics of a room likely has a GUI and a mechanism for persistence, but its real focus is upon the mathematics of the model.

As I further classify different kinds of object-oriented projects, two other common issues appear, all of which are orthogonal to, although not completely divorced from, my earlier classification:

- Distributed systems   A system whose GUI, data, or computational elements are physically distributed

- Legacy systems   An older, potentially moldy, system that must be preserved for any number of economic or social reasons, yet must also coexist with newly-developed elements.

In general, the more complex a system, the more likely it is to be distributed.* Also, the more important a system is to the business, the more likely it is to have to coexist with legacy systems that it extends or will eventually replace.

Combining these first three genres of software with the last two yields two general classifications of software, for which there are some uniquely identifiable practices and rules:

- Information management system   A system centered around a (usually distributed) domain model, upon which user applications are built, and which itself lives on top of a database layer, and a communications layer.

- Real time systems   A system whose behaviors are tightly constrained by time and/or space.

Finally, across both of these general classifications, it is common to find one other kind of identifiable software system:

---

* Furthermore, the most distributed a system, the more likely it is to be complex.

- Framework   A microarchitecture that provides an incomplete template for applications against a specific domain.

An examination of the recommended practices and rules for any one of these eight kinds of systems would itself warrant an entire book. Therefore, in the remaining sections, I do not pretend to cover them in complete depth, but I examine some of the more important practices that seem to distinguish successful object-oriented projects in each of these domain.

WHAT THEY DON'T TEACH YOU IN PROGRAMMING CLASS

In just the past two or three years, the rules of software development have changed radically. Whether or not your particular organization might be playing by these new rules is entirely a different matter.

> What are some of the new rules of software development successful organizations must live by?
> - A drive toward more end-user programmability
> - A movement away from monolithic applications and toward systems grown from the integration of many smaller components
> - Increased expectations of radically greater functionality, delivered under radically shorter schedules

These are the forces that continue to make software development really very hard.

If one contrasts a few of the major genres of software, the implication of these forces becomes very clear. Figure 7-1 illustrates this point. Here I show that the closer a system is to being user-centric, the more applicable are non-programming tools such as GUI builders. Similarly, the closer a system is to being data-centric, the more applicable are any of a number of database builders.

This suggests an important practice that I find followed by every successful object-oriented project:

P 122

Do not write code unless you absolutely, positively must. Wherever possible, employ application builders or frameworks that focus on a particular domain, but be sure to center them around some object-oriented architecture that gives them a context and that glues them together.

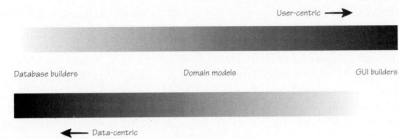

Figure 7-1 Forces in Software Development

Application builders and frameworks can be found for every subdomain wherein there is very well-defined set of big architectural patterns. Thus, database builders are possible not only because the underlying theory of relational databases is well-understood, but also because the behaviors common to database management (transactions, navigation, querying, reporting, and security, to name a few) are sufficiently well-defined that it is possible to write programs that carry out these common things. Similarly, GUI builders and user interface frameworks are both possible and desirable, because the fundamental elements of graphical user interaction (for example, buttons, windows, controls, and properties) are now fairly well-understood, and besides, doing GUI programming by hand is very tedious.[*]

The key to all this programming-without-programming is a codification of the abstractions and mechanisms that constitute a particular mature domain. Therefore, what I cannot advise you on here are systems in domains that are not mature. In such cases, creativity must be allowed to run rampant, and new rules must be made up as you go along.

> I worked with a large telecommunications company whose TV commercials at the time were touting all the wonderful things consumers would be able to do in the future, like reviewing a virtual blueprint while lounging on the beach.[‡] Their marketing organization was continuously dreaming up new ideas. Their development organization was continuously in disarray, because it did not have a clue how the company was going to deliver on all of those promises.

---

[*] GUI design is still more of an art than it is a science, although the past few years have led the world to a relative consensus on the kinds of visualizations (such as buttons, text boxes, and scroll bars) and the kinds of user gestures (namely, pointing, clicking, dragging, and dropping) that are both relevant and common. New kinds of visual metaphors continue to be advanced (for example, tabbed folders in dialog boxes, and divided notebooks in user windows), and as these reach general acceptance, they become something that can be automated.

[‡] I will not tell you which company this was, but I will tell you that, at the time, just about every telephone or cable company in the United States and Europe was running such an ad. By the way, it may be my personal bias, but I am still unclear why anyone would want to work intensely while lounging on the beach.

Even given the flexibility of software, a team's ability to execute is the limiting factor. In a sense, then, there is a very real envelope of possibility in software, beyond which an organization's ability to successfully and consistently deliver breaks down. This is why the eight genres of software are important: they all represent examples of large, mature architectural patterns, whose presence serves to extend this envelop by codifying certain domains.

Where do these kind of large architectural patterns come from? Kruchten suggests that every software architect uses some combination of theft, method, and intuition.[*] In novel or unprecedented systems, method, followed closely by intuition, dominates. In classical systems, theft (more politely known as reuse) dominates. In a very real sense, then, each of the eight categories of software I have described represent the theft of ideas that are known to have worked.

USER-CENTRIC SYSTEMS

The demand for applications with graphical user interfaces has exploded during the past few years, fueled by the maturation of windowing environments for workstations and especially for personal computers. GUIs and object-oriented technology go hand in hand, largely because visual idioms such as windows and buttons lend themselves very well to an object-oriented perspective. In fact, the history of graphical user interfaces can trace many of its roots back to the pioneering work done in Smalltalk, whose environment inspired the Apple Macintosh operating system and Microsoft's Windows as well.

Graphical user interfaces are thus nothing new, although the GUI wars continue to flare up from time to time.[‡] However, the good news is that across all of the dominant windowing environments, there is remarkable consensus in the kinds of visual idioms (such as buttons and icons) and user gestures (such as pointing and clicking as well as dropping and dragging) that are important. There continues to be improvement in the art of this domain, as applications are driven to more dynamic kinds of interaction (involving new visual idioms such as video clips, for example). The fact that there is growing stability in this domain is thus welcome news, but this good news is countered by the high expectations of end users, many of whom are used to powerful visual metaphors, and thus demand the same kinds of mature features in custom software applications as they have in mass-market software that serves a huge class of users and has had literally years to evolve.

---

[*] Kruchten, P. 1995. "Mommy, Where Do Software Architectures Come From?" *17th International Conference on Software Engineering Workshop on Architecture,* Seattle, Washington.
[‡] Arguing about the relative technical merits of Motif, Windows, or the Macintosh is a great way to start a fight among techies.

An organization, in the business of providing information management solutions to its customers, found itself constantly frustrated with its end users. Although much of its work involved reengineering old, character-based mainframe applications, many of the ultimate end users were already PC-savvy, and could not understand why it was so hard for the development team to deliver a beautiful, full-functioning graphical interface that was exactly like what was on their computers at home. This imbalance of expectations versus what was possible led to a tremendous ill-will between the end users and development staff, which was only neutralized once the development team found its rhythm and begin to produce more mature user interfaces.

There is a rule I use to help people set expectations:

Unless you can do so by theft or other extreme forms of reuse, the cost of building a fully-functioning, well-integrated GUI-intensive system is somewhere around $50,000 for each unique window.

R 65

Why is building user-centric systems so difficult, despite the relative stability of this domain? Simply put, it is because user interface design is still more of an art that it is a science: the psychology of human/computer interaction is a topic that not every developer will or can master. Furthermore, the forces that shape the requirements for user-centric systems are not always rational:

Another organization (a different one from the previous example) was in the process of moving all of its applications off its mainframe, and onto a distributed, client/server topology. In the old system, users interacted through character-oriented, block-structured terminals. In the new system, users would interact through a modern, graphical windowing environment. The development team encountered unexpected resistance from its end users, who flatly rejected any interface that did not have the look and feel of a character-oriented, block-structured terminal: they were used to it, and they simply did not want to change. The development team eventually overcame these objections by planting some well thought-out prototypes in the hands of key (and vocal) users. These early prototypes concentrated on providing a few creature comforts to these end users that automated some of their more tedious and error-prone tasks. Once these key influencers were hooked, the rest of the end user community eventually came around and began to interact with the development team in positive ways.

So, as you build a user-centric system, expect to be pulled by impossible demands from users who want perfectly beautiful GUIs yesterday, and at the same time, expect to be dragged down by Luddites who reject anything that looks different. What is a team to do?

My experience is that all of the previous practices and rules apply, with the following variations:

P 123

When crafting a system in which user interaction dominates, develop a style guide that codifies the application's common look and feel, and validate that model through a series of early prototypes that are released quickly and regularly to end users in a controlled manner.

P 124

When crafting a system in which user interaction dominates, explicitly decouple the GUI from the domain model, and use GUI builders and frameworks wherever possible.

This second practice likely needs some more explanation, best illustrated by an example:

A development organization selected a graphical application builder to craft its new family of applications. It quickly became very productive, and developers were able to generate running applications that carved out a large part of the graphical interaction. However, as they got deeper and deeper into development, it became increasingly difficult to add anything new or to make changes to existing semantics. The resulting system was very fragile, because the underlying GUI code was scattered everywhere, as was all the code that modeled the system's business rules.

The point here is that, even in the presence of GUI builders and frameworks, an application must still have a strong sense of architecture. Specifically, a user-centric architecture typically has three dominant layers, listed from top to bottom:

- Classes that provide the system's look and feel
- Classes the map the GUI layer to the domain model
- Classes that denote the domain model

This layering represents a strong and deliberate separation of concerns between the visualization of the objects in a domain and a statement of the domain itself. Thus, the top two layers generally consist of objects that have a clear visual analog and that are responsible for responding to events (such as clicking, dragging, and dropping). Because these objects are event driven, development is largely a matter of attaching code to each event. In user-centric applications, this layer is often very thick:

> In user-centric applications, approximately 50% of the code will be asso-
> ciated with the look and feel; much of this code need not be handwrit-
> ten, but instead can be provided by GUI builders.

R 66

There is another, very pragmatic reason for separating the domain model from the classes that provide its visualization. As I explain in the previous chapter, in user-centric applications, a system's look and feel changes far more rapidly than its underlying model. Thus, by decoupling the two, it is possible to migrate the system to more advanced forms of user access, while keeping intact its core.

DATA-CENTRIC SYSTEMS

Data-centric systems are characterized by the presence of webs of data, whose schema is relatively stable compared to its content (which may change rapidly) and its size (which may grow to large proportions). I speak of webs of data, because in most interesting data-centric systems, strong semantic connections exist among different kinds of data, and most applications serve to either navigate those associations or to preserve their integrity. In such systems, issues of scale, consistency, performance, and security tend to dominate.

The fact that data-centric systems are so pervasive has spawned a subculture of computer science, namely, the study of databases, and in particular relational databases. Database development tends to focus on the entities that comprise a particular domain, together with the relationships among them. Now that sounds an awful lot like object-oriented practice,[*] but there is one fundamental difference: traditional approaches to data-centric systems are best described as "data-first" whereas object-oriented development is best described as "behavior-first."

> When crafting a data-centric system, do not consider the application's
> data only; consider its behavior as well.

P 125

There is nothing intrinsically evil with a data first approach. However, taken to the extreme—as it too often is— this traditional practice tends to lead to the development of stovepipe architectures, as I describe in Chapter 1. Why is this so? One important consequence of a data first philosophy is that data becomes explicitly decoupled from the rules that dictate the manipulation of that data. Thus, as new applications are built up, each one ends up having to replicate those rules. Then, as the rules change, each application ends up adapting to

---

[*] In fact, entity-relationship (ER) approaches to database design provide a reasonable starting point for doing domain modeling in object-oriented systems.

those new rules at different rates because of the latency involved in sweeping through an organization's large suite of applications. This yields the growth of nearly-independent columns of applications grown on top of the more-slowly changing data. Explicitly coupling an object's data and behavior in object-oriented systems directly mitigates this problem, by localizing these rules and attaching them directly to their associated data. As these rules change, they have to be changed in only one place. Furthermore, new rules can be created as adaptations of existing rules, an approach that is facilitated by inheritance in object-oriented systems.

One other social consequence of a data-first philosophy, especially in larger organizations, is that it encourages the creation of data fiefdoms in which critical data assets are controlled by relatively independent data base administrators, who—because of the very existence of their roles—tend to defend access to their data at all costs, even if it results in some pretty silly consequences for the business as a whole.

One large organization was stumbling in the market place for a variety of reasons, not the least of which was the inability of its sales force to keep up with the rapidly changing nature of the company's many product offerings. The root of the problem was that each business unit had its own way of collecting and distributing sales information, which was, of course, incompatible with every other business unit's approach. One of the goals of reengineering this system in an object-oriented fashion was the hope that these internal inconsistencies would go away. Indeed, the development team was quite successful in developing an object-oriented domain model of the entire business, and in record time at that. It did all the right things: it validated the model against real scenarios, and it even built some prototypes of the architecture. However, the project ultimately failed for political reasons. Without going into all the messy details, suffice it to say that one business unit staged a successful palace revolt for control of the architecture, and thereupon threw away the unified domain model that was simpler and self-consistent and continued with a relentless defense of its data schema.

I do not mean to paint an unfair picture of database administrators, but if you view the world as a sea of database tables, then every problem looks like a database problem, which often it is not. An object-oriented perspective takes a radically different view of the world, as summed up in the following practice:

P 126

When crafting an object-oriented system for which data dominates, focus upon the creation of a domain model first, and then treat any associated underlying database as simply a mechanism that provides transparent persistence for the objects in the domain model.

This practice has two very important implications. First, it pushes the details of data storage down to the lower layers of a system's architecture so that applications that live on top of the domain model can be constructed relatively independently of the details surrounding any particular database technology. Second, this practice offers the development team considerable degrees of freedom to chose alternative database mechanisms as performance requirements dictate, without rending the semantics of the entire system. Accordingly, object-oriented systems constructed in this manner tend to yield applications that are smaller and simpler.

Following this practice, data-centric architectures typically exhibit a three-tiered architecture, whose layers are listed from top to bottom:

- Classes that access and manipulate the domain model
- Classes that denote the domain model
- Classes that provide persistence for the domain model

In this context, what exactly does transparent persistence mean? To put it simply, from the perspective of a client that lives on top of the domain model, this means that you can create or modify an object, and it will stick long after the client goes away. In principle, this is not exactly rocket science: the simplest model of object persistence streams out the state of an object to a table upon writing, and then streams in the state of the object when reading. This is of course an oversimplification of the problem,* but it is the case that the details of such a mechanism can be hidden from view. With such an approach, one thing that should not be hidden from the full view of a domain model's clients is a mechanism for transactions, as I introduce in Chapter 2. Transactions are a concept that is borrowed from traditional database technology but applies equally well to the problem of ensuring consistent updates to an object-oriented domain models whose objects are semantically connected.

Thus, it is reasonable to approach the design of a data-centric system by devising a thin object-oriented layer on top of a more traditional relational database technology. This approach is attractive because it leverages the existence of a mature technology (namely, relational databases) yet still permits the core of a system to be cast in object-oriented terms.

An emerging alternative technology is that of object-oriented database management systems (OODBMS), which provide a model of persistence that maps directly to an object-oriented view of the world. Most OODBMSs permit a developer to devise an object-oriented domain model, specify which classes of objects are persistent and which are not, and then store and retrieve persistent objects seamlessly, either by simply touching an object or by explicit operations supplied only for persistent objects.

---

* The larger problem involves issues of object identification, the mapping of 1 to N and M to N associations, the mapping of subclasses and superclasses to tables, mechanisms for change notification, the tradeoffs between lazy and pessimistic updating, and approaches to caching.

OODBMSs and relational database management systems (RDBMS) have different strengths and weaknesses, and it is these very differences that make one or the other more appropriate, depending upon the exact nature of the domain being modeled. OODBMSs excel in their ability to navigate easily around the objects in a domain model. For example, in a customer tracking system, a query such as "given a customer, give me its last order, then give me its common shipper, then return to me the last time they sent a shipment" is handled easily by an OODBMS (an RDBMS would have to carry out multiple joins to respond to such a query). On the other hand, RDBMSs excel in their ability to deal with issues of scale and with queries on collections. For example, in the same customer tracking system, an RDBMS can more easily handle queries such as "give me all the shippers who sent a delivery between these two dates."

How does one decide? Most of the successful projects I encounter tend to following this practice:

P 127

> For most cases, it is reasonable to approach the design of a data-centric system by devising a thin object-oriented layer on top of an RDBMS. If the performance of navigating around the domain model is the central concern, consider providing persistence through an OODBMS.

I use the following rule to guide my decision in this matter:

R 67

> For the same volume of data, moving from flat files to an RDBMS involves an increase in storage by a factor of 3, but with vastly superior performance in querying and updating. For the same volume of data, moving from an RDBMS to an OODBMS involves an increase in storage by a factor of 1.5 but with better performance for navigating around a model.

COMPUTATION-CENTRIC SYSTEMS

Computation-centric systems generally fall into one of two categories: they either involve a lot of hairy mathematics, or they typically involve the automation of a process that interacts with real objects in the real world. Either way, in computation-centric systems, the number of different kinds of objects in a domain is generally small, compared to the complexity of the algorithms that transform those objects.

The problem with traditional computation-centric systems is that they tend to be very fragile. Because the dominant problem in such systems is more algorithmic than anything else, system developers tend to craft architectures that center around processes instead of the objects that are affected by such processes. This approach—which is distinctly not object-oriented—tends to yield systems that, once built, people are afraid to touch.

> One organization built embedded systems for automobiles which covered everything from optimizing the fuel/air mixture for the engine, to monitoring the status of turn signals, to controlling the inside temperature for the passengers. Although the systems themselves were not horribly complex, the problem was vastly complicated by the fact that they had to work for a multitude of different car models released every year around the world. In addition, an error could result in the recall of tens of thousands of cars, which made the development organization very, very risk aversive. In the process of beginning to migrate its work from assembly language to object-oriented technology, the organization discovered that in current releases, a large fraction of its code was dead, meaning that it would never be executed in any car under any conditions. It seems that the development team was so afraid to touch anything that worked once, that although the requirements changed over time, the team failed to realize that some of its work had become irrelevant.

It is hard to generalize for a genre of software that covers so many different kinds of systems, but the following practice seems to help:

> When crafting a computation-centric system, reify any interesting algorithms, either by attaching them as operations upon a particular class of objects, or by inventing agents responsible for carrying out these operations through the collaboration of several objects.

P 128

To reify means to treat something as an object. For example, using traditional techniques, one might think of an algorithm for compressing a stream of data (a classical input/process/output filtering problem). However, in object-oriented terms, I would probably abstract the problem by defining a class that denotes the stream of data, a set of classes that denotes the different kinds of data in the stream, and then an agent responsible for looking at that stream of objects and transforming it into a more compressed representation. This is overkill, you might say, and in some cases, you would be right—not everything in the world should be thought of an object. However, if there were opportunities for reusing parts of this algorithm, the object-oriented approach would offer some advantage. In particular, suppose my problem demanded that I adapt the compression algorithm to new, unanticipated kinds of data (for example, video data instead of audio data, which exhibits a quite different frequency spectrum). In traditional approaches, I would likely have to tear my algorithm down and start all over. In an object-oriented approach, I would be able to tweak my algorithm without tearing it apart, typically by providing new classes whose operations modified some behavior earlier defined. The difference is subtle but striking: the use of inheritance permits a team to introduce new behaviors without disturbing old ones.

Following this earlier practice, computation-centric architectures typically exhibit three dominant layers, which I list from top to bottom:

- Classes whose objects act as agents responsible for carrying out algorithms that involve the collaboration of several other objects
- Classes that model the objects transformed by the system
- Classes to which higher level objects delegate certain more primitive responsibilities, so that common behaviors can be localized and thus reused

In computation-centric systems, performance is often the central concern, and so it is reasonable to worry about the impact that reifying an algorithm might have. To ease your fears, I find that the following rule applies:

R 68

In most object-oriented programming languages, the cost of calling a polymorphic operation upon an object is about 1.5 times that of calling a procedure in a non-object-oriented language. However, that figure drops to parity (that is, one to one) if strong typing permits that polymorphic operation to be resolved to a specific instance.

Furthermore:

R 69

All things being equal, an object-oriented system and an equivalent non-object-oriented system will perform just about the same. If well-architected, the object-oriented system can be about 10 to 20% faster, because of better locality of reference and an overall smaller size.

DISTRIBUTED SYSTEMS

Distributed systems represent a different kind of factoring in the genres of software I have described thus far because ultimately almost every real system is amenable to some degree of distribution. Distribution is thus in its own right worthy of study, because it introduces a level of complexity all of its own.

In the simplest sense, a distributed object-oriented system is one whose objects are all logically part of a single domain model, yet physically may be spread across a network of machines. This implies, therefore, an equivalent distribution of processes that animate these objects. In more complex systems, distribution may involve the migration of objects and processes from one machine to another over time.

> An organization was tasked with building a real time information management system for air traffic control that exhibited all of the classical characteristics of a distributed system. Specifically, the system modeled the movement of aircraft from one air space to another. As a given aircraft moved into a new airspace, control would be passed off to another operational site. For performance and reliability reasons, these real-world movements were paralleled by the physical movement of objects in the underlying software system. Although this made the underlying mechanisms more complicated, it made the task of building applications easier because of this clear separation of concerns.

Distributed systems have always been important, but they have become even more pervasive over time, given the economics of hardware and networks, and the increasing globalization of many businesses. In practice, distribution may take several forms. At one extreme, a system may be distributed across a set of loosely-coupled processors that are geographically distributed yet connected by high bandwidth networks. At the other extreme, a system may be distributed across a set of tightly coupled processors sharing the same address space. In the first extreme, problems of interprocess communication among heavy weight processes dominates; in the second extreme, problems of synchronization among light weight threads dominates. Either way, distributing an already complex system adds yet more complexity.

Consider this spectrum in a different way: in the simplest case, a system may not be distributed all, meaning that every piece of the application resides on a single processor. Clearly, one can improve performance by running the system on a faster processor, but there is a practical limit to the throughput of such an approach. In the next most typical case, a system might be distributed across a client/server architecture, in which the top layers of the object-oriented architecture are mapped to the client, and the bottom layers to one or more servers. This approach eliminates many of the bottlenecks of a non-distributed architecture, but it is incrementally more complex, and introduces other issues, such as the replication of shared objects and the synchronization of the concurrent clients. In the most sophisticated case, a system may be distributed across a set of companion machines with peer-to-peer communication paths established, such that an object or a process can live anywhere on the network, and in fact migrate as necessary for purposes of load balancing and machine failure. This approach offers the potential for the highest throughput and the ability to adapt to changing conditions, yet is vastly more complicated, and hence has its practical limits.

For many object-oriented systems that can reasonably be distributed, a straightforward client/server form of distribution is sufficient. In fact, this flavor of distribution is so common that it has lead to the commercialization of middleware software whose responsibility is to hide the nasty details of distribution from the rest of an application.[*]

P 129

> When possible, use standard commercial middleware to provide your system's distribution mechanisms. If you find (through early prototyping) that these off-the-shelf products are not mature enough for you to bet you project on,realize that your primary alternative is to write your own middleware.

Of course, writing your own middleware layer adds complexity. However, in many cases it is possible to make enough simplifying assumptions such that the incremental risk is acceptable.

In the context of distributed object-oriented systems, one very powerful middleware abstraction is that of an object request broker (ORB). ORBs are sort of the plumbing of a distributed system, and ultimately have responsibility for two basic behaviors:

- Object registration   The problem of unique object identity across address spaces

- Object distribution   The problem of sending messages to a distant object

Using ORBs as a basic architectural building block leads to a model of distribution that is really quite straight forward. For example, consider one object sending a message to another object. From the outside, this looks like a typical method dispatch from one object to another. Under the sheets in the middleware, however this turns into a request to an ORB, which locates the object in the network, given its unique identity. If the object is indeed local, the message passing proceeds as usual. If the object is remote, however, the ORB establishes a proxy, packs the message for transmission across the network, ensures its delivery, unpacks the message at the side of the remote object, and then completes the connection.

A common approach to the implementation of ORBs is the use of remote procedure calls (RPCs), which represent a fairly stable and proven technology. The function of an ORB is to hide the details of such a mechanism and to add the behaviors associated with object registration and distribution.

---

[*] Most notable in this domain is the emergence of standards for CORBA (Common Object Request Broker), as defined by the Object Management Group (OMG).

Assuming a network of moderate bandwidth, an ORB built on top of a remote procedure call mechanism can support around 1000 messages per second.

Across a well-balanced network, distributing an object introduces a time overhead of about 10 to 20%.

R 70

How does one best approach the development of a distributed system? In practice, I find that most successful projects follow this path:

R 71

When crafting a distributed system, start with a stable non-distributed domain model. In the context of executable artifacts, study the patterns of communication among objects in the model and then map them to the network so that fine-grained object interactions happen locally and coarse-grained interactions are distributed.

P 130

LEGACY SYSTEMS

Coping with legacy systems poses a special challenge, largely because business issues—not technical ones—end up dominating.

A company grew by acquisition over the past decade. As a result, its information systems were in disarray, with each acquired business having its own system. In practice, a customer order would wind its way through about a dozen different automated systems, from the time the order was placed until the service was delivered and the customer billed. From the board of director's 35,000-foot view of the problem,* it looked like a simple matter of replacing the disparate systems with one corporate system. Down in the trenches, however, migrating from a traditional mainframe system to a more object-oriented system was painful, because progress was greatly constrained by the requirement to support ongoing company operations.

Indeed, the very reason that an organization might even consider to preserve, migrate, or possibly throw away a legacy system is entirely economic. If the real costs or even the opportunity costs of keeping a legacy system alive are sufficiently high, this condition can generate so much inertia in the organization that it may threaten to drag it down completely. Of course, many organiza-

---

* Some parties involved in this project suggested that the board had more like a 100,000-foot view of the problem, which was in itself a problem.

tions do not have the luxury of just throwing away old systems and starting over. Most mission-critical systems either represent such a large capital investment in software or they are so critical to ongoing operations that they cannot be easily discarded.

This is a wicked problem for many organizations: there is high risk in doing nothing (because of the high costs of maintaining the legacy system, coupled with its inflexibility), but there is also high risk in starting all over from scratch (because there is no room for error, and certainly no second chance). For this reason, and rightfully so, many organizations take the approach of trying to move to object-oriented technology with the additional requirement of having to coexist with certain legacy systems for a period of time.

Let there be no doubt: moving your development team toward a brave, new object-oriented world but having to look back over your shoulder for peaceful coexistence with legacy systems, greatly complicates the situation.

Having to coexist with a legacy system requires 50 to 100% more effort than if your team could proceed with a green field development.

R 72   This is a technology-neutral rule: developing a fresh, new system, unencumbered by any mistakes of past systems vastly simplifies the development problem, no matter what technology you employ. This suggests the following practice:

Where possible, outsource all of your legacy system maintenance.

P 131   In many cases that practice is simply not possible, thus the following practice kicks in:

If your development work must coexist with legacy systems, first define an object-oriented architecture as you would like the world to be, then carve off the piece covered by each legacy system. Encapsulate those
P 132   pieces by defining a thin object-oriented layer that separates each legacy system from the rest of the architecture.

This practice tends to yield the following architecture, whose layers are listed from top to bottom:

- Classes that make up the core object-oriented architecture
- A thin set of classes that resolve the impedance mismatch between the object-oriented architecture and the legacy systems
- The non-object-oriented legacy systems

The motivation for this layering is that it prevents any legacy system from warping a more solid architecture, which is intentionally designed to last for a long time. Given this solid base, then, it is possible for the development team to absorb and then replace legacy systems one at a time, starting with the long hanging fruit that is easy to pick, until the entire system is transformed.

INFORMATION MANAGEMENT SYSTEMS

Information management systems represent a broad class of applications, but no matter what their particular domain, they all share some very common characteristics. In particular, most such systems are all hybrids: they look a lot like a user-centric system and a data-centric system bashed together, with a fair amount of distribution, a modest amount of legacy, and a sprinkling of computation-centric characteristics thrown in. As a result, all of the general practices and rules from the last six chapters, together with the special rules described above, apply.

Thus, if you think that information management system development is a bit of a schizophrenic activity, well, then you are right. However—and I do not mean to oversimplify or trivialize the complexity of such systems—most information management systems have a very simple three-tier architecture, whose layers I list from top to bottom:

- Classes that provide access to and visualization of objects in the domain model
- Classes that denote the domain model
- Classes that provide for the persistence and distribution of objects in the domain model

There is nothing magical about this architecture: it represents a very balanced distribution of responsibilities, and so is well-matched to object-oriented development. The top layer encompasses the user-centric part of the system. The middle layer captures the vocabulary of the problem space, together with the business rules that regulate the behavior of the objects in this domain. The bottom layer is the technology layer which encompasses the non-domain-specific mechanisms for storing and distributing objects.

There are a number of common variations on this basic architecture, all of which involve the placement of the domain model and its associated business rules. At one extreme is the fat client, in which the top two layers of the architecture live on client machines, and the server exists simply as a data repository responsible for transparent persistence. At the other extreme is that of the fat server, in which the bottom two layers of the architecture live on a server and the top layer resides on the clients which are responsible only for the user-centric aspects of the system. Of course, there are any number of points in between, and deciding where to draw that point is one of the most important strategic decisions the development team will make. Figure 7-2 illustrates the tradeoffs involved in this decision process.

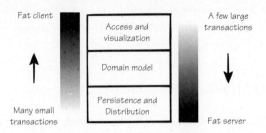

Figure 7-2   The Spectrum of Client/Server Architectures

No matter where this point is drawn, one practice remains central to all successful object-oriented information management systems:

P 133

The center of gravity of an object-oriented information system should be its domain model. Get this model right, and your task will be much easier; get this model wrong, and abandon all hope.

I have a number of rules to guide your way. First:

R 73

In well-balanced object-oriented information management systems, applications will be relatively tiny, encompassing less than a third of the delivered system. The bulk of the system should reside in the system's domain model and infrastructure.

This is a hard rule for traditional developers to accept, but it represents another practice common among successful object-oriented systems:

P 134

In crafting information management systems, treat each application as a restricted porthole through which users can view and manipulate the objects in the underlying domain model.

Continuing:

R 74

In most modest-sized information management systems, the underlying domain model will consist of about 100 to 200 classes and will take about 6 to 8 weeks to develop. On top of that model, there will be about 30 to 50 fundamental scenarios that encompass most of the interesting business functions.

This rule exposes the fact the scenario-based analysis is fundamental to the construction of object-oriented management systems. Why is this so? The short answer is that business processes are easily described in an object-oriented manner, such as by using scenario diagrams illustrated in Chapter 3.

An organization was in the midst of a company-wide business process reengineering activity that would ultimately reshape its entire business. Because these changes had a very direct impact upon the company's information systems assets, the software development organization was made a fundamental part of the reengineering effort. As the company began to redefine the work flow of its business units, the development team found that it could easily take these business processes and cast them into object-oriented models. After it had analyzed a modest percentage of these new work flows, the team also found it was possible to derive a domain model against which all these scenarios played. The development team ultimately took these models and used them to devise the system's architecture

This example illustrates the specific life cycle found in object-oriented information management system development. The general practices and rules described earlier still apply, but with a slightly different emphasis:

- Begin analysis by enumerating and then elaborating upon the fundamental scenarios that define the business.

- Continue analysis by validating these scenarios through prototypes and vigorous user review.

- Proceed into design by evolving a unified domain model, both on paper and as executable artifacts.

- Continue design by exploring the events that impact the domain model, the queries and reports that extract information from the model, and the life cycles of key classes of objects.

- Conclude design with an exploration and then a statement of policy regarding all of the technology issues, such as the treatment of persistence, transactions, security, and look and feel.

- Conduct the evolution of the project by managing against a stream of executable releases, each of which adds substance to the basic architecture and increasingly carries out more system functions.

In building an industrial-strength information management system, do not be surprised to find the need for a mixture of technologies. In fact, none of the commercial system of substance I have worked with were ever homogeneous either in terms of language or of platform. Thus, it was at first startling to walk into a project and find some proprietary database engines on the back end, some C++ acting as glue for the middleware, and a sprinkling of Visual Basic, Smalltalk, and proprietary application development languages on the front end. Although homogeneous approaches simplify the development process somewhat, there are often pragmatic economic pressures that will lead a complex system to this multiplicity of technologies. There is a very real risk in any system that this lack of homogeny will drag a project down, but the key to mitigating this risk is, not surprisingly, focusing upon the creation of a sound software architecture.

REAL TIME SYSTEMS

Real time means different things to different people, but it is at least fair to say that all real time systems involve behavior for which there are significant constraints upon time and (quite often) space. Different domains involve different scales of time, which suggests the following spectrum:

- Non-real time   Behavior of the system is largely unconstrained by time, although all processing must take reasonable amounts of time and space.

Examples of non-real time applications include the batch printing of cable television bills and the rendering of complex shaded three-dimensional models for special effects in a movie. The time scale of such applications often encompasses several hours of clock time.

- Near real time   Behavior of the system is somewhat constrained by time, often according to the pace of human cognition or the time scale of slowly changing physical events.

Examples of near real time applications include reservation systems and information kiosks at theme parks, special sporting events, or resorts. Here, the time scale of such applications is bounded by the limits of human patience: if the system takes longer than a second or two to complete a data base query, the customer will likely move on. Similarly, applications that track the migration of animals (such as bears) tagged with radio transponders need only sample every few minutes or so: bears are not particularly speedy animals, and besides, what is important in such application is not the precise location of every individual animal, but rather general migratory trends.

- Real time   Behavior of the system is very constrained by time, often according to the pace of human reaction or the time scale of rapidly-changing physical events.

Example of real time applications include air traffic control systems, certain video games, patient monitoring systems, building security systems, applications for the control of chemical processes, and test instrumentation. Time scales vary even within this category, but typically such real time systems involve behaviors that require responses to within a few microseconds. In less demanding real time systems, this time scale may involve responses on the order of milliseconds; in more demanding ones, the time scale may be on the order of nanoseconds.

• Hard real time   Behavior of the system is seriously constrained by time; furthermore, the behavior of the system must be deterministic especially in the face of heavily loaded conditions.

Examples of hard real time systems include flight control systems for inherently unstable aircraft and embedded devices such as pacemakers. Because of the requirement for predictability, this is a very special breed of applications that often demands serious mathematical analysis, a ruthless passion for raw performance, and an utter intolerance of failure.*

Space is often a concern in real time systems for two broad reasons. First, storage management of large virtual address spaces is inherently unpredictable, and such unscheduled performance hits cannot be tolerated by most real time systems. For this reason, many real time systems aggressively avoid the use of heap space. Having to reboot a pacemaker because your application corrupted its heap space is not a particularly good idea. Second, especially in embedded applications, program size equals weight. You cannot reasonably tag a bear with a device that requires a gigabyte hard drive; similarly, every memory chip in a satellite has some mass, and the cost of throwing any mass into orbit is non-trivial.

Because of these severe demands upon time and space, real time development breeds its own subculture, which is quite distinct from most information management systems. For this reason, it is useful to consider how real time demands warp the general practices and rules presented in the last six chapters. To begin, the good news is that, even in the most demanding real time applications, it is rare that 100% of a system is real time. This is important, because it means that the development team can devise a sound architecture, isolate its hot spots, and then deliberately seek out and destroy every inefficiency, usually by making local changes instead of rending the fabric of the entire design.

Continuing, there are some general rules I use when scoping a real time object-oriented system:

---

* The failure of many kinds of hard real time systems can directly lead to loss of human life. The ultimate sign of a systems failure in real time systems is the presence of lawyers who have to sort out the damage.

R 75

> A single operation dispatched at any one level of a system will expand to about 10 to 20 operations dispatched at the next level down.

This is fairly typical of object-oriented systems, as I explain in Chapter 4: in the context of an outwardly-visible scenario, each object will do some work and then delegate the rest of the work to the other objects with which it collaborates. Clearly, application of this rule suggests building real time systems that are not very thick, meaning that the path from outwardly visible behavior to internal behavior is very short.

R 76

> On a 486/33 class machine, it is possible to dispatch about 100,000 Smalltalk messages per second.

Furthermore:

R 77

> All things being equal, a given Smalltalk application will run about 1.5 to 2 times slower than an equivalent C++ application, and the C++ application will tend to run about the same speed as an equivalent C application.*

Bringing these rules together yields the conclusion that object-oriented technology is quite adequate for most real time systems. Indeed, many real time systems fail, not because they are too slow, but because their complexity was so overwhelming they were never finished. Object-oriented technology helps here as well by spreading out the risk of developing such complex systems, thus increasing the chance that they will be finished.

Cast in object-oriented terms, most real time systems tend to track the following architecture, whose layers are again listed from top to bottom:

- Classes that represent the sensors and actuators that connect with the real world
- Classes that carry out the system's control strategy
- Classes that support the other two domains, typically by providing needed services (for example, persistence) or by providing an internal model of the real world

Most real time systems follow one of two different kinds of control strategies. The two most common patterns are frame-based and message-driven systems.

In frame-based real time systems, time is divided into a set of frames; in more complicated systems, there may be subframes as well. Within each frame

---

* This rule is not meant to imply any condemnation of Smalltalk, by the way. What Smalltalk may lack in execution speed compared to C++, it makes up for in ease of development.

of time, regular work is allocated such that important processing takes place every frame, and less critical processing is shared through slots allocated in alternate frames of time. For example, in a data acquisition system, one might sample a motion sensor every frame and a temperature sensor every tenth frame. This turns out to be an easy model to objectify and deliver as a framework. Basically, there exists one central object that manages frame processing. Each frame is itself an object whose behavior is dispatched by this one central object. Each frame object is responsible for carrying out the processing demanded of that frame, which typically involves the collaboration of other lower level objects. Different kinds of frames may be represented by different kinds of objects

Message-driven systems focus upon event processing and are best suited to situations wherein events must be handled opportunistically. To objectify this model, one typically defines a set of event classes, one central object responsible for detecting and then dispatching events, and then a series of classes responsible for handling individual events or sets of events.

Under either control strategy, the tracing of events through a system and the specification of the lifetime of certain objects are both very important activities. As I introduce in Chapter 3, an object-oriented approach again helps here by providing a means of modeling finite state machines (in the context of classes), which is a particularly expressive way of modeling reactive systems.

> An organization was tasked with constructing the guidance system for a semi-autonomous submarine, used for deep sea exploration. The development team began by modeling the sensors and actuators on board the submarine, and then it proceeded by studying various scenarios of the submarine in action. This analysis led to the creation of a number of finite state machine models for different classes of objects relevant to the system. Since the hardware development lagged the software development, these models proved useful in simulating the entire system in operation.

This example begins to illustrate the specific life cycle found in object-oriented real time system development. Again, the general practices and rules described in the previous chapters still apply, but there is a subtly different emphasis during analysis and design:

- Early in analysis, enumerate the external events that drive the system
- Classify these events into groups of related kinds of events
- For every interesting set of events, develop a scenario that expresses the desired behavior of the system
- As part of architectural design, select a control strategy and then model the behavior of certain key classes as finite state machines

Stated in the form of a practice, this life cycle of successful projects can be summarized as follows:

P 135

> When crafting a real time system, focus upon designing for functionality first and for local performance second.

In this light, the iterative and incremental nature of the object-oriented development life cycle is particularly important when crafting a real time system. Early in the life cycle, the development team typically does not know enough to fully understand where the performance bottlenecks will arise in the system. By analyzing the behavior of incremental releases via histogramming or other such techniques, the team can better understand how to tune the system over time. As evolution proceeds, the specific performance requirements associated with a real time system may demand that some of the pure structures designed earlier have to be compromised slightly. Do not be surprised by these pragmatics: in the real world, one must often sacrifice beauty for efficiency, and this is exactly why one finds data base designers having to denormalize their schemas. For real time systems, this often means the following kinds of local changes:

- Flatten class hierarchies
- Eliminate polymorphism where possible
- Balance the allocation of active objects to processors

This first change tends to reduce the overhead of one subclass instance invoking operations of its superclass and so on. This trades off reuse for speed. The second kind of change involves changing virtual member functions to non-virtual member functions, thus yielding a static binding to an operation. This trades off flexibility for speed. The third change involves organizing active objects such that those that communicate tightly are physically close together. By reifying processes, it is possible to defer this kind of load balancing to late in the development cycle, yet at the same time it does not compromise the semantic integrity of the system.

FRAMEWORKS

Frameworks are in a sense the ultimate product of object-oriented technology, offering promises for reuse in the large. A framework is a kind of microarchitecture that codifies a particular domain, yet provides suitable knobs, slots, and tabs that permit a development team to adapt it to any number of specific applications within a given range of behavior. When carried out properly, frameworks can yield results that are almost magical:

A multinational banking organization set out to build a series of frameworks that each codified a particular aspect of the business. It took a significant investment to mature these frameworks, but once they were stable, the development organization found that projects that would have required one to two years to complete could now be deployed after only about 6 months of development.

In a very real way, a framework serves to codify the language of a particular domain. Thus, it is reasonable to consider crafting a framework for any domain that is sufficiently stable and well-defined. However, this is not nearly so easy as it sounds. In fact, my experience suggests the following cruel rule:

> About 80% of all framework projects fail.

The reality is, a development team will likely fail if it sets out to craft a framework from scratch. The most successful frameworks seem to come from harvesting results and generalizing experiences from earlier successful systems in the same domain.[*] Thus, another rule applies here:

R 78

> You have to build at least three or more applications against a framework (and then throw them away) before you can be reasonably confident that you have built the right architecture for that domain.[‡]

R 79

Deploying a good framework involves far more than simply writing good code. Indeed, one of the main reasons most such projects fail is because they deliver frameworks that are brilliant and profound but that are utterly unapproachable. To be useful, a framework must be understandable, and its patterns must be simple and explicit. For that reason, most successful framework projects involve a large measure of documentation, which serves to record the framework's architecture and communicate its patterns of use to its clients.

The architecture of every good framework is comprised of at least two components: a set of classes that capture the vocabulary of a particular domain and a control policy that orchestrates the instances of those classes. In fact, it is the existence of a flow of control that distinguishes a simple class library from a framework. Simply stated, a class library provides services that clients can only use or invoke, but a framework provides places that clients can plug into to complete the framework, and the framework in turn calls upon the services of these clients.

---

[*] One of my colleagues expressed it best by noting that the best frameworks are built upon the dead bodies of earlier systems.

[‡] Rebecca Wirfs-Brock, *private communication*.

This, then, is the challenge of building good frameworks. Codifying a domain's vocabulary is the easy part, but figuring out where the framework's slots and tabs should be is the hard part, and this is an activity that is best done in conjunction with real use to validate the placement of these templates. Make the framework too rigid, and you end up limiting the degrees of freedom clients have. Make the framework too flexible, and you overwhelm clients with too many degrees of freedom. Indeed, one of the main reasons so many framework projects fail is that the resulting products are entirely unapproachable.

P 136

Approach a framework project much like you would any other complex application for that same domain: first concentrate upon getting the architecture right, and only then through use determine how that framework can best be generalized.

In this manner, today's complex systems can become tomorrow's frameworks, upon which a development team may craft yet more complex applications.

Epilogue

In these seven chapters, I have covered the expanse of pragmatic software development issues that address what it takes to turn cool ideas into reality. If you remember just two things from this book, I hope they are the following:

- Software development is difficult
- Object-oriented technology helps

Is object-oriented technology mature enough upon which to build industrial-strength systems? Absolutely. Does this technology scale? Indeed. Is it the sole technology worth considering? No way. Is there some better technology we should be using in the future? Possibly, but I am clueless as to what that might be.

It is dangerous to make predictions, especially in a discipline that changes so rapidly, but one thing I can say with confidence is that I have seen the future, and it is object-oriented. Perhaps someday, our industry will find a breakthrough technology that completely changes the rules and makes software development infinitely easier. I hope so because I have more cool ideas that I want to turn into reality than I can fit into a lifetime. A select few may discover those breakthroughs; some will choose to wait for these breakthroughs. The successful ones will acknowledge the reality that, while waiting for these breakthroughs, there are a lot of things that can be built with the methods and tools at hand, and so shoulder their load and press forward.

My hope is that this book has helped to lighten your load.

Summary of Recommended Practices

CHAPTER 1   First Principles

P 1   Management must actively attack a project's risks, otherwise they will actively attack you.

P 2   Involve real users throughout the software development process; their presence is a constant reminder why and for whom the software is being crafted.

P 3   Where possible, do not bind your project to any single-source technology, but if you must (such as when that technology offers some compelling advantage even in the face of its risk), build firewalls into your architecture and process so that your project will not unravel even if the technology does.

P 4   To be successful, the software development team must be ruthless: every technical decision must contribute to satisfying a system's essential minimal characteristics. Any decision that is counter to these characteristics must be rejected; any decision that is neutral to these characteristics must be considered a luxury.

P 5   An architecture-driven style of development is usually the best approach for the creation of most complex software-intensive systems.

P 6   A successful object-oriented project must be both focused and ruthless, but it must also not be blind to opportunities for simplifying its problem by identifying general solutions that can be specialized to solve its particular problem.

P 7   Crafting good abstractions is difficult, and furthermore, there is no such thing as a perfect abstraction. Successful projects realize this, and they are not afraid continually to improve their abstractions as they learn more about the problem they are trying to solve.

P 8   Remember that the class is a necessary but insufficient means of decomposition. For all but the most trivial systems, it is necessary to architect the system not in terms of individual classes, but in the form of clusters of classes.

P 9   To be successful, an object-oriented project must craft an architecture that is both coherent and resilient and then must propagate and evolve the vision of this architecture to the entire development team.

P 10   To reconcile the need for creativity with the demand for rigor, a successful object-oriented project must apply an incremental and iterative process, which rapidly converges upon a solution that meet's the system's essential minimal characteristics.

CHAPTER 2   Products and Process

P 11   For the object-oriented project, remember that the primary unit of decomposition is the class, not the algorithm.

P 12   Every class in an object-oriented system should map to some tangible or conceptual abstraction in the domain of the end user or the implementer. Actively challenge all classes that fail this test.

P 13   Distribute the behavior in an object-oriented system in two ways: up and down class hierarchies, representing the generalization/specialization of responsibilities, and across peer classes that collaborate with one another.

P 14   Craft architectures so that they encompass all the abstractions relevant to the given domain together with all the mechanisms that animate these abstractions within that domain.

P 15   For the larger object-oriented project, remember that the primary unit of decomposition is the class category, not the individual class.

P 16   Remember that a class rarely stands alone. Thus, especially when considering the dynamics of a system, concentrate on how certain groups of objects collaborate so that common behavior is handled through common mechanisms.

P 17   The architecture of a well-structured, object-oriented system denotes its logical and physical structure, forged by all the strategic and tactical decisions applied during development. Be certain to make all strategic decisions explicitly with consideration for the tradeoffs of each alternative. Similarly, do not neglect the myriad of tactical decision that must be made: establish tactical policies for the project, and put controls in place so that these policies are followed consistently.

P 18 Seek to build simple architectures, wherein common behavior is achieved through common mechanisms.

P19 Early in the development process, agree upon a set of idioms that your team will use to write its code. Document these decisions in the form of a style guide, and enforce these idioms through the use of tools (which unequivocally demand conformance) and through walkthroughs (which achieve convergence through peer pressure and mentoring).

P 20 During architectural design, agree upon a set of mechanisms responsible for providing the system's central behavior that results from collaborations of objects. Validate these mechanisms with prototypes, document these decisions in the form of an architecture document, and enforce these mechanisms through the use of tools and walkthroughs.

P 21 Where possible, employ existing mature frameworks in your system. If such frameworks do not exist, and if you expect to build a family of programs for your domain, consider creating your own framework.

P 22 In deciding what tangible artifacts to develop beyond the software itself, the successful project must consider all those elements that contribute to reducing risk, provide points of control for management, and help to ensure conceptual integrity in the architecture.

P 23 Institute a process that reconciles the macro and micro life cycle. This approach allows an organization to "fake" a fully rational development process and provides a foundation for at least the defined level of software process maturity.

CHAPTER 3   The Macro Process

P 24 The macro process of the object-oriented project should comprise the successive refinement of the system's architecture.

P 25 The activities leading up to every evolutionary release in the macro process should be risk-driven: first assess the project's highest risks, and then direct the project's resources in such as way as to mitigate those risks.

P 26 In the context of continuously integrating a system's architecture, establish a project's rhythm by driving to closure certain artifacts at regular intervals; these deliverables serve as tangible milestones through which management can measure the project and then meaningfully exert its control.

P 27 Enter into conceptualization only when the project's risks are relatively high or when it is necessary to forge an initial bond between the customer and development organization; otherwise, press forward directly into analysis.

P 28 During conceptualization, focus upon establishing the project's vision by quickly developing a fairly broad yet shallow executable prototype. At the end of this phase, throw the prototype away, but retain the vision. This process will leave the project with a better understanding of the risks ahead.

P 29 After establishing the goals and a firm schedule for the delivery of a prototype, the best things management can do during conceptualization is to get out of the way.

P 30 The most effective prototypes generated during conceptualization are those built by a small team, consisting of the system's architect and perhaps one or two other developers who collectively continue their engagement through analysis and design.

P 31 During analysis, focus upon developing a model of the system's desired behavior by examining various scenarios that represent threads of activity typically cutting across different parts of the system.

P 32 In the creation of a domain model during analysis, focus only upon those classes that make up the central vocabulary of the problem domain. If the removal of any one particular class does not make the model collapse, remove it, because it is not important to the analysis.

P 33 When creating a domain model, focus mainly upon the associations among its classes, and identify their meaning and (where appropriate) their cardinality. Rarely worry about identifying inheritance relationships this early in the life cycle, unless it is really central to the problem domain.

P 34 Interview domain experts and end users to establish the vocabulary of the problem space. First through techniques such as CRC cards, and then more formally through scenario diagrams, capture their understanding of the scenarios that define the system's behavior.

P 35 If you find your project getting bogged down in analysis, bring in an outside mentor to conduct a CRC card exercise that forces users and developers to talk to one another again about important scenarios. Hide this group away from the rest of the organization, and do not release them until progress is made in breaking this mental logjam.

P 36 Organize the web of scenarios that defines a system along two dimensions: first clump them in use cases according to major system functions, and then distinguish between primary scenarios (that represent a fundamental kind of behavior) and secondary ones (that represent variations on the theme of primary ones, often reflecting exceptional conditions).

P 37 Develop executable prototypes during analysis only for noble reasons, not as an excuse to accelerate coding. Noble reasons include exploring areas of human interaction (such as for experimenting with the application's look and feel) or investigating novel abstractions and algorithms (such as studying the dynamics of a control system).

P 38 Analysis is best conducted by a small team, ideally made up of a core group consisting of only 4 to 6 people including the system's architect, one or two analysts/senior developers, one or two domain experts or end users, and a member of the quality assurance/testing team.

P 39 During design, build an executable architectural release that forces you to consider the pragmatics of all important interfaces and all important collaborations.

P 40 If the dominant risk to the success of your system involves the technology, attack design with a vertical slice through the architecture. If the dominant risk is instead the logic of the system, take a horizontal slice.

P 41 During design, explicitly specify the system's microarchitecture, including its idioms, mechanisms, and frameworks.

P 42 Just do it. Resist the urge to delay building something real until you know all there is to know about your problem; by then it will be too late, and the problem will likely have changed anyway.

P 43 During design, focus the creation of an architecture on three things: interfaces, the intelligent distribution of responsibilities throughout the system, and the exploitation of patterns of collaboration that make the system simpler.

P 44 During design, the architect should first consider how to adapt existing frameworks before setting out to build an architecture from scratch.

P 45 During design, explicitly select, validate, and then document the common idioms and mechanisms that shape the system and bring it conceptual integrity.

P 46 Aggressively seek out ways to avoid writing code. Where it makes sense, adapt existing frameworks or use application builders.

P 47 Toward the end of the design phase, establish the rhythm of a project that drives it to the end of its scheduled life cycle by planning for a series of intermediate releases, each of which grows the architecture from the inside out.

P 48 Design is best conducted by a small team made up of the project's very best people, principally including an architect and one or two other developers. As the complexity of the project grows, this group should be supplemented by a few other developers (who mainly concentrate upon certain technology areas), a toolsmith (responsible for the team's development environment), a member of the quality assurance/testing team (responsible for the project's quality program), and perhaps a writer (who manages the project's documentation).

P 49 The design phase should be drawn to a close only once the team has delivered an architectural release whose bones are healthy enough and whose risks are sufficiently understood such that it would be willing to bet the future of the project on it.

P 50 When designing, always keep in mind that this is an engineering problem. Do not become obsessive about finding perfect solutions (they are an illusion) but equally, do not assume away all of the hard parts of your problem (they will come back to haunt you). Strive for *adequate* solutions that resolve the competing technical, social, and economic forces that shape your particular problem.

P 51 During evolution, beat a steady rhythm that allows the team to first approach each new risk with caution but then, once identified as real, to attack each risk with due and deliberate haste.

P 52 During evolution, refine each new release so that it adds more flesh to the bones of the previous one. Choose where to expand each release according to the highest risk at hand.

P 53 Remember that prototypes are meant to be thrown away or cannibalized; especially in the presence of fierce schedule pressure; resist the urge to build a prototype, bless it, and then declare it as production quality. Doing so may offer the project a short term gain, but assuredly this decision will come back to haunt you.

P 54 Carry out the development of each new release during evolution as one or more spins of the micro process.

P 55 During evolution, aggressively focus a main line of developers on the next release, but hedge your bets by allocating a few resources for exploring areas of risk. Preserve the project's rhythm by the planned incorporation of the results of these investigations into future releases.

P 56 During evolution, carry out unit testing of all new classes and objects, but also apply regression testing to each new complete release.

P 57 During evolution, maintain a regular release schedule as much as possible. All things being equal, shift functionality rather than schedules, but never ever let functionality creep out of the picture altogether.

P 58 During evolution, minor changes can be handled by the owner of the affected classes. Modest changes should be handled by collaboration among the abstractionists who own the corresponding class categories with a sign off by the architect. Major changes should first be validated by a tiger team lead by the system's architect and then incorporated by collaboration with all of the system's class category owners.

P 59 Throw away a little as you go along, so you do not have to throw it all away at the end.

P 60 Don't panic. No matter how broken your system is, the world will still go on. The worst thing management can do is overreact and spread hysteria throughout the team; the rational thing management can do is assess the damage, pick up the broken pieces, and develop an intelligent plan for reestablishing the project's rhythm.

P 61 Organize tiger teams as the need arises to attack some risk in the project. Explicitly create such a team with clear goals as to its mission, scope, and schedule, then disband the team when its work is done.

P 62 Never throw an interim release over the wall to a customer: not only will you get large amounts of low quality feedback, but you will eventually alienate all of your customers by forcing them to do the testing your team should have done in the first place. Therefore, when exposing releases to end users during evolution, be certain to set expectations as to what each release does and does not do.

P 63 Evolution should be drawn to a close only when the functionality and quality of the releases are sufficient to ship the product to an average customer who requires little or no hand-holding to use the system.

P 64 During evolution, use a bug tracking system to identify the minority of classes and collaborations of classes that are the source of the majority of the system's errors. Conduct design walkthroughs against each of these key abstractions to work on improving their quality.

P 65 During evolution, seek to stabilize key architectural decisions as early as possible. In particular, track the stability of the key classes and clusters of classes in the system that encompass its domain model and essential mechanisms.

P 66 If you find your application getting too complex, add more classes.

P 67 If the cost of ownership of a software system is greater than the cost of developing a new one, then the most merciful course of action is metaphorically to put the aging system out to pasture or, as conditions dictate, either to abandon it or to shoot it.

CHAPTER 4   The Micro Process

P 68 The micro process of the object-oriented project should comprise the overlapping waves of discovery, invention, and implementation.

P 69 Use the macro process to control the activities of the project as a whole; use the micro process to iteratively carry out these activities and to regulate the future conduct of the macro process.

P 70 Remember that identifying classes and objects is fundamentally an engineering problem, not a theoretical one. Seek to find a set of abstractions that are good enough, and let the iterative nature of the object-oriented development process provide a mechanism of natural selection that forces these abstractions to become better as the project unfolds.

P 71 Use scenarios to drive the process of identifying classes and objects; CRC card techniques are particularly effective at getting interested parties together to work through scenarios.

P 72 Do not let the internals of an abstraction leak out to its externals. When considering the semantics of classes and objects, there will be a tendency to explain how things work; the proper response is "I don't care."

P 73 Start with the essential elements of any notation and apply only those advanced concepts necessary to express details that are essential to visualizing or understanding the system that cannot otherwise be expressed easily in code.

P 74 Sometimes, the best way to solve a problem is to expand it. If you find yourself getting stuck in the complexity of a scenario, add more classes.

P 75 Good class design requires an intelligent distribution of responsibilities. Specifically, operations that may be used by a set of peer classes should be migrated to a common superclass, possibly by introducing a new intermediate abstract class. Operations that may be used by a disjoint set of classes should be encapsulated in a mixin class. Operations that are unique to specific classes or that represent specializations of other operations should be pushed lower in a class hierarchy.

P 76 Employ pattern scavenging as an opportunistic activity to seek out and exploit global as well as local commonality. Ignore this practice and you run the high risk of architectural bloat which, if left untreated, will cause your architecture to collapse of its own sheer weight.

P 77 Responsibilities and operations that are neither simple nor clear suggest that the given abstraction is not yet well-defined. An inability to express a concrete header file or other kinds of formal class interfaces also suggests that the abstraction is ill-formed, or that the wrong person is doing the abstracting.

P 78 While identifying the relationships among classes and objects, seek to discover common patterns of relationship, and invent ways to exploit these patterns. Specifically, maximize the connections among things that are semantically related, and minimize the connections among things that are semantically distant and that are subject to change.

P 79 Start identifying the relationships among abstractions by considering their associations first. Once these are reasonably stable, begin to refine them in more concrete ways.

P 80 Seek to build logically cohesive and loosely coupled abstractions. Abstractions that are clumsy to use or to implement represent a failure to properly identify the right semantics or the right relationships for a given abstraction.

P 81 Encourage pragmatic engineering decisions: implementing classes and objects means moving to practical abstractions.

P 82 Remember that successful developers seek to write small amounts of quality code, rather than massive amounts of mediocre code. Thus, during implementation, aggressively search for parts to reuse; if you find some that are close to your needs, spend the effort to make them just right.

CHAPTER 5   The Development Team

P 83 Remember that software development is ultimately a human endeavor.

P 84 Organize your core development team among three groups: an architect who is responsible for the system's overall structure, abstractionists who manage the system's microarchitecture, and application engineers who implement and assemble the classes and mechanisms found in the system.

P 85 Choose an architect who possess a vision large enough to inspire the project to great things, the wisdom born from experience that knows what to worry about and what to ignore, the pragmatism necessary to make hard engineering decisions, and the tenacity to see this vision through to closure.

P 86 Select abstractionists who are skilled at identifying, specifying, and implementing classes and mechanisms that are germane to the domain and to the implementation.

P 87 Assemble the implementation team from application engineers who love to code and who are able to turn abstractions into reality.

P 88 Surround your core development team with people responsible for the daily care and feeding of the project's artifacts.

P 89 Treat the architect and the project manager as peers; they should effectively be joined at the hip.

P 90 Do not confuse the roles of project management and development; they encompass very different activities. Remember that a team's architects, abstractionists, and application engineers are responsible for designing software and that the project manager is responsible for designing the team of software developers.

P 91 Executing a project in a technically flawless manner is a laudable goal, but never forget for whom you are building the system.

P 92 Assign someone to act as a liaison between the core development team and its clients, especially its patrons and end users.

P 93 Organize your development team so that its center of gravity lies within a tight grouping of the project manager, architect, abstractionists, and application engineers.

P 94 Control the conceptual integrity of your system by assigning responsibility of each class category to exactly one abstractionist and assigning responsibility of the overall structure to exactly one architect.

P 95 As the complexity of your problem rises, grow a layer of middle level development management by letting abstractionists act as the architects of their piece of the system. Retain the role of the system architect to preserve a simplicity and harmony that cuts across all of these microarchitectures.

P 96 Staff your project in three overlapping waves. The architect leads the charge, the team's abstractionists follow, and the mass of application engineers provide the main body of resources.

P 97 Recognize that applying the object-oriented paradigm requires a change in attitude. Allow sufficient time for your team members to mature in their roles. Every developer must have the time to reach some "aha" experience.

P 98 Before you bet your company on object-oriented technology, completely carry out a pilot project that lets you validate your expectations and tune the technology and your organizational culture to one another.

P 99 To rapidly jell your team and level set its members' skills, conduct an intense boot camp that immerses everyone into the technology. This practice can have an impact along many dimensions, not the least of which is helping grow the team by providing a shared experience.

P 100 Do not forget to transition your management. Bring them to an understanding of the different products and process inherent in object-oriented technology by exposing them to other projects, letting them run a pilot project, giving them formal training, and mentoring them.

P 101 Rotate tiger team assignments to give developers a break from the grind of main-line development and so that developers have a chance to stretch their skills.

P 102 Do not neglect the physical setting. Put related projects down the hall from one another. Arrange cubicles so that they all open to a common work area. Install a vending machine or a library or even a pinball game or video game so that developers have a chance to separate themselves from their computers and talk with one another.

P 103 Invest some time and resources into developing an infrastructure that rewards and cultivates your developer's talents.

P 104 Avoid writing code in the first place, but if you have to choose a language, do so based upon its expressiveness, approachability, acceptance, and staying power in the market place, and the existence of a third-party industry that feeds that market. Most importantly, consider the cost of ownership of software written in that language versus another one.

P 105 Validate your tool set early (the software equivalent of kicking the tires before you buy). Try out the complete tool set that you intend to use for production development as early in the life cycle as possible.

CHAPTER 6   Management and Planning

P 106 Make it the development team's responsibility to aggressively seek out risk and to question all assumptions. Similarly, make it management's responsibility to judge these issues without passion and prejudice, weighed against the project's essential minimal characteristics.

P 107 Introduce object-oriented practices to your organization in the form of a pilot project that affords the team the opportunity to fail.

P 108 Maintain a running list of your project's top ten risks, and use this list to drive each release.

P 109 Remember that the response to every risk is ultimately a business decision, not necessarily a technical one. Figuratively speaking, this means that sometimes you must shoot the engineer.

P 110 In the successful project, remember that planning is a continuous activity that is driven by risk factors and that focuses on the control of key artifacts.

P 111 Shield your developers from any and all distractions that keep them from their primary mission, namely, writing quality software.

P 112 Calibrate the productivity of your team in a pilot project. Continuously recalibrate it at every release during evolution.

P 113 Institute a policy of automated regression testing, tied to each release.

P 114 Focus formal reviews upon the most complex classes as well as these mechanisms (involving collaborations of classes) that are of greatest strategic importance to the architecture.

P 115 Especially for user-centric systems, write your system's reference manual and user guide early in the development process. This not only forces end users to become involved in the development process, it also forces developers to build friendly systems, since user-visible behavior that is difficult to explain is probably the wrong behavior to provide.

P 116 Treat a requirements document not as a statement of objective, unchangeable fact, but rather as a living contract between the users and the developers of a system. As a contract, a requirements document infers obligations of both parties and are open for negotiation.

P 117 Provide a simple architecture document that describes the essential structural patterns that permeate the system. Evolve this document so that it tracks the evolving architecture, and use this document as a means of architectural control.

P 118 Make documentation an essential, albeit a secondary, artifact. Concentrate upon those documents whose creation and evolution helps drive the project to closure and serves either as a means of project control or as a measure of the project's health.

P 119 If you find your project in crisis, above all, do not panic. Immediately conduct a software triage that identifies the project's showstoppers and the top two or three risks to the life of the project. Appoint small tiger teams to drive these risks to the ground, and in parallel, get the rest of the team focused on recovering its rhythm.

P 120 If your development schedule is slipping yet your deployment schedule is inflexible, do not try to make up time by forcing your developers to work even harder; it will exacerbate the problem. Rather, acknowledge reality, regain control of the architecture, and either relax the schedule constraint or relax the system's required functionality. To do neither is pure folly.

CHAPTER 7   Special Topics

P 121 Remember that sometimes you have to break the rules; some risks to the success of your project may be so daunting, you may have to make up new rules along the way. Realize, of course, that in so doing, you will always be trading off one set of risks for another.

P 122 Do not write code unless you absolutely, positively must. Wherever possible, employ application builders or frameworks that focus on a particular domain, but be sure to center them around some object-oriented architecture that gives them a context and that glues them together.

P 123 When crafting a system in which user interaction dominates, develop a style guide that codifies the application's common look and feel, and validate that model through a series of early prototypes that are released quickly and regularly to end users in a controlled manner.

P 124 When crafting a system in which user interaction dominates, explicitly decouple the GUI from the domain model, and use GUI builders and frameworks wherever possible.

P 125 When crafting a data-centric system, do not consider the application's data only; consider its behavior as well.

P 126 When crafting an object-oriented system for which data dominates, focus upon the creation of a domain model first, and then treat any associated underlying database as simply a mechanism that provides transparent persistence for the objects in the domain model.

P 127 For most cases, it is reasonable to approach the design of a data-centric system by devising a thin object-oriented layer on top of an RDBMS. If the performance of navigating around the domain model is the central concern, consider providing persistence through an OODBMS.

P 128 When crafting a computation-centric system, reify any interesting algorithms, either by attaching them as operations upon a particular class of objects, or by inventing agents responsible for carrying out these operations through the collaboration of several objects.

P 129 When possible, use standard commercial middleware to provide your system's distribution mechanisms. If you find (through early prototyping) that these off-the-shelf products are not mature enough for you to bet you project on, realize that your primary alternative is to write your own middleware.

P 130 When crafting a distributed system, start with a stable non-distributed domain model. In the context of executable artifacts, study the patterns of communication among objects in the model and then map them to the network so that fine-grained object interactions happen locally and coarse-grained interactions are distributed.

P 131 Where possible, outsource all of your legacy system maintenance.

P 132 If your development work must coexist with legacy systems, first define an object-oriented architecture as you would like the world to be, then carve off the piece covered by each legacy system. Encapsulate those pieces by defining a thin object-oriented layer that separates each legacy system from the rest of the architecture.

P 133 The center of gravity of an object-oriented information system should be its domain model. Get this model right, and your task will be much easier; get this model wrong, and abandon all hope.

P 134 In crafting information management systems, treat each application as a restricted porthole through which users can view and manipulate the objects in the underlying domain model.

P 135 When crafting a real time system, focus upon designing for functionality first and for local performance second.

P 136 Approach a framework project much like you would any other complex application for that same domain: first concentrate upon getting the architecture right, and only then through use determine how that framework can best be generalized.

Summary of
Rules of Thumb

CHAPTER 1 First Principles

R 1 If the majority of the projects in your organization are obsessively short term, calendar-driven projects, there is something very, very wrong, indeed. Radical changes in the organization's software development process are in order, before the company or its people are ruined.

R 2 If 90% or more of your system's requirements are expected to be stable over the software's lifespan, then applying a requirements-driven policy has a fair chance of yielding a reasonably optimal solution. Anything less than this degree of stability requires a different development approach to achieve a tolerable value for the system's total cost of ownership.

R 3 If your project has more writers than programmers, or if the cost of updating your documentation is greater than the cost of making a change to your software, then your project has certainly fallen into the black hole of documentation-driven development.

R 4 If even a single human life were to be jeopardized by the failure of your software system, a quality-driven approach to development should be considered.

CHAPTER 2 Products and Process

R 5 Every class should embody only about 3-5 distinct responsibilities.

R 6 A single class hierarchy is suitable for only the most simple application; every other system should in general have exactly one hierarchy of classes for every fundamental abstraction in the model.

R 7 If your system has only a few classes, then class categories are generally architectural overkill. If, however, your system has more than about 50 to 100 classes, to manage the growing complexity, you must decompose your system in terms of class categories, not just individual classes.

R 8 The typical class category will consist of a dozen or so classes.

R 9 Most object-oriented systems require less than 10 to 20 central mechanisms.

R 10 The typical developer will only be able to absorb a few dozen new idioms, and thus the best style guides are simple, averaging about 30 pages, and serve to document idioms important to the project.

R 11 The best architecture documents are simple, averaging far less than 100 pages, and they serve to document the key class structures and mechanisms important to the project.

R 12 A framework does not even begin to reach maturity until it has been applied in at least three or more distinct applications.

R 13 70% of the classes in a system are relatively easy to discover. 25% of the classes emerge during design and implementation. The remaining 5% are often not found until maintenance.

R 14 In most projects, there are typically only about 3-5 tangible artifacts beyond the software itself that are truly central to risk reduction, management control, and conceptual integrity. Most of these artifacts begin to show up fairly early in the life cycle.

CHAPTER 3   The Macro Process

R 15 If there is not a single organization chart posted around your office, your software project likely needs to be nudged in the direction of more formality; if your programmer's desk drawers have several such charts, your software project likely needs to be nudged in the opposite direction, toward more informality.

R 16 A project's risk starts reaching critical proportions once you begin to change more than two factors relative to existing practices (such as the team, the technology base, the platform, the method, the tools, the development language, and system's requirements).

R 17 For projects of modest complexity whose full life cycle is about one year, the conceptualization phase typically lasts about one month.

R 18 For projects of modest complexity, expect to find a few dozen use cases, an order of magnitude more primary scenarios, and an order of magnitude more secondary ones.

R 19 For projects of modest complexity, expect to discover about 50 to 100 classes in the domain model of a system which represents only those key abstractions that define the vocabulary of the problem space.

R 20 For projects of modest complexity whose full life cycle is about one year, the analysis phase typically lasts about one to two months.

R 21 The analysis phase should be drawn to a close once the team has elaborated approximately 80% of a system's primary scenarios along with a representative selection of the secondary ones. Elaborate upon any more, and your analysis will likely reach diminishing returns; elaborate upon any fewer, and you will not have a sufficient understanding of the desired behavior of the system to properly understand the risks.

R 22 For most systems of modest or greater complexity, focus design on a broad sweep, covering some 80% of the breadth and about 20% of its depth.

R 23 For projects of modest complexity whose full life cycle is about one year, the design phase typically lasts about one month and rarely exceeds two months.

R 24 Even the most unusual application should be able to steal at least 10% of its implementation from existing simple frameworks, such as for domain-independent data structures. More mature organizations should be able to avoid writing about 30% of their whole system from scratch. The most mature organizations – those which have invested the resources necessary to develop a domain-specific framework that offers them a competitive advantage – can see in the steady state the ability to avoid writing 60% or more of their applications.

R 25 Since most object-oriented systems require less than 10 to 20 really central mechanisms, during design focus on the 5 to 7 mechanisms that have the most sweeping implications to the evolving implementation or that represent the highest risk to the success of the project.

R 26 For most projects, plan on about five (plus or minus two) intermediate releases during evolution.

R 27 Never engage a core design team larger than about 7 to 10 people; anything bigger is almost impossible to manage. If the sheer complexity of your project demands it, however, break your project into several teams of a dozen or so people, but still coordinate their activities under the control of a single core design team.

R 28 For each critical mechanism in the architecture and for every framework intended to be used in the system, create a tiger team who drives that pattern to closure within about 1 to 5 days (or 1 to 5 weeks for the more complicated frameworks).

R 29 Pragmatically, strive toward an 80% solution. Achieving a 100% solution requires exponentially more effort, and the last 20% of functionality (typically representing the dark corners of a system's behavior) is often not commensurate with the required effort (often because you misunderstood the problem in the first place). Additionally, your risk of failure is much, much higher. Setting and making an 80% solution is far better than setting out for a 100% solution and achieving a 0% one.

R 30 For a modest-sized project, plan for a new release every 2 to 3 months. For more complex projects, plan for a new release every 6 to 9 months.

R 31 For projects of modest complexity whose full life cycle is about one year, the evolution phase typically lasts about nine months.

R 32 A change that affects just a handful of classes is minor (and typical). A change that affects the basic structure of only one or two class categories has a modest impact (and is not uncommon). A change that effects the basic structure of three or more class categories is major (and should be rare in healthy projects).

R 33 With each iteration, if you throw away less than 10% of your work, you are not throwing away enough; if you throw away more than 20%, it probably means you are not integrating enough of your prototypes into the final product (your actual mileage may vary).

R 34 If at your first iteration you find you must trash more than 30% of your work, this is a sign that your architecture has never really achieved a stable state.

R 35 During evolution, a full 80% of the team should be focused on pumping out each new release. The remaining 20% or so should be assigned to secondary tasks that attack new risks and that prepare the ground work for the next series of releases.

R 36 The typical tiger team has from one to three members, with one and one-half being a median size.

R 37 80% of the errors in an object-oriented system will be found in 20% of its classes.

CHAPTER 4 The Micro Process

R 38 Most good responsibilities can be written with approximately a dozen-words; any more, and you probably should divide the responsibility; far fewer, and you probably need to combine responsibilities.

R 39 Most interesting classes will, on the average, have about a dozen operations. It is not unusual to find classes with only one or two operations, particularly if they are subclasses. Finding classes with statistically far more operations is not in itself a bad thing, but it is a warning sign that perhaps you have underabstracted.

R 40 Be sensitive to balance. As a rule, good architectures are composed of forests of classes, rather than trees of classes, wherein each hierarchy is generally no deeper than 5±2, and no wider than 7±2 at each intermediate node.

R 41 Adapting a class or mechanism that is just 5 - 10% off from your needs is a no-brainer: do it without question unless there are extenuating circumstances. Adapting an abstraction that is 20 - 30% off from your needs requires a bit more consideration: do it if you expect you will be able to reuse it in one or two more additional ways. Abstractions that are 50% or more off from your needs are not likely candidates for reuse: but if you find a number of such near-misses, then you have the wrong set of components, and so you ought to reconsider their microarchitecture before you move on.

R 42 Most individual operations associated with a class can be implemented in a dozen or so lines of code. It is not unusual to find some implementations that require only one or two lines of code. If you find implementations that require a hundred or more lines of code, then you have done something very wrong.

CHAPTER 5 The Development Team

R 43 Hyperproductive developers are, on the average, 4 to 10 times more productive than the average developer.

R 44 Hyperproductive developers constitute less than about 1 or 2% of the entire developer population.

R 45 A small object-oriented project can be carried out with a team of only 1 or 2 people. A slightly larger project requires around five people. A modestly-sized project requires a development team of dozen or two. A team developing a moderately complex project will typically reach a peak staff of around 50. Projects of geopolitical scope may require the efforts of a few hundred developers.

R 46 Approximately 10% of the development team should be a full or part time member of the architecture team. About 30% of the team are abstractionists. Application engineers constitute about 50% of the whole team. The remaining 10% serve in supporting roles.

R 47 Although your project may be an economic success, you have failed your end users if you require a technical support team an order of magnitude larger than your core development team.

R 48 In a well-balanced project, 1 out of 7 developers is a full time or part time member of the architecture team. In smaller projects, 1 in 12 is satisfactory, since communication within the team is easier.

R 49 If your project is of modest risk, set aside about 10% to 15% of your development resources for tiger teams.

R 50 For most projects, the median size of a tiger team is one or two people. The median lifetime of a tiger team is one or two weeks.

R 51 All other things being equal (and they never are), your first object-oriented project will likely cost you 10% - 20% more resources (people and/ or schedule) than your usual non-object-oriented projects. By the time you hit your second or third project, if you have done things right, you should see a need for 20% - 30% fewer resources than traditional staffing would suggest.

R 52 It takes about one month for a professional programmer to learn the syntax and semantics of an object-oriented programming language such as C++ or Smalltalk. It takes about 6-9 months for that same developer to really embrace the object paradigm.

R 53 It takes about one month for a professional programmer to become adept with a simple class library. It takes about 6-9 months for that same developer to become really proficient with a much larger framework (for example, the Smalltalk environment). This rate is not linear; rather it is exponential, relative to the complexity of the framework.

R 54 Given a random selection of professional developers, about 10-15% will just never get it. In other words, they will never be able to make the transition to object-oriented stuff.

R 55 When staffing a new object-oriented project, 2/3 of the team can come from traditional projects, and 1/3 should be "outsiders" already exposed to objects. Increase the number of traditional developers, and you slow down the technology transfer process; increase the number of outsiders, and you run the risk of leaving the traditional developers behind.

R 56 Figures vary, but the tool cost (hardware and software) for the typical developer in the United States, neutral to object-orientation, averages somewhere around 25% of labor costs plus burden. For example, a development shop paying an average of $60,000 per year burdened costs should spend about $15,000 per developer per year.

R 57 The use of an incremental development environment can reduce turn around times by a factor of 10 to 100.

R 58 Simple tools often yield an 80% solution; solving the last 20% generally makes the tool much more clumsy and costly.

CHAPTER 6 Management and Planning

R 59 A strong warning signal that you have misplanned or misscheduled your project is the observation that most of your team is working a steady 60 to 80 hour work week. For most projects, an occasional hard week is to be expected. For some critical projects, several such weeks can be tolerated. For all projects, overtime as a common practice is not only unsustainable, it is an indication of severe management malpractice.

R 60 For your team's first object-oriented project, take the schedule you would have planned with traditional development, and inflate it by 10-30%.

R 61 In the steady state, plan for your object-oriented project to require 10-50% fewer resources than traditional practices. Expect your development schedules to stay the same (but with increased functionality and quality) or be slightly compressed (but at the same level of functionality as tradition would provide).

R 62 In a modest size project, a typical architecture review will take one or two days scheduled every quarter. Other reviews will take an hour or so, and these are scheduled as needed.

R 63 The usefulness of a formal review is inversely proportional to the number of people attending beyond five.

R 64 Most successful projects spend about 5-10% of their development resources on both internal and external documentation.

CHAPTER 7   Special Topics

R 65 Unless you can do so by theft or other extreme forms of reuse, the cost of building a fully-functioning, well-integrated GUI-intensive system is somewhere around $50,000 for each unique window.

R 66 In user-centric applications, approximately 50% of the code will be associated with the look and feel; much of this code need not be handwritten, but instead can be provided by GUI builders.

R 67 For the same volume of data, moving from flat files to an RDBMS involves an increase in storage by a factor of 3, but with vastly superior performance in querying and updating. For the same volume of data, moving from an RDBMS to an OODBMS involves an increase in storage by a factor of 1.5 but with better performance for navigating around a model.

R 68 In most object-oriented programming languages, the cost of calling a polymorphic operation upon an object is about 1.5 times that of calling a procedure in a non-object-oriented language. However, that figure drops to parity (that is, one to one) if strong typing permits that polymorphic operation to be resolved to a specific instance.

R 69 All things being equal, an object-oriented system and an equivalent non-object-oriented system will perform just about the same. If well-architected, the object-oriented system can be about 10 to 20% faster, because of better locality of reference and an overall smaller size.

R 70 Assuming a network of moderate bandwidth, an ORB built on top of a remote procedure call mechanism can support around 1000 messages per second.

R 71 Across a well-balanced network, distributing an object introduces a time overhead of about 10 to 20%.

R 72 Having to coexist with a legacy system requires 50 to 100% more effort than if your team could proceed with a green field development.

R 73 In well-balanced object-oriented information management systems, applications will be relatively tiny, comprising less than a third of the delivered system. The bulk of the system should reside in the system's domain model and infrastructure.

R 74 In most modest-sized information management systems, the underlying domain model will consist of about 100 to 200 classes and will take about 6 to 8 weeks to develop. On top of that model, there will be about 30 to 50 fundamental scenarios that encompass most of the interesting business functions.

R 75 A single operation dispatched at any one level of a system will expand to about 10 to 20 operations dispatched at the next level down.

R 76 On a 486/33 class machine, it is possible to dispatch about 100,000 Smalltalk messages per second.

R 77 All things being equal, a given Smalltalk application will run about 1.5 to 2 times slower than an equivalent C++ application, and the C++ application will tend to run about the same speed as an equivalent C application.

R 78 About 80% of all framework projects fail.

R 79 You have to build at least three or more applications against a framework (and then throw them away) before you can be reasonably confident that you have built the right architecture for that domain.

Glossary

abstractionist A person responsible for class and class category design. An abstractionist is charged with evolving and maintaining the system's microarchitecture.

analysis An early phase of development, focused upon discovering the desired behavior of a system together with the roles and responsibilities of the central objects that carry out this behavior.

application engineer A person responsible for implementing the classes and mechanisms invented by the architect and abstractionists and who assembles these artifacts into small program fragments to fulfill the system's requirements.

architect The person or persons responsible for evolving and maintaining the system's architecture. Ultimately, the architect gives the system its conceptual integrity.

architecture The logical and physical structure of a system, forged by all of the strategic and tactical design decisions applied during development. A well-structured object-oriented architecture consists of a sea of classes together with the mechanisms that animate those classes.

artifact A tangible product of the development process.

behavioral prototype An intermediate release of software used to explore alternative designs or to further analyze the dark corners of a system's functionality. Prototypes are distinctly not production-quality artifacts; hence, during the evolution of a system, their ideas but not their substance are folded into production architectural releases.

ceremony The practices and rituals that a project uses to develop systems. A high ceremony project has a very formal process and lots of rules about how things should be analyzed, designed, documented, and tested. A low ceremony project has very few rules and depends entirely upon the skills of its individual team members.

class A set of objects that share a common structure and a common behavior.

class diagram A diagram that is used to show the static existence of classes, class categories, and their relationships.

collaboration The cooperation of a set of classes or objects, working together to carry out some higher-level behavior. The resulting behavior is not the responsibility of any one abstraction, rather, it derives from the distributed responsibilities of the community. Mechanisms represent collaborations of classes.

computation-centric system A system whose focus is upon the transformation of objects that are interesting to the system.

conceptualization The earliest phase of development, focused upon providing a proof of concept for the system and characterized by a largely unrestrained activity directed toward the delivery of a prototype whose goals and schedules are clearly defined.

cost of ownership The total cost of developing, maintaining, preserving, and operating a piece of software.

data-centric system A system whose focus is upon preserving the integrity of the persistent objects in the system.

design An intermediate phase of development, focused upon inventing an architecture for the evolving implementation and specifying the common tactical policies that must be used by disparate elements of the system.

discovery The activity of investigation that leads to an understanding of a system's desired behavior and performance.

distributed system A system whose GUI, data, or computational elements are physically distributed.

domain model The sea of classes in an system that serve to capture the vocabulary of the problem space; also known as a conceptual model. A domain model can often be expressed in a set of class diagrams whose purpose is to visualize all of the central classes responsible for the essential behavior of the system, together with a specification of the distribution of roles and responsibilities among such classes.

essential minimal characteristics The primary characteristics of a system, such as time to market, completeness, and quality, against which economic decisions can be made during development.

evolution A later phase of development, focused upon growing and changing the implementation through the successive refinement of the architecture, ultimately leading to deployment of the production system.

framework A collection of classes that provide a set of services for a particular domain; a framework exports a number of individual classes and mechanisms which clients can use or adapt. Frameworks are a kind of pattern that provides reuse in the large. Thus, a framework constitutes a microarchitecture that provides an incomplete template for applications within a specific domain.

idiom An expression peculiar to a certain programming language or application culture, representing a generally accepted convention for use of the language. Idioms are a pattern that represent reuse in the small.

implementation The activity of programming, testing, and integration that leads to a deliverable application satisfying a system's desired behavior and performance.

inertia A measure of the willingness and capacity of an organization to change. High inertia organizations are ultra-conservative and abhor risk. Low inertia organizations thrive on risk and are usually the earliest adopters of new technology.

information management system A system centered around a (usually distributed) domain model upon which user applications are built and which itself lives on top of a database layer that provides persistence, together with a communications layer that provides distribution.

invention The activity of creation that leads to a system's architecture.

iteration A product baseline, carried out through through the application of the micro process.

mechanism A structure whereby objects collaborate to provide some behavior that satisfies a requirement of the problem; a mechanism is thus a design decision about how certain collections of objects cooperate. Mechanisms are a kind of pattern that represent the soul of a system's design.

legacy system An older, potentially moldy system that must be preserved for any number of economic or social reasons, yet must also coexist with newly developed elements.

microarchitecture The patterns from which a well-structured object-oriented system is composed.

object Something you can do things to. An object has state, behavior, and identity; the structure and behavior of similar objects are defined in their common class.

pattern A common solution to a problem in a given context. A well-structured object-oriented architecture typically encompasses a range of patterns, from idioms to mechanisms to frameworks.

phase Any of the major divisions of the macro process (conceptualization, analysis, design, evolution, and maintenance), encompassing a set of iterations each with a common economic objective.

rational process The development life cycle that leads from a statement of requirements to an implementation, achieved through a series of development phases whose purpose, products, activities, agents, milestones, and measures of goodness are well-defined and under opportunistic control.

real time system A system whose behaviors are tightly constrained by time and/or space.

responsibility Some behavior for which an object is held accountable; a responsibility denotes the obligation of an object to provide a certain behavior and occasionally the delegation of that behavior to some other object.

release A stable, self-complete, and executable version of a system, together with any other peripheral elements necessary to use that release. Releases may be intermediate, meaning that they are meant only for internal consumption, or they may represent deployed versions, meaning that they are meant for external consumption.

role The face that an object or a class presents to the world. The same object may play different roles at different times and thus logically present a different face each time. Collectively, the roles of an object form the object's protocol.

scenario An instance of a use case that signifies a single path through that use case. A primary scenario represents some fundamental system function; secondary scenarios represent variations on the theme of a primary scenario, often reflecting exceptional conditions.

scenario diagram A diagram that is used to used to show the dynamics of scenarios and mechanisms, both involving the collaboration of several classes or objects. A scenario diagram highlights a flow of events and messages over time. Scenario diagrams include object message diagrams (which focus on messages dispatched among collaborating objects) and message trace diagrams (which focus on the flow of messages over time).

strategic decision A development decision that has sweeping architectural implications.

state machine diagram A diagram that is used to show the dynamics of individual classes, in terms of the events that impact them, the actions they give out in response, and the states that they may be found in over their lifetimes.

system function Any of the really large behaviors that constitute a business domain or subject area.

tactical decision A development decision that has local architectural implications.

use case A named region of a system's behavior; a given use case denotes some function or business process.

user-centric system A system whose focus is the direct visualization and manipulation of the objects that define a certain domain.

Bibliography

This highly selective bibliography records my favorite books that collectively cover the full range of issues germane to the management of successful object-oriented projects. I have included works that have influenced my way of thinking, as well as references that offer a complete treatment of specific topics, including software architecture, risk management, quality assurance, and the psychology of software project management. I have also included references to detailed case studies about a number of object-oriented projects.

Alexander, C. 1979. *The Timeless Way of Building*. New York, New York: Oxford University Press.
>A strikingly wise book on the theory of architecture. Although Alexander is not a software architect, his ideas apply to the crafting of well structured object-oriented systems.

Berard, E. 1993. *Essays on Object-Oriented Software Engineering*. Englewood Cliffs, New Jersey: Prentice Hall.
>A very approachable examination of the impact of object-oriented technology to a project's infrastructure, including requirements analysis, documentation, and testing. Berard is not timid in expressing his views of what works and what does not.

Booch, G. 1994. *Object-Oriented Analysis and Design with Applications*. Redwood City, California: Benjamin/Cummings.
>The central source for the notation and process described in *Object Solutions*. *OOAD* examines the theoretical underpinnings of all things object-oriented, and offers a comprehensive reference to a unified method of object-oriented analysis and design. *OOAD* also provides an exhaustive bibliography of object-oriented technology.

Brooks, F. 1975. *The Mythical Man-Month*. Reading, Massachusetts: Addison-Wesley.
>A classic that should be required reading for every manager and programmer. Brook's profound insights are directly applicable to contemporary object-oriented projects. I reread this book every year, just for inspiration.

Charette, R. 1989. *Software Engineering Risk Analysis and Management*. New York, New York: McGraw-Hill.
>A practical study on the nature of risk in software engineering. Charette offers a candid discussion of the kinds of risks inherent in software development,

approaches to risk analysis (encompassing identification, estimation, and evaluation), and the tasks of risk management (namely, planning, control, and monitoring).

DeGrace, P. and Stahl, L. 1990. *Wicked Problems, Righteous Solutions: A Catalog of Modern Software Engineering Practices.* Englewood Cliffs, New Jersey: Yourdon Press.
> An often whimsical yet unmistakably practical guide to the process of software development. DeGrace and Stahl cover the gamut of life cycle models, ranging from the traditional waterfall life cycle to more incremental and iterative processes, with a number of esoteric approaches (such as scrum development and the Hollywood model) thrown in for good measure.

DeMarco, T. and Lister, T. 1987. *Peopleware.* New York, New York: Dorset House.
> Understanding the human element of a software project. DeMarco and Lister present their collective wisdom regarding the very difficult problem of managing a diverse team of very human programmers.

Gamma, E., Helm, R., Johnson, R., and Vlissides, J. 1995. *Design Patterns: Elements of Object-Oriented Architecture.* Reading, Massachusetts: Addison-Wesley.
> A profound book that introduces the theory and practice of patterns as microarchitectures in object-oriented systems. Gamma et al have codified around two dozen patterns typically found in well structured object-oriented software.

Goldberg, A. and Rubin, K. 1995. *Succeeding with Objects: Decision Frameworks for Project Management.* Reading, Massachusetts: Addison-Wesley.
> A guide to developing a process for managing object-oriented projects. This book serves as a metamodel for *Object Solutions*; rather than being directly prescriptive, Goldberg and Rubin take lessons learned from 39 case studies and derive a framework that projects may adapt to build their own process.

Grady, R. 1992. *Practical Software Metrics for Project Management and Process Improvement.* Englewood Cliffs, New Jersey: Prentice Hall.
> Everything you always wanted to know about software metrics, but were afraid to ask. Drawing from his extensive experience, Grady shows how metrics may be applied as a management tool to improve software quality and advance the organization's development process.

Gilb, T. 1988. *Principles of Software Engineering Management.* Reading, Massachusetts Addison-Wesley.
> A central work on software project management. Gilb's book provides a very approachable compendium of pragmatic guidelines for virtually every software management issue, including requirements specification, evolutionary planning, and the inspection process.

Harmon, P. and Taylor, D. 1993. *Objects in Action: Commercial Applications of Object-Oriented Technologies.* Reading, Massachusetts: Addison-Wesley.
> Proof that object-oriented technology works. Harmon and Taylor survey 19 successful projects and examine the lessons learned from each.

Humphrey, W. 1989. *Managing the Software Process.* Reading, Massachusetts: Addison-Wesley.
> The seminal reference dealing with the maturity of software development organizations. Humphrey's classic and sometimes controversial work provides a standard against which all software processes may be measured.

Jones, C. 1994. *Analysis and Control of Software Risks*. New York, Englewood Cliffs, New Jersey: Prentice-Hall.

> Mitigating risks in a software project. Jones takes a very pragmatic view of the software development process, and offers a wealth of advice for improving the quality of software as well as the other artifacts of a project.

Lorenz, M. and Kidd, J. 1994. *Object-Oriented Software Metrics*. Englewood Cliffs, New Jersey: Prentice Hall.

> Measuring the object-oriented project. Lorenz and Kidd suggest a number of useful measures substantiated by field experience and suitable for project sizing and scheduling as well as for measuring a program's complexity and quality.

Love, T. 1993. *Object Lessons: Lessons Learned in Object-Oriented Development Projects*. New York, New York: SIGS Books.

> Further proof that object-oriented technology works. Love examines a number of commercial applications, and offers predictions for the future of objects.

Maguire, S. 1994. *Debugging the Development Process*. Redmond, Washington: Microsoft Press.

> An examination of the issues that go into building teams and keeping projects on track. If one measures success by revenue, then Maguire's book provides some useful insights into how software development is conducted at one very successful company, namely, Microsoft.

McConnell, S. 1993. *Code Complete: A Practical Handbook of Software Construction*. Redmond, Washington: Microsoft Press.

> A comprehensive examination of the tactical issues that go into crafting a well-engineered program. McConnell's work covers such diverse topics as architecture, coding standards, testing, integration, and the nature of software craftsmanship.

Meyer, B. and Nerson, J. 1993. *Object-Oriented Applications*. Englewood Cliffs, New Jersey: Prentice-Hall.

> Additional proof that object-oriented technology works. Meyer and Nerson examine seven diverse object-oriented applications.

Parnas, D. and Clements, P. 1986. A Rational Design Process: How and Why to Fake It. *IEEE Transactions on Software Engineering* vol. SE-12(2).

> The primary inspiration for the process described in Object Solutions. Parnas and Clements' marvelously pragmatic paper demonstrates how a project can reconcile the art and science of software development

Pinson, L. and Wiener, R. 1990. *Applications of Object-Oriented Programming*. Reading, Massachusetts: Addison-Wesley.

> Still more proof that object-oriented technology works. Pinson and Wiener examine six different applications implemented in a variety of programming languages.

Rechtin, E. 1991. *Systems Architecting: Creating and Building Complex Systems*. Englewood Cliffs, New Jersey: Prentice-Hall.

> An intensely pragmatic book about crafting all kinds of complex systems. Rechtin, himself a highly experienced architect, offers over a hundred heuristics for systems architecting.

Schulmeyer, G. and McManus, J. 1992. *Handbook of Software Quality Assurance.* New York, New York: Van Nostrand Reinhold.

> Everything you always wanted to know about software quality assurance, but were too busy coding to ask. Schulmeyer and McManus have assembled an unparalleled collection of contributions from many of the pioneers and practitioners in the field.

Shaw, M. and Garlan, D. 1996. *Software Architecture.* Englewood Cliffs, New Jersey: Prentice-Hall.

> An introduction to the field of software architecture. Shaw and Garlan provide a pragmatic study of a number of big architectural patterns.

Taligent's Guide to Designing Programs: Well-Mannered Object-Oriented Design in C++. 1994. Reading, Massachusetts: Addison-Wesley.

> Another comprehensive examination of the tactical issues that go into crafting a well-engineered program. This guide is full of practical advice on building industrial-strength frameworks in C++.

Taylor, D. 1990. *Object-Oriented Technology: A Manager's Guide.* Reading, Massachusetts: Addison-Wesley.

> A wonderfully gentle yet complete introduction to object-oriented technology. If the mere mention of "class" and "object" causes you to tremble and brings you fear, uncertainty, or doubt, read Taylor's book immediately

Webster, B. 1995. *Pitfalls of Object-Oriented Development.* New York, New York: M & T Books.

> A guidebook to avoiding the dangers that lie on the path of object-oriented technology. Webster draws upon his extensive experience to offer pragmatic advice on rescuing projects in crisis, as well as starting projects off in the right direction.

Weinberg, G. 1988. *Rethinking Systems Analysis and Design.* New York, New York: Dorset House.

> How to analyze and design in an imperfect world. Although Weinberg's conceptual framework is drawn from structured methods rather than object-oriented ones, his observations on the pragmatics of analysis and design are relevant to all production-quality systems.

Witt, B., Baker, T., and Merritt, E. 1994. *Software Architecture and Design: Principles, Models, and Methods.* New York, New York: Van Nostrand Reinhold.

> How to craft resilient frameworks that can be implemented predictably. Witt et al discuss architectural principles that derive from a fusion of object-oriented and structured methods.

Yourdon, E. 1994. *Object-Oriented Systems Design.* Englewood Cliffs, New Jersey: Prentice Hall.

> Understanding the managerial and cultural side of object-oriented technology. Yourdon addresses topics such as project management, configuration management, testing, tools, and technology transfer.

Index

abstraction, 27-28, 39, 97, 160-161, 165-166
  dictionary, 163, 168
  harvesting, 211
abstractionist, 173, 195, 197-198
  activities, 197
  definition, 303
active management, 30
Ada, 83, 85, 168, 220
adaptability, 39
adult supervision, 5
Airlie Software Council, 238
Alexander, Christopher, 35
algorithmic decomposition, 38
amorphous blob, 133
analysis, 77-78, 161
  activities, 100
  agents, 105
  definition, 303
  domain, 100
  measures, 107
  milestones, 107
  paralysis, 102
  products, 88
  purpose, 86-87
  team, 208
analyst, 166, 199, 202
application development environment,
  51, 53, 222
application engineer, 166, 173, 195,
  198-199

activities, 198
definition, 303
specialities, 199
archeologist, 209
architect, 35-36, 42, 59, 125, 166, 195, 197,
  200
  activities, 196
  definition, 303
  skills, 196
architecture, 45, 54-55, 63, 117, 254, 275
  architecture-driven, 21
  artifacts, 110
  baselined, 109
  behavior first, 257
  canonical, 51
  changes, 141, 146-149
  client/server, 268
  coherent, 28
  computation-centric, 262
  conceptual integrity, 208
  control, 208, 272
  data first, 257
  data-centric, 259
  definition, 303
  design, 108
  dimensions, 44
  document, 50, 241-243
  executable, 111
  firewall, 8, 232
  footprint, 128

horizontal slice, 111-112
importance, 38, 221
information management, 267
infrastructure, 51
legacy, 266
object-oriented, 28
pattern, 118
planning, 117, 120
real time, 272
remembrance, 36
requirements-driven, 15
resilience, 28
reusable, 10
review, 238
simplicity, 48, 127
soul, 42
stability, 127, 149
stovepipe, 15, 128, 257
successive refinement, 133, 158, 232, 234
team, 208
three-tier, 267
user-centric, 256
vertical slice, 111-112
vision, 25, 28
well-structured, 43, 48, 53-54
architecture-driven project, 11, 19-21
artifact, 54-61, 63, 75, 159, 234
architecture, 110
central, 63
definition, 303
intangible, 60-61
organization, 233
tangible, 60-61, 110
association, 97, 177, 179
assumptions, 230
attribute, 170

Beck, Kent, 92, 167
behavior, 39, 45, 86, 92, 166-167, 170, 257, 270-271
localization, 24
temporal, 94
behavioral prototype
definition, 303
Belady, Les, 151
benefits of object-oriented technology, 23

big bang integration, 234
blindsided by technology, 5, 7-8
Boehm, Barry, 77
boot camp, 217
breaking the rules, 250
Brooks, Fred, 82
bug
hunt, 239
tracking, 146
business
case, 76
decision, 229, 233

C++, 44, 48, 83, 85, 108, 149, 168, 174, 213, 217, 220, 269, 272
vs Smalltalk, 149
calendar-driven project, 11-13
calibrating, 231, 236
capital resources, 219
predictability, 227
ceremony
definition, 303
high, 207, 241
low, 207, 241
change, 141, 146-149
rate, 232
resilience, 23
rules, 250
chutzpah, 144
civil engineering, 196
class, 39, 92, 94
adaptability, 39
as a unit of decomposition, 38
association, 177, 179
attribute, 170
behavior, 39, 45, 167
category, 44-45, 112
classification, 163
collaboration, 41-43, 45, 92, 94, 175-179, 182
definition, 303
discovery, 62
extensibility, 39
hierarchy, 43-44, 179
identifying, 162, 165
implementation, 181-182
insufficient, 28, 38

isolated design, 169, 171
  necessary, 28, 38
  operation, 40, 171
  perfect, 27
  protocol, 98, 170-171, 182
  quality, 39-41
  relationships, 175, 178
  representation, 167
  responsibilities, 39-41, 160, 167, 169,
      171, 173, 183
  semantics, 167
  separation of concerns, 39, 256
  well-designed, 39
class diagram, 64, 96, 111-112, 168, 176
  definition, 303
client/server architecture, 268
CLOS, 220
cluster, 44, 179
COBOL, 85, 195, 214, 220
COCOMO, 58
code, 54-56, 63
cohesion, 180
collaboration, 41-43, 45, 92, 94, 175-179,
    182
  definition, 303
combat coding, 12
Common Object Request Broker
    (CORBA), 264
communication, 160
completeness, 10
complexity, 4-5, 170, 190, 211, 237, 251, 276
computation-centric system, 251, 260-262
  definition, 304
conceptual integrity, 28, 106, 208
conceptualization, 77-78
  activities, 4
  agents, 4
  definition, 304
  measures, 86
  milestones, 86
  products, 82
  purpose, 80
configuration management and version-
    control (CMVC), 223
constraint, 11, 233, 271
construction, 76
context, 88, 101

continuous integration, 75
control, 273
Coplien, Jim, 207
core team, 194
Cortese, A., 51
cost of ownership, 10, 151, 221, 241
  definition, 304
costing, 229, 236
coupling, 180
cowboy programmer, 189
CRC cards, 92, 94, 101, 165, 168, 178, 217
creativity, 29, 67, 122, 152
crisis, 73, 102, 142, 192, 230, 244-245
culture, 11, 25-26, 218
Cunningham, Ward, 62, 92, 165
cyclic process, 76

data, 54, 56-57, 257
data-centric system, 250, 257, 259
  definition, 304
database, 258
  object-oriented (OODBMS), 259-260
  relational, 260
  relational (RDBMS), 259
decision
  business, 229, 233
  retracting, 11
  strategic, 9, 47
  tactical, 9, 47
  technical, 229, 233
decomposition, 28, 38
  by algorithm, 38, 261
  by class, 38, 261
defect, 146
  defect density, 145
  defect discovery rate, 145
deployment, 129
  team, 208
design, 54-55, 77-78, 161
  activities, 115
  agents, 125
  definition, 304
  document, 241, 243
  measures, 127
  milestones, 127
  products, 109
  purpose, 108

tactical, 55
team, 208
developer, 158-160, 193
heroic, 189
hyperproductive, 189-190
interchangeable, 192
development
environment, 51, 53, 222
growing a team, 217
process, 36
rules, 252
team, 187
diagram
class, 96, 111-112
message trace, 94-95
object message, 88, 95, 124
scenario, 94-95
state machine, 99
dictionary of abstractions, 163, 168
discovery, 61-62, 87-88, 159, 162, 164,
167, 174
definition, 304
Disney, Walt, 89
distributed
object management, 51-52
system, 251, 262-265
distributed system
definition, 304
distribution of responsibilities, 40-42, 98,
117, 127, 160, 167, 169, 171, 173
documentation, 17, 49-50, 54, 58, 60, 200,
203, 229, 241
ancillary, 240
architecture, 50, 241-243
purpose, 239
reasons, 240
requirements, 241-242
style guide, 126
user, 240
documentation-driven project, 11, 16-17
domain
analysis, 100
domain model, 51, 53, 88, 96-98, 258, 268
definition, 304
domain-independent framework, 51, 53
domain-specific framework, 51

dynamic structure, 109

Ecclesiastes, 187
Eiffel, 220
elaboration, 76
elegance, 37
entity-relationship (ER) modeling, 97, 257
essential minimal characteristics, 10, 23
definition, 304
estimates, 54, 58, 211
event, 46
evolution, 77-78, 123, 161
activities, 136
agents, 142
definition, 304
measures, 144
milestone, 144
products, 132
purpose, 129
exception, 46
extensibility, 10, 39

failure, 18
fear, 26-27
in projects, 5, 227
innocent lies, 160
opportunity, 230
fault tolerance, 10
fear, 26-27, 249
Feynman, Richard, 3
firewall, 8, 232
first principles, 3
focus, 9, 229, 235
Foley, M., 51
footprint, 128
form, 86
frame-based mechanism, 272
framework ,41, 50-51, 114, 159, 252-253,
274-275
definition, 304
frictionless environment, 230
function, 100
point, 87, 137

Gamma, Eric, 50
Gaston, 249

generalization/specialization, 179
Gilb, T., 6
graphical user interface (GUI), 46, 51, 53, 253-254

habits of successful project, 25, 73
hard real time system, 271
Hawthorn effect, 211
heroic programming, 189
hierarchy, 43-44, 179
high-ceremony, 207, 241
high-fidelity scenario, 92
human interfaces, 54, 56, 58

idiom, 48-49, 114-115, 121
    definition, 304
implementation, 61-62, 159, 167, 174, 181-182
    definition, 304
    language, 4, 220-221
    team, 208
inception, 76
industrial-strength software, 37, 232, 269
inertia, 232
    definition, 304
information management system, 251, 267, 269
    definition, 304
infrastructure, 51, 59, 218
innocent lies, 160
integration, 75, 200, 202, 234
    continuous, 130
intelligent classification, 163
interface, 112
invention, 61-62, 118, 159, 164, 167, 174
    definition, 305
iteration, 142
    definition, 305
iterative and incremental life cycle, 25, 29, 42, 73, 158, 239

Jacobson, Ivar, 88
jelling, 217
joint application development (JAD), 101
Jones, Capers, 54-55, 63, 75
Jones, Indiana, 227

Kidd, Jeff, 174
Kruchten, Philippe, 43, 61, 136, 181, 195-196, 254

legacy system, 251, 265-266
    definition, 305
librarian, 200, 204
life cycle, 63
    discovery, 61-62
    implementation, 61
    information management, 269
    invention, 61-62
    iterative and incremental, 25, 29, 42, 73, 158, 239
    real time, 273
    release, 76
    rhythm, 72
    spiral, 77
    waterfall, 14, 77
localization
    of behavior, 24
    of structure, 24
Lorenz, Mark, 174
low-ceremony, 207, 241
low-fidelity scenario, 92

MacApp, 41-42
Machiavellian practices, 214
Macintosh, 254
macro process, 67, 71, 73, 75, 158, 188, 227
    activities, 78
    conceptual model, 78
    phases, 77
    rhythm, 79
    staffing, 212
magic, 201, 239
maintenance, 77-78, 161
    activities, 152
    agents, 153
    measures, 153
    milestones, 153
    products, 152
    purpose, 151
management, 29, 75, 211, 227
    active, 30
    central task, 10

frictionless, 230
growing a team, 218
process, 160
role, 229
team, 58
Marasco, Joe, 136
measuring, 229, 237
mechanism, 45, 49, 114-115, 121-122, 160,
    166, 174
    definition, 305
    events, 46
    exceptions, 46
    frame-based, 272
    graphical user interface (GUI), 46
    identifying, 165
    message-driven, 272
    messaging, 46
    MVC, 42, 176
    networking, 46
    object distribution, 46
    object migration, 46-47
    persistence, 46, 49, 259-260
    process management, 46
    storage management, 46
    transactions, 46
mentoring, 217, 238
message trace diagram, 94-95
message-driven mechanism, 272
messaging, 46
method, 63-64, 74
    Booch, 65
    Jacobson, 65
    OMT, 65
methodology, 74
    one minute, 74
metrics
    abstraction, 184
    analysis, 107
    cohesion, 180
    complexity, 237
    conceptualization, 86
    coupling, 180
    design, 127
    evolution, 144
    identifying classes, 166
    maintenance, 153
    quality, 237

relationships, 180
semantics, 173
 size, 237
stability, 237
micro process, 67, 136-137, 157-158, 188,
    227
    agendas, 160
    phases, 161
microarchitecture, 114, 208, 274
    definition, 305
mid-course correction, 140
middleware, 264
milestone, 75, 160
model-view-controller (MVC), 42, 176
modeling, 86, 104
    association, 97
    entity-relationship, 97, 257
    object-oriented, 25
Mongolian horde principle, 192
monitoring, 229, 237
Moo, Barbara, 231
Motif, 254

near real time system, 270
networking, 46, 51
Nike®, 117, 157
non-real time system, 270
notation, 64, 168
    class diagram, 64, 168, 176
    roles, 64
    scenario diagram, 64, 168, 177
    state machine diagram, 64, 168, 177

object, 98
    definition, 305
    distribution, 46, 264
    island, 175
    migration, 46-47
    protocol, 98, 170-171, 182
    registration, 264
    reify, 261
object message diagram, 88, 95, 124
Object Request Broker (ORB), 264
object-oriented
    architecture, 28, 38
    benefits of technology, 23
    database, 259

database (OODBMS), 260
  limitations, 190
  method, 64
  modeling, 25
  technology, 28
Objective-C, 220
OLE, 138
one minute methodology, 74
operating system, 51
operation, 40, 171
opportunistic process, 76, 161, 172
Orr, Ken, 74-75
over-architect, 128

panic, 142
Parnas, David, 9, 76, 158
patron, 204
pattern, 3, 48
  big architectural, 118
  definition, 305
  framework, 50-51, 114, 252-253
  idiom, 48-49, 114-115, 121
  importance, 114
  mechanism, 45-46, 49, 114-115, 121,
    160, 174
  organizational, 207
  real time, 272
  scavenging, 104, 169, 172
  specification, 109
people, 188, 191
perfect class, 27
performance, 10, 65
peripheral team, 194
persistence, 45-46, 49, 51, 259-260
  object store, 52
phase
  definition, 305
  macro process, 77
  micro process, 161
Picard, Jean Luc, 71
pilot project, 216, 231
plan
  project, 54, 58, 63
  release, 109, 115, 123
  task, 125
  test, 54, 58, 63, 115

planning, 58-59, 63, 100, 117, 120, 169, 227,
    229, 233, 235
  continuous, 233
policy
  tactical, 116, 120, 123
pond scum, 215
portability, 10
postmortem, 245
practices
  abstraction, 27, 39, 97, 163, 167, 180-181
  abstractionist, 198
  analysis, 105
  application engineer, 199
  architect, 4, 119, 197, 200
  architecture, 28, 44, 48, 112, 117, 149
  architecture-driven, 21
  associations, 97, 177
  assumptions, 230
  attacking risk, 6
  bug tracking, 146
  calibration, 236
  changes, 141
  class category, 45
  collaboration, 45
  complexity, 150, 170
  computation-centric, 261
  conceptual integrity, 208
  conceptualization, 4, 80, 82
  control, 160
  cost of ownership, 151
  CRC cards, 102, 165
  creativity, 29
  crisis, 244
  data-centric, 257-258, 260
  decomposition, 28, 38, 45
  design, 125, 127, 129
  distribution, 264-265
  distribution of responsibilities, 42
  documentation, 240, 244
  domain model, 97
  evolution, 131, 133, 145-146
  expansion, 170
  framework, 50, 114, 119, 276
  identifying classes, 165
  idiom, 48, 114
  information management, 268

infrastructure, 218
integration, 75
involving users, 7, 204-205
language, 221
legacy, 266
macro process, 73
maintenance, 151
mechanisms, 50, 114
micro process, 137, 159
microarchitecture, 114
Nike approach, 117
notation, 168
organization, 195, 200, 207
panic, 142
pattern, 114, 121
perfection, 129
pilot project, 216, 230
planning, 233
pragmatism, 181
process, 67
project manager, 200
prototyping, 4, 50, 82, 84, 105, 135
real time, 274
relationships, 175, 177
release, 125, 133, 137, 140, 144
requirements, 241
responsibilities, 117, 171
reuse, 122, 252
review, 238
rhythm, 125, 139
rigor, 29
risk, 73, 113, 139, 233
risks, 232
rules, 250
ruthlessness, 26
scenarios, 91, 103
simplicity, 173, 183
single-source technology, 8
stability, 149
staffing, 212
strategic decision, 47
structure, 47
tactical decision, 47
team, 230, 235
testing, 140, 238
throwing away, 141
tiger team, 143, 218

tools, 224
transition, 214-215, 217-218
user-centric, 256
users, 101
vocabulary, 101
workplace, 218
predictability, 67, 227
Price-S, 58
primary scenario, 90-91, 103
process, 35, 37, 42, 64-65, 158
    activities, 78
    and people, 188
    cyclic, 76, 161
    defined, 65
    development, 36
    disease, 234
    dogma, 234
    forcing closure, 139
    human endeavor, 191
    information management, 269
    initial, 65
    iterative and incremental, 25, 29, 42,
        73, 158, 239
    Machiavellian, 214
    macro, 67, 73
    managed, 65
    management, 46, 160
    mature, 76
    maturity, 65-67, 80
    micro, 67, 136
    opportunistic, 76, 161, 172
    optimizing, 65
    phases, 77
    pragmatic, 161
    rational, 9, 63
    real time, 273
    repeatable, 65
    rhythm, 79
    roles, 65
    tailoring, 234
    technical, 160
product manager, 204
products, 35, 37, 54-61, 63
    abstraction, 168
    analysis, 88
    architecture document, 241-243
    central, 63

conceptualization, 82
design, 109
design document, 241, 243
diagram, 168
dictionary of abstractions, 163, 168
evolution, 132
executable code, 181
intangible, 60-61
maintenance, 152
requirements document, 241-242
review, 238
specification, 168, 176
tangible, 60-61
throwing away, 235
programming-without-programming, 253
project
  abandoning, 11, 245
  architecture-driven, 11, 19-21
  artifacts, 54-61, 63
  calendar-driven, 11-13
  chutzpah, 144
  crisis, 73, 102, 142, 192, 230, 244-245
  culture, 11, 25-26
  documentation-driven, 11, 16-17
  essential minimal characteristics, 10, 23
  experiences, 250
  focus, 9, 229
  frictionless, 230
  habits of successful, 25, 73
  healthy, 72-73, 142, 146
  high-ceremony, 207, 241
  honor, 193
  immaturity, 227
  inertia, 232
  large, 4, 106, 126, 191, 210
  low-ceremony, 207, 241
  management, 29
  mid-course correction, 140
  pilot, 216, 230-231
  plan, 54, 58, 63
  planning, 59
  postmortem, 245
  predictability, 67
  process, 37
  products, 37, 54-61, 63

quality-driven, 11, 17-19
reasons for failure, 5, 227
reasons for success, 22, 24
releases, 76
requirements-driven, 11, 13-16
rhythm, 72-73, 76, 158
risks, 81, 231
ruthlessness, 11, 25-26, 227
scheduling, 59, 84, 236
selfish interests, 227
small, 4, 106, 191, 210
stability, 67
staffing, 59, 106, 190, 192-193, 216
successful, 250, 252
unconstrained, 215
unhealthy, 73, 205
uniqueness, 79
unsuccessful, 250
project manager, 195, 199-200
  activities, 201
  kinds, 229
  quest, 227
  skills, 201
protocol, 98, 170-171, 182
prototype, 50, 84, 105, 128, 132, 134-135, 143
  behavioral, 303
  cannibalize, 82
  elements, 134
  goals, 84
  honorable reasons, 135
  rabid, 27
  rapid, 118

quality, 10, 23, 37, 39-41, 237
  predictabilty, 227
quality assurance, 106, 200, 202
quality assurance team, 125
quality-driven project, 11, 17-19

rabid prototyping, 27
radio silence, 244
rapid application development (RAD), 118
rational process, 9, 63
  definition, 305

reactive systems, 104
real time system, 251, 270, 272-274
    definition, 305
regression testing, 140, 238
reify, 261
relational database (RDBMS), 259-260
relationships, 175, 178
relaxing constraints, 11, 233
release, 76, 124-125, 137, 139-140
    definition, 305
    interim, 144
    intermediate, 125
    plan, 109, 115, 123
    stream, 132
remote procedure call (RPC), 264
representation, 167, 170
requirements, 10, 54, 56, 63
    contract, 241
    document, 241-242
    living, 241
    scenario-based, 57
    traceability, 15
requirements-driven architecture, 15
requirements-driven project, 11, 13-16
resilience to change, 23
responsibility, 39-41, 92, 94, 160, 183
    definition, 305
    distribution, 40-42, 98, 117, 127, 160,
        167, 169, 171, 173
retracting decisions, 11
return on investment, 159, 211
reuse, 23, 119, 252
review
    architecture, 238
    peer, 238
rhythm, 73, 76, 79, 125, 131, 158
rigor, 29, 64
risk
    assessment, 88, 98, 109
    attacking, 6, 75
    factors, 231
    management, 4-6, 54, 73, 81, 113, 139,
        159, 227, 229, 231-232
    top ten, 232
role
    definition, 305
Royce, Walker, 66, 234

rules
    80% solution, 129
    analysis, 100, 107
    architecture documentation, 50
    artifacts, 63
    balance, 180
    breadth, 113
    calendar-driven, 13
    changes, 141
    class, 174
    class category, 45
    complexity, 113, 116
    conceptualization, 84
    data-centric, 260
    depth, 113
    design, 116
    developers, 189-190
    development environment, 222
    discovery, 62, 97
    distribution, 265
    documentation, 17, 241
    domain model, 97, 268
    errors, 145
    estimation, 211
    evolution, 136, 142
    formality, 80
    framework, 51, 214, 275
    hierarchy, 44
    human life, 18
    idiom, 49
    implementation, 184
    informality, 80
    information management, 268
    iteration, 142
    legacy, 266
    mechanism, 121
    OODBMS, 260
    operations, 184
    organization, 195, 208
    people, 191
    perfection, 129
    performance, 262, 272
    polymorphism, 262
    RDBMS, 260
    release, 134
    requirements stability, 16
    resources, 237

responsibilities, 170
reuse, 119, 183
review, 238
risk, 81, 209
scenario, 107
scheduling, 84, 100, 116, 134, 236
staffing, 126, 142, 191, 216
team, 195, 235
tech support, 206
throwing away, 141-142
tiger team, 126, 144, 209-210
tools, 219, 224
transition, 214
use cases, 90
user-centric, 257, 265
ruthlessness, 11, 25-26, 227

scaleability, 10
scavenging, 104
scenario, 57, 87-89, 124, 166, 172, 268
benefits, 92
definition, 305
diagram, 168
high-fidelity, 92
informal, 95
low-fidelity, 92
planning, 100, 169
primary, 90-91, 103
secondary, 90-91, 103
scenario diagram, 64, 95, 177
definition, 305
scheduling, 59, 84, 229, 233, 236
predictability, 227
pressures, 244
slipping, 245
secondary scenario, 90-91, 103
Selic, B., 61
separation of concerns, 39, 256
simplicity, 24, 127
single-source technology, 8
size, 237
Smalltalk, 27, 42, 44, 83, 149-150, 168, 174,
   201, 217, 220, 254, 269, 272
   vs C++, 149
software
   complexity, 4-5
   cost of ownership, 10, 151, 221, 241

development method, 63-64
elegance, 37
errors, 145
failure, 18
forces, 253
industrial-strength, 37, 232, 269
meltdown, 244
middleware, 264
never sleeps, 202
new, 81
pervasiveness, 4
quality, 37
triage, 244
weight, 16
software archeologist, 209
Sommerville, Ian, 151
special topics, 249
spiral life cycle, 77
stability, 67, 76, 88, 127, 146, 237
staffing, 59, 190-192, 212, 216, 229, 236
   mindset, 193
state machine diagram, 64, 99, 168, 177
   definition, 306
static structure, 109
storage management, 46
storyboard, 89
   purpose, 89
stovepipe architecture, 15, 128, 257
strategic decision, 9, 47
   definition, 306
Stroustrup, Bjarne, 213
structure, 39, 109
   dynamic, 109
   localization, 24
   static, 109
style guide, 49, 126
success
   definition, 22
   reasons for, 22, 24
successive refinement, 133, 158, 232, 234
supplemental team, 194
SWAT team, 106
system
   administrator, 200, 203
   builder, 253
   computation-centric, 251, 260-262
   data-centric, 250, 257

distributed, 251, 262-265
framework, 252, 274-275
hard real time, 271
information management, 251, 267, 269
legacy, 251, 265-266
near real time, 270
non-real time, 270
real time, 251, 270, 272-274
user-centric, 250, 254, 256, 265
system function, 87, 100, 137
definition, 306

tactical
decision, 9, 47
design, 55
policy, 116, 120, 123
tactical decision
definition, 306
team, 187-188, 215
abstractionist, 195, 197-198
analysis, 208
analyst, 199, 202
application engineer, 195, 198-199
architect, 195-197, 200
architecture, 208
boot camp, 217
calibrating, 231, 236
complexity, 190
core, 194
culture, 189
deployment, 208, 233
design, 208
development, 217
documentation, 200, 203
fluid, 210
focus, 235
implementation, 208
incentivizing, 235
inertia, 232
infrastructure, 218
integration, 200, 202
jelling, 217
large, 188, 190
librarian, 200, 204
management, 58, 218
mentoring, 217, 238
middle management, 211

organization, 188, 195, 206-207, 215
patron, 204
peripheral, 194
product manager, 204
project manager, 195, 199-201
quality assurance, 106, 125, 200, 202
radio silence, 244
ruthlessness, 11, 25-26
scale, 210
scheduling, 235
shielding, 235
small, 188, 190
staffing, 212
subgroups, 207
supplemental, 194
SWAT, 106
system administrator, 200, 203
tech support, 204
testing, 106, 125
tiger, 106, 122, 126, 138, 143, 208
tools, 219
toolsmith, 200, 203
training, 216
transition, 214
users, 204
tech support, 204
technical decision, 229, 233
technologist, 37
technology transfer, 212
test
plan, 54, 58, 63
testing, 229, 237, 239
bug hunt, 239
criteria, 115
regression, 140, 238
team, 106, 125
unit, 140
three-tier architecture, 267
tiger team, 106, 122, 126, 138, 143, 208
time-to-market, 10, 23
tools, 219-224
toolsmith, 125, 200, 203
traceability
requirements, 15
training, 216
transaction, 46
transition, 76, 214

triage, 244

unit testing, 140
UNIX, 51
use case, 57, 87-89, 172
    definition, 306
    web, 91, 103
user-centric system, 250, 254, 256, 265
    definition, 306
users, 92, 204
    attitudes toward, 205
    creativity, 152
    documentation, 240
    involvement, 7

vision, 76
Visual Basic, 269

waterfall life cycle, 14, 77
well-designed class, 39
well-structured architecture, 43, 48, 53-54
white board, 102
wicked problem, 219, 266
Windows, 51, 254
Wirfs-Brock, Rebecca, 275
workplace, 218